SOUTHWESTERN COLLEGE LIBRARY

3 3200 00172 59

D0438786

5-16-01

Real Estate Rainmaker®

Successful Strategies for Real Estate Marketing

HD
1375
R466
2000

Dan Gooder Richard

SOUTHWESTERN
COLLEGE
Library
CHULA VISTA
CALIFORNIA

JOHN WILEY & SONS, INC.

New York • Chichester • Weinheim • Brisbane • Singapore • Toronto

This book is printed on acid-free paper. ∞

Copyright © 2000 by Dan Gooder Richard. All rights reserved.

Published by John Wiley & Sons, Inc.

Published simultaneously in Canada.

Real Estate Rainmaker®, 3-Step Rainmaker Lead System®, and **Gooder Group®** are registered trademarks of The Gooder Group, Inc., Fairfax, VA. All Rights Reserved.

REALTOR® is a registered trademark of the National Association of REALTORS®.

No part of this publication may be reproduced, stored in a retrieval system or transmitted in any form or by any means, electronic, mechanical, photocopying, recording, scanning or otherwise, except as permitted under Sections 107 or 108 of the 1976 United States Copyright Act, without either the prior written permission of the Publisher, or authorization through payment of the appropriate per-copy fee to the Copyright Clearance Center, 222 Rosewood Drive, Danvers, MA 01923, (978) 750-8400, fax (978) 750-4744. Requests to the Publisher for permission should be addressed to the Permissions Department, John Wiley & Sons, Inc., 605 Third Avenue, New York, NY 10158-0012, (212) 850-6011, fax (212) 850-6008, E-Mail: PERMREQ @WILEY.COM.

This publication is designed to provide accurate and authoritative information in regard to the subject matter covered. It is sold with the understanding that the publisher is not engaged in rendering professional services. If professional advice or other expert assistance is required, the services of a competent professional person should be sought.

Library of Congress Cataloging-in-Publication Data:

Richard, Dan Gooder, 1947–

   Real estate rainmaker : successful strategies for real estate
marketing / Dan Gooder Richard.
      p.   cm.
   Includes index.
   ISBN 0-471-34554-7 (cloth : alk. paper)
   1. Real estate business—Marketing.   2. Real estate agents.
3. Real estate business—United States—Marketing.   4. Real estate
agents—United States.
   HD1375.R466   2000
   333.33′068′8—dc21   99-23926

Printed in the United States of America.

10 9 8 7 6 5 4 3 2

To Synnöve,
whose love and support make it all possible
and worth it.

Contents

Foreword by Laurie Moore-Moore   *xi*

Acknowledgments   *xiii*

Introduction   *xv*

PART ONE

3-STEP RAINMAKER LEAD SYSTEM

1 Nine Deadly Truths That Could Kill Your Business   3

Truth #1: Most Customers Call Only One Real
   Estate Agent   3
Truth #2: Predatory Giants Have Declared War on
   Your Customer   5
Truth #3: Inevitable Roller Coaster of Sales Cycles
   Creates Feast or Famine   6
Truth #4: Focusing on Sellers Is No Longer Enough   6
Truth #5: Profits Will Continue to Be Squeezed   8
Truth #6: Advertising Property Drives Prospects to
   the Competition   8
Truth #7: Prospects Are Taking a Longer Time to
   Be Ready   11

Truth #8: Database and Demographic Aging Demand
   Customer Replacement   12
Truth #9: Geographic Farming Doesn't Work Anymore   13
Rainmaker Chapter 1 Summary   14

2 A Better Way: All You Do Is Close   15
Hail, the Rainmaker!   15
Nine Strategies to Becoming a Rainmaker   16
Rainmaker Chapter 2 Summary   32

PART TWO

STEP 1: CREATE CUSTOMERS
WITH LEAD GENERATION

3 Media Strategies to Win in Any Market   35
Understanding the Direct-Response Lead
   Generation System   35
Four Fundamental Truths of Customer-Direct Marketing   36
Maximize Your Media Pie   37
Seven Rainmaker Secrets to Successful Media Strategies   39
Costly Media Mistakes to Avoid   49
Rainmaker Chapter 3 Summary   52

4 Offer Strategies That Attract Prospects
Like a Magnet   53
Nine Rainmaker Strategies to Increase Results with
   Response Offers   54
Seminars Make a Powerful Offer   57
Costly Mistakes to Avoid with Your Offers   67
Rainmaker Chapter 4 Summary   69

5 Creative Strategies to Beat the Competition
Every Time   71
Creating an Identity for Your Practice   71
Confusing Corporate Identity with Personal Identity   72
Four Rainmaker Strategies to Increase Creative Results   76
Costly Creative Mistakes to Avoid   84
Rainmaker Chapter 5 Summary   86

PART THREE

STEP 2: CAPTURE CUSTOMERS WITH PROSPECT FOLLOW-UP

6 **Customer Conversion Strategies to Maximize Sales**   89
   Today's Leads Are Tomorrow's Sales   90
   Why the Competition Quits   92
   Triple Your Business with Effective Follow-Up   93
   Five Rainmaker Strategies to Effective
      Prospect Follow-Up   94
   Rainmaker Chapter 6 Summary   110

7 **Shooting Fish in a Barrel**   111
   Convert Prospects into Shoppers with a Preferred
      Customer Program   112
   Seven Sure-Fire Preferred Customer Services   113
   A Final Tip   119
   Rainmaker Chapter 7 Summary   120

PART FOUR

STEP 3: KEEP CUSTOMERS WITH LONG-TERM CONTACT

8 **Customer Retention Strategies for Optimum Profits**   123
   Understanding New Customers versus
      Lifetime Customers   124
   Follow the Example of FedEx   125
   Minimize New Customer Acquisition Costs   126
   Maximize Lifetime Customer Value   127
   Knowing What Works Makes Getting More Easy   128
   Four Secrets to Perfect Customer Care (and More
      Word-of-Mouth Referrals)   128
   Nine Rainmaker Strategies to Maximize Long-Term
      Contact Referrals   132
   Rainmaker Chapter 8 Summary   142

9 **Creating a Perpetual Referral Machine**   **143**

Four Rainmaker Strategies to Cultivate
    Endless Referrals   144
Costly Long-Term Contact Mistakes to Avoid   156
Win the War for Control of the Customer   158
Rainmaker Chapter 9 Summary   158

PART FIVE

WRITING A MARKETING PLAN IN
SIX EASY MORNINGS

10 **Morning #1: Benchmarks**   **161**

Keeping It Simple   162
Starting with What You Did Last Year   163
Learning about a Marketing Expenses Benchmark   163
Tracking Your Prospecting Activities   168
Completing a Benchmark Worksheet for Your
    Prospecting Activities   170
Rainmaker Chapter 10 Summary   173

11 **Morning #2: Objectives**   **175**

Warming Up   175
Crafting Your *Real Estate Rainmaker* Mission Statement 176
Exploring Your Objectives   179
Ranking Your Personal *Real Estate Rainmaker*
    Marketing Objectives   182
Rainmaker Chapter 11 Summary   186

12 **Morning #3: Customers**   **187**

Targeting the Customer Segments You Want   189
Understanding What Motivates Your Target Customers 196
Studying Your Competition   198
Rainmaker Chapter 12 Summary   200

13 **Morning #4: Strategies**   **201**

Knowing the Difference between Objectives
    and Strategies   201
Using the Five Tests for Strategy Selection   203
Brainstorming Solutions to Problem Objectives   205

Ranking Your Personal Strategic Action Plan   207
Rainmaker Chapter 13 Summary   208

14 **Morning #5: Budget**   **209**
Learning How Much You Should Invest   210
Understanding a Transaction-Based Budget   212
Using the Database Customer-Value Technique   213
Building a Zero-Base Budget   214
Adjusting for Exceptions to the Rules   216
Rainmaker Chapter 14 Summary   218

15 **Morning #6: Case Studies**   **219**
Four *Real Estate Rainmaker* Case Studies   219
Assembling Your *Real Estate Rainmaker* Marketing Plan   237
Rainmaker Chapter 15 Summary   240

PART SIX

GROWING YOUR PRACTICE TO SELL

16 **Building a *Real Estate Rainmaker***
Trophy Database   **243**
Building a Trophy Database Is Your Top Job   243
Assembling Invaluable Customer Information   246
Five Rainmaker Strategies to Grow Your Practice   252
Rainmaker Chapter 16 Summary   257

17 **Exit Strategies to Cash In or Cash Out**   **259**
Be Paid to Walk Away   260
Costly Mistakes to Avoid When Selling a Practice   262
Four Rainmaker Exit Strategies   269
Mergers and Acquisitions   277
Rainmaker Chapter 17 Summary   278

18 ***Real Estate Rainmaker* Resource Guide**   **279**

Afterword by Steve Murray   *303*

Index   *305*

About the Author   *317*

Foreword

All sales begin with marketing. Doing business without marketing is like winking in the dark. You know you're doing it, but nobody else knows.

In these tumultuous times, it's critical for every real estate professional to have a touchstone of certainty in this sea of change. What is needed is a solid, basic, never changing, fundamental focus, a focus on the customer.

Technology may multiply the flow of information. Consolidation may steadily enlarge giant competitors. Profitability may demand ever higher personal production and ever more transactions completed in less time. But rising above all the tumult of change is the need of the customer for service. Service to cut through the flood of information to find what's important. Service to reduce the time and costly mistakes that lurk in the home buying and selling process. Service to add value and exceed the client's expectations. Service worth telling others about.

But sales and service never get a chance unless marketing first creates a prospect, unless marketing converts a prospect into a customer appointment, and unless marketing retains a past client as a referral source. Every salesperson needs a marketing system to help generate more leads and more sales for less cost. Without a marketing system, a terrible thing happens. Nothing.

The problem is knowing what marketing works and what doesn't without having to reinvent the wheel with costly mistakes. The challenge is knowing the key components of a marketing model that can be put into practice immediately and built upon throughout an entire career. The need every salesperson faces today is to create a coherent marketing system from Day 1 that doesn't put you out of business in the meantime with wasteful hit-and-miss (mostly miss) experiments.

Dan Gooder Richard has observed and been a part of real estate marketing for more than 20 years. His is a unique perspective—not one shaped by a single market or brand philosophy or media. Anyone connected to real estate for their livelihood, agents and brokers alike, will be enriched by the store of knowledge in these pages. I'm confidant the *Real Estate Rainmaker* system will work for you.

Laurie Moore-Moore
Co-editor, REAL Trends, Inc.

Acknowledgments

More than twenty years ago, I started my career fresh out of journalism graduate school at the University of Missouri–Columbia wanting to be a publisher and in search of an industry. Real estate became my home in 1979 when Laurie Moore-Moore and Wes Foster hired me as the first director of marketing for Long & Foster, Realtors in the Washington, D.C. market.

The knowledge and experience gained at Long & Foster and in the years since 1984 at Gooder Group, publishing marketing materials for real estate, make up the core of this book. Upon that core, what truly enriches this work is the accumulation of great insights from all the numerous people who shared their own ideas about real estate marketing along the way. Without their help, this book would not be possible. To all those who took time from their busy schedules and shared their ideas in person, in writing, and in seminars, thank you. Among those I want to thank specifically are the following:

Joe Amidei	Chuck Bode	K. C. Butler
Bill Barrett	Bob Bohlen	Howard Brinton
Dave Beson	Brian Buffini	Lisa Burridge
Gladys Blum	Maria Bunting	Marilynn Cedarstrom

Jack Cotton

Ray Covington Jr.

Pat Dearing

Tony DiCello

Mike Ferry

P. Wesley Foster Jr.

Allen F. Hainge

Ed Hatch

LeRoy Houser

Larry Kendall

Laurie Moore-Moore

Joyce Caughman Morris

Steve Murray

Forrest Pafenberg

Zac Pasmanick

Craig Proctor

John and Geri Rinehart

Ralph Roberts

Walter Sanford

Bill and Peggy Sloan

Bill Sparkman

Joe Stumpf

Pat Wattam

Pat Zaby

No project of this length is possible without the finishing work. I would also like to thank the staff at Gooder Group, who kept the show on the road while I stayed home most mornings for a year to write and edit; my agents at Altair Literary Agency, Nicholas Smith and Andrea Podelsky, whose Valentine's Day first critique was lovingly insightful and not a massacre; my former managing editor at Gooder Group, Carol Boyd Leon, whose edits always make me look good; my brother, Randy Richard, whose computer savvy saved the day more than once; my mother, Adrienne Richard, whose novels and poetry inspired me to take on this project; my brother, Jim Richard, who taught me how to fish where the fish are; my grandfather, Leslie MacDonald Gooder, whose family name in publishing I still carry on; my intellectual property attorney, Susan C. Chaires; my production staff at Publications Development Company of Texas; my production manager at John Wiley & Sons, Linda Indig; and my discerning and patient editor at John Wiley & Sons, Mike Hamilton. Many thanks; I couldn't have done it without you.

Dan Gooder Richard

Introduction

Imagine a real estate practice . . .

. . . where your income is three times what it is today because you spend most of your time closing listings and buyer's agreements, not prospecting or processing.

Imagine a real estate practice . . .

. . . where your productivity averages 30, 50, 100 real estate transactions per year, not the national average of 12, because you generate an endless stream of qualified leads.

Imagine a real estate practice . . .

. . . where tracking prospect calls is so precise that media selection and target-marketing choices reduce your advertising expenses by 50%.

Imagine a real estate practice . . .

. . . where the marketing cost per transaction is 40% less because more than half your business comes through word of mouth from past clients and a referral network, as you've cultivated customer relationships for life, not just one deal.

Imagine a real estate practice . . .

. . . where prospect inquiries are converted into customer presentations 100% of the time, because trained assistants take the calls and systematically follow up as long as it takes to get the appointment.

Imagine a real estate practice . . .

. . . where you close the customer more than 75% of the time because your staff has presold the customer on you with a preappointment commitment system so effective you can focus totally on the customer's needs, not on selling yourself.

Imagine a real estate practice . . .

. . . where your support systems and staff are so well trained you could take a vacation or work only four days a week and still cash in a six-figure income year after year.

Imagine a real estate practice . . .

. . . where the value of your customer database guarantees you financial independence whenever you want to cash out, because other practitioners recognize how much your steady stream of business would be worth to them.

I'm Dan Gooder Richard.

I've spent my career making the phones ring for real estate professionals. For over 20 years, I've helped thousands of real estate agents generate more leads to grow their businesses.

In the 1970s, real estate practitioners mostly used "Jack in the Beanstalk" prospecting—they threw some classifieds or newsletters out the window and hoped some neighborhood homeowners called to list or buy a house. We called it "farming."

Today, real estate professionals need a new approach. You need a powerful system that multiplies your personal efforts and generates more prospects and closes more deals at the lowest cost. In short, you need to be a systematic *Real Estate Rainmaker*®. People depend on you to create business. Whether you depend on yourself as a sole practitioner doing it all or you have a partner or a team of assistants, if you don't make it happen, the practice fails. You are the rainmaker. Without you closing a steady flow of prospects, the business withers and everything dies.

Making matters even more pressing today, constantly squeezed profit margins demand ever more production, higher volumes, more deals, a bigger slice of the pie. You're not alone. Everybody in the industry is in the same boat. The demand for ever higher sales production has fundamentally altered how real estate services must be marketed at the beginning of the new millennium.

Fortunately, there is a better way. By drawing on proven laws of marketing and the insights of other industries, I've boiled down the solution into an easy 3-step systematic approach to lead management. The system begins and ends with lead generation. In between, the secret to beating the competition is careful prospect follow-up and long-term contact. The *3-Step Rainmaker Lead System*® is designed to deliver a steady stream of leads to the rainmaker. Then, your only job is to close.

Exactly how to generate more leads and more sales is the subject of this book. The heart of the technique is our trade-marked *3-Step Rainmaker Lead System.* The system requires you, like a grizzly bear hunting a salmon, to stay focused on your customer—not on your product, not on your ego, not on your company—as you lock onto solving the problems and servicing the needs of your customer. You might call it "give and get" prospecting. Give them good service, and you'll get more business. In today's world of real estate, rainmakers who above all else preserve the value and quality of their relationship with the customer are the true winners.

How to Use This Book

Real Estate Rainmaker is organized into six parts. Part One: *3-Step Rainmaker Lead System* paints the landscape of problems every rainmaker faces in today's market and solutions every rainmaker can use. Then, Part Two: Lead Generation extensively details the critical first step of customer creation in the *3-Step Rainmaker Lead System.* Part Three: Prospect Follow-Up outlines the second step in the system, where rainmakers make the most sales with customer conversion. Part Four: Long-Term

Contact shows you step three, where you increase referrals and maximize profits with customer retention.

Part Five: Writing a Marketing Plan in Six Easy Mornings takes you through a simple process for writing your own marketing plan. Part Six: Growing Your Practice to Sell details the nuts and bolts of building a Trophy Database and developing exit strategies to cash in a six-figure income or cash out with a nice nest egg toward financial independence. The Resource Guide in Chapter 18 is an invaluable collection of proven marketing tools never before assembled in one place, including the essential contact information to find what you need easily.

Read straight through or jump to the chapter that addresses your particular interest. However you use this book, the *3-Step Rainmaker Lead System* will show you the way to become a successful rainmaker.

Let's get started.

ONE

3-STEP RAINMAKER
LEAD SYSTEM

Nine Deadly Truths That Could Kill Your Business

> The first guy
> gets the oyster.
>
> The second gets
> the shell.
>
> Old marketing maxim

Truth #1: Most Customers Call Only One Real Estate Agent

Above all else, today's real estate salespeople who want to expand their practice face one fundamental truth: Most customers use the first salesperson they contact. To confirm this fact, my company, Gooder Group, sponsored several questions on the National Association of REALTORS® (NAR) 1998 survey of ten thousand home buyers and sellers, *Home Buying and Selling Process.* The survey asked: "How many real estate agents did you contact before you selected one to help you buy (sell) your home?" The answer was astonishing (see Table 1.1).

Most consumers only contacted one agent. (When you include talking to a second agent, the percentage of all respondents who talked to only two agents soars to 80%!) Statistically speaking, most consumers perceive all real estate agents to be pretty much alike, or assume one salesperson is probably just about as good as the next.

As practitioners, we think of real estate as a profession. We spend careers studying and getting higher designations. We are

---

Table 1.1
Percent of Customers Who Contacted
Only One Agent before Agent Selection

Prospect	Percent Who Contacted One Agent
All respondents	58
All sellers	63
Repeat buyers	61
First-time buyers	54
Resale home buyers	58
New home buyers	60

Source: National Association of REALTORS®

---

constantly striving to be better than the salesperson following us. We know that not all real estate agents are created equal. But to the majority of consumers looking for an agent, we are all perceived to be the same—and the consumer's perception is all that counts. Naturally, we must give professional service and satisfy our customers' needs. But in the beginning—when our customers are making their critical first contact to select an agent—we all look pretty much alike.

What does this trend mean to rainmakers? It means no matter how much we work at being better than the competition, how much we try to be different, how much effort we give to standing out from the crowd—the secret to getting more business is to get more leads. This immutable law of marketing is why there is a direct relationship between the number of prospects you have and your income. Real estate is a business of leads. If you don't have leads, you don't have business.

Because most consumers are satisfied with the first real estate agent they call, to get their business YOU must be the one they call first.

After all, if you are a skilled salesperson and can close one deal, you have the sales skill to close two or twenty or fifty or one hundred transactions. All you need is the opportunity. As the baseball saying goes, "All I need is more trips to the plate.

Sooner or later, I'll hit a home run." But without trips to the plate, you will never hit a home run. Without some playing time, you'll never score. That's why generating leads—before the competition—is the critical first strategy of the *Real Estate Rainmaker* system.

Truth #2: Predatory Giants Have Declared War on Your Customer

Real estate is a mature industry; that is, almost no customers go unserved. Today, REALTORS® are involved in 81% of all home transactions; the rest are FSBOs, builder sales, Real Estate Owned (REO) by institutions, and estate sales. To gain market share, competitors today must prey on other competitors' customers. Because being first is critical to survival, getting the customer to call them first is not lost on giant competitors from affinity groups to franchises to megabrokerages to lenders.

Some of the largest competitors are created through consolidation. Many industries besides real estate, from health care and accounting to funeral services and retail, have experienced a similar "big-eats-small" consolidation trend. The consolidators' strategy is always the same: Gobble up companies through mergers and acquisitions. Offer discounted prices or rebates to capture customers and drive out the competition. Cross-sell more profitable noncore ancillary services to a customer base interested in one-stop shopping. Success for these giant consolidators—and for the little guy—lies in their relationship with a satisfied customer, in branding the customer's mind with the benefits of working with one source.

In this new predatory world, many individual practitioners drop out, as declining NAR membership shows. Only those who understand how to beat the giant consolidators to the mind of the customer will survive and thrive. They will capture a larger slice of the pie, enjoy increased profits, and ultimately take advantage of lucrative opportunities to sell their practice.

Truth #3: Inevitable Roller Coaster of Sales Cycles Creates Feast or Famine

Markets fluctuate. Down markets follow up markets. Up markets follow down markets. The roller coaster is as inevitable as the business cycle. The timing is always a surprise, but the result is the same: feast or famine.

To compound this business trend, sales agents have their own personal production roller coaster. At the top, they are busy with more prospects than they can handle—but no time to prospect. When those prospects close, the salesperson crashes to the bottom with no prospects, no leads, and no money. Debts and desperation drive them to find four or five new prospects. The cycle continues. Perhaps an attendee at one of my workshops best summed up the insidious symptom of a personal boom-and-bust cycle. Asked when he markets himself, he said, "When I don't have anything better to do."

Both these macro and micro business trends are the principal killers of most sales careers in real estate today. Each downturn weeds out those who haven't learned how to survive the inevitable market and personal production fluctuations.

Truth #4: Focusing on Sellers Is No Longer Enough

In the 1970s and 1980s, there was a saying: "Control the listings and you control the market." That approach had two benefits.

First, when a listing was taken, the property was advertised. The ads and yard sign and open houses and just-listed mailers generated calls from buyers. In short, a listing created its own buyer market. Marketing was simple: Farm to get listings; advertise properties to get buyers.

Second, once a listing was placed into the Multiple Listing Service (MLS), effectively every agent in the market went to work to sell it to their active buyers. Naturally, a listing agent could handle far more sellers than buyers simultaneously. Buyers had to be chauffeured around and shown properties—on average, eighteen different homes in the NAR's survey! No wonder some successful listers said they could coordinate as many as seven listings in the same time required to work with only one buyer. Buyers were high maintenance "time drains." Yet, the commissions for listing and for selling were about the same.

Clearly, the old approach to marketing success was to focus on listing, not selling.

Unfortunately, in the 1990s, two trends endangered the listing-only focus. First, brokers responded to higher commission splits by shifting the cost of property advertising and marketing to sales agents. Now, listings became more expensive to carry and less lucrative for agents.

A second trend was the explosion of the Internet and its ability to provide virtually universal public access to property information—once the exclusive domain of real estate professionals. In this new cyberworld, the old model of charging a single, seller-paid percent-of-sale commission for a bundled package of real estate services—many provided free to the buyer—came under attack by savvy home sellers.

Finally, in the 1990s, the trend toward buyer's agency leveled the playing field somewhat. At last, having a buyer under agreement gave you some protection against buyers walking into an open house blindly and flushing all your work with them down the drain.

Now it is possible to put prospects on an automatic update system that notifies them of new listings that fit their criteria and turn buyers loose with a list of properties to drive by. All the buyers do is call you when they want to inspect a house inside or get more than thumbnail information.

The upshot of these changes is the marketing pendulum is swinging back toward a balanced approach. No longer is marketing solely focused on generating sellers. Now buyers are a significant target of consumer-direct marketing. If your business plan calls for balanced growth, then generating buyers as well as sellers will be an important component of your *Rainmaker Lead System*.

Truth #5: Profits Will Continue to Be Squeezed

We've seen this threat for several years. Expenses for everything from salaries to advertising to technology to insurance and litigation keep rising faster than home prices. At the same time, sellers and buyers are demanding lower commission rates. Nationally, the average commission rate per transaction side has fallen from 2.9% in 1992 to 2.8% in 1997, according to NAR statistics. As commissions have decreased, referral fees of 30%, 35%, even 45% have appeared to affinity groups, referral networks, relocation management companies, advance marketing firms, and in-house broker business development operations. Making the squeeze worse is the occasional need to throw in a sweetener from your own pocket at the last minute to keep a deal together, whether it is to pay for a minor repair or pick up the tab on a warranty. No matter how you cut it, the bottom line is not pretty. Profits—and your net income—are being squeezed.

Truth #6: Advertising Property Drives Prospects to the Competition

We spend our sales lives matching customers with product. Property focus is fine for sales. But for marketing, where the all-important goal is to generate prospects *before* they call the competition, trying to generate leads with property advertising right alongside the competition's product is a frustrating mistake. Although property advertising is a traditional source for keeping the duty desk busy and will always be with us, for a proactive rainmaker, property advertising has lost its effectiveness. The problems are many.

Look-alike property ads in a customer-centered world. Scan the ads every day in any newspaper or home magazine. They all look alike. And they are the biggest single waste of marketing dollars for most real estate professionals. The reason is simple. Property ads create maximum competition for a prospect's attention. It's also why very few buyers actually use ads to find the house they buy: only 8% used a newspaper advertisement to find their house, and 3% used a home book/magazine, according to NAR's buying and selling survey. Property advertising is a mirror of the reason why so many agents fail at real estate: Too many agents wait for business to come to them. They are passive. To beat the pack, today's rainmaker must be aggressive, proactive, reach out to identify prospects before the competition, and build rapport first.

Reluctant prospect mindset. Property advertising puts the prospect into a negative mindset. Prospects naturally perceive the advertiser as more interested in selling them something (the house) than in helping them personally. That's why prospects that call on property ads are reluctant to give their personal information. This means agents waste time fielding the calls with little or no prospect information to show for the lost time and money.

Too late to appeal. One of the reasons the prospect's mindset is negative is because property ads appeal to a "shopper," not a prospect. Simply said, product advertising is too late in the customer cycle to generate receptive prospects. Typically, moments before you receive an ad call, the prospect called the previous ad, and after you hang up, he or she turns the page and dials another agent. No wonder many calls are worthless. Often, prospects are already working with another agent, or someone such as the duty agent takes the call, or you're in the field and prospects don't leave a message.

The Internet makes it worse. The Internet's virtual MLS of all properties is driving a trend toward unassisted transactions and makes traditional property advertising even less effective as a lead generator. With almost all properties advertised continuously on the Internet, cyber-savvy do-it-yourself prospects no longer need to ask about "unadvertised" properties or request a comprehensive MLS property search. Thus, old follow-up door openers are closed when all properties are at a go-it-alone prospect's fingertips with a click of a mouse.

Limited prospect appeal. Probably the single biggest reason property advertising is less effective is its limited appeal. Turn to the classified section of your newspaper where houses for sale are listed. Read ten ads in your neighborhood. Draw a circle around the houses that appeal to you and mark an X through the ads that don't appeal to you. Like most folks, you'll find many ads are wasted because you as a prospective buyer had no interest in those specific properties or prices or locations. If prospects are not interested in your *specific* product, they skip over the ad and go on. Valuable money is lost because prospects don't call those ads. No question you could service *every* prospect's needs—if you only knew who the prospects were. What is lacking in all property advertising by its nature is a compelling direct-response offer with universal prospect appeal.

Too many ads, not enough time. Not only does property advertising produce hit-or-miss results—after all, not every prospect reads every ad on every page—but how do you choose the right advertising medium? With more and more media to choose from with more and more channels and publications and websites and promotional offers, everyone is inundated. Have you ever tried to stay current with just your industry reading? It's virtually a full-time job.

From a marketer's viewpoint, this problem is called market fragmentation. As more media compete for the customer's attention, fewer customers are using any one particular medium. Thus, it is growing ever more difficult to reach the mass market with mass media. If you use only one medium, you reach only that slice of the fragmented market that is using that one medium. To reach a larger slice of the pie, you need to use a larger number of media. The more different media you use for your marketing, the greater the market share you will generate. In today's fragmented media market, you must have a comprehensive media plan to reach a steady stream of new customers.

Truth #7: Prospects Are Taking a Longer Time to Be Ready

Another challenge to real estate professionals is that different customers are ready to be active at different times. The natural consumer life cycle can take a blink of an eye or it can take years from nonprospect (completely satisfied) to suspect (possible future interest) to prospect (self-identified interest) to shopper (someone actively shopping) to customer (signed listing agreement or buyer's agreement).

All too often, when a prospect contacts a salesperson today, that prospect is "not ready yet." You promise to stay in touch. Next week, another prospect contacts you. Now you have two prospects: the new one and the old one. You stay in touch, but neither the new one nor the old one is ready now. Next week, another couple comes to your open house. They are really hot to trot. You dedicate every ounce of your attention to the third prospects' ready-now needs. Follow-up on the "oldest" prospects slips through the cracks. Understandable, but disastrous.

My company, Gooder Group, analyzed more than 3,000 e-mail requests for special reports our subscribers received through our Rainmaker E-Leads Internet service from active home buyer and seller prospects. When asked "When do you want to move?" prospects answered:

- 31% wanted to move in 1–3 months.
- 25% wanted to move in 4–6 months.
- 27% wanted to move in 7–12 months.
- 17% wanted to move in more than 1 year.

The point is many prospects have a very long buying horizon. In our study, 44% planned to move in six months or more after contacting an agent. Confirming this trend, NAR's buyer survey showed resale buyers search an average of three and a half months and new home buyers search almost four months before they decide on a house. The long horizon trend is a double challenge. On the one hand, rainmakers must get prospects to call them first—before the prospect calls anyone else. On the other hand, rainmakers must be prepared to follow up until the prospect buys or dies. That may take months. Follow-up is the price we must pay to eliminate the competition when we beat them to a prospect.

Truth #8: Database and Demographic Aging Demand Customer Replacement

Recently, my wife and I revisited southern California, where we were married in 1983. We went to "our" beach for a picnic and to revisit where we had practiced our vows. To our surprise, the beach was gone. Instead of a one hundred-foot strand of barefoot sand, all that remained was a barren rocky shoreline. We asked a surfer what had happened. He said some experts think sand mining in rivers up the coast depleted the source of beach sand. For eons, sand washed down the rivers into the ocean and the waves deposited it on the downcoast beach. Without the renewable source of sand, the waves simply washed the rocks and gravel clean. We were dismayed.

The same threat affects every real estate agent's customer base. If your practice doesn't have a constant influx of fresh new customers, the old customers (and everybody they know) will steadily age beyond their home buying years, move away, or die off, only to leave you with a barren rocky practice. Because the primary home buying age group is 30–45, once you've been in the business for fifteen years, your customers will have grown older and have fewer and fewer interested friends to refer for your services. To have a healthy, balanced practice in today's market, roughly 40% of a rainmaker's customer base should be lead-generated new business, 40% should be referrals, and 20% should be repeat customers. Demographic trends, coupled with simply wearing out a picked-over customer list, demand a constantly refreshed customer base to produce a growing practice. Looking for 100% referral is a prescription for disaster.

Truth #9: Geographic Farming Doesn't Work Anymore

Not only are your customers aging, but the entire population of the United States is aging as well. This means prospects are moving less often. Recently, a survey of repeat home buyers by Chicago Title discovered that the average length of ownership in the United States today is 11.9 years. Put that into marketing terms and it translates into a meager homeowner turnover rate of about 8% annually nationwide. Of course, some hot streets and hot markets turn over faster, but some are slower. Today, it's not uncommon for turnover to be 5% or less in some neighborhoods.

Given the trend of lower and lower turnover, simple geographic prospecting, that is, prospecting every contiguous neighbor in an area, doesn't produce the results it once did. Today's rainmaker must give up the atom bomb technique of dropping marketing on everybody and move to a laser beam approach of targeting specific households that are most likely to move soon or have expressed an interest by recently responding to consumer-direct advertising.

If You Are in a Hole, Quit Digging

Given the absolute requirement to be called first; given the intense competition for customers; given the feast-or-famine roller coaster of sales cycles; given reduced margins; given a balanced focus on buyers and sellers; given the need to use universally appealing response-oriented advertising; given the need to work with the prospect's life cycle, not against it; given a constant need for new customers; and given the need to replace farming with database marketing—real estate in the new century needs new solutions to the old problem of generating leads.

Fortunately, there is a better way.

RAINMAKER CHAPTER 1 SUMMARY

Nine Deadly Truths That Could Kill Your Business

- ▶ Truth #1: Most Customers Call Only One Real Estate Agent.
- ▶ Truth #2: Predatory Giants Have Declared War on Your Customer.
- ▶ Truth #3: Inevitable Roller Coaster of Sales Cycles Creates Feast or Famine.
- ▶ Truth #4: Focusing on Sellers Is No Longer Enough.
- ▶ Truth #5: Profits Will Continue to Be Squeezed.
- ▶ Truth #6: Advertising Property Drives Prospects to the Competition.
- ▶ Truth #7: Prospects Are Taking a Longer Time to Be Ready.
- ▶ Truth #8: Database and Demographic Aging Demand Customer Replacement.
- ▶ Truth #9: Geographic Farming Doesn't Work Anymore.

A Better Way:
All You Do Is Close

~~~~~~~~~~~

"Do you know what
a Rainmaker is?

Bucks will be
falling from
the sky."

Deck Booker
(Danny DeVito), *The
Rainmaker* (movie)
~~~~~~~~~~~

Hail, the Rainmaker!

Long, long ago in ancient Greece, Zeus, the Father of the Gods, was also the god of rain. Because little rain falls in Greece and on its islands, every drop could spell the difference between life and death. According to legend, the solution for the desperate Greeks on the Saronic Islands was to have Aikos appeal to Zeus in the heavens through Aikos' mother, Aigina, who was one of Zeus' hundreds of mistresses. Zeus, being Father of the Gods, granted Aikos' request and sent rain. Aikos, the young rainmaker, was a hero to the Greeks.

A similar theme plays out among the Navaho in the southwestern United States. There, the people turn to the shaman—or rainmaker—to appeal to the gods for rain. The success of the shaman is the success of the people, whose crops and livestock depend on regular rain. Believers have faith the shaman's appealing prayers are the reason the rain falls.

In a modern approach, airplanes have been used to "seed" the atmosphere with condensation-forming chemicals. The theory is the chemicals will attract moisture to form a cloud that

15

will grow heavy enough to release rain. Many scientists believe this technique works.

Today's real estate professional is in a similar position. All the people in the enterprise—even if it's an enterprise of one—depend on the rainmaker to make it rain, to generate business. Without those life-giving leads, the business will die. Generating a deluge of new business is the rainmaker's highest responsibility. After all, more leads mean more sales. In short, the rainmaker is the god-shaman-pilot who gives life to a real estate practice.

Nine Strategies to Becoming a Rainmaker

Rainmaker Strategy #1: Concentrate on Marketing, Sales Will Follow

Real estate has evolved from a sales business to a marketing business. Failing to understand the difference between marketing and sales can be a big mistake. To illustrate, I'm told 150,000 alligators live in the New Orleans area. Every year, there is an alligator hunting season. To hunt, you must get a license and you can keep only the big ones over 18 inches long. Of course, the ol' boys only want to catch the big ones, because they get about $10 a foot for alligator hide and about $15 a pound for alligator meat. As they say, "The bigger the gator, the better."

The hunt is the interesting part. First, the ol' boys get some giant hooks and stout lines. Out in the bayou they bait these hooks. There are chicken baiters and bacon baiters, and each claims the other's bait wouldn't attract a fly in a garbage dump.

The one invariable technique they all use is to loop the line carefully over a strong tree limb and position the hook 18 inches above the water, then tie off the extra coil of line with a rubber strip. Exactly 18 inches is critical. The reason is an alligator can only reach out of the water according to the size of its snout and the length of its legs. At 18 inches, the little gators can't get the hook, only the big gators can reach the bait. Next morning, the ol' boys check their lines. If they've got a gator, they pull it in next to the boat, club it in the head, and wrestle it into the boat.

For real estate professionals, the lesson of this story illustrates the fundamental difference between marketing and sales. Marketing's job is to make the phone ring, to generate the lead, to get prospects through the door and compel them to ask for an appointment. Marketing is the hook, the line, and the sinker. Marketing is the bait you use. Marketing is where you place the hook, how many inches from the water, and under which tree. Marketing is testing different techniques until you know your alligator customer so well you think like an alligator.

The job of sales, on the other hand, is to knock them on the head, get them in the boat, and not let them go until they buy something.

The fundamental difference between marketing and sales is that marketing is attracting and sales is convincing. These are two distinct, separate functions that go together like hand and glove. When marketing does its job well, all sales has to do is close.

Probably the biggest single mistake most real estate salespeople make is not understanding the difference between marketing and sales. To be a successful rainmaker today, your first strategy must be to concentrate on marketing and sales will follow.

Rainmaker Strategy #2: Make Your Relationship with Customers Job One

Most customers are no different from you and me. They want:

- High-quality service at the lowest possible price.
- Ready access to information on their terms and in their time.
- Representation that puts their interests first, whether selling or buying.

The rainmaker's Job One is to probe deeper into customers' minds to find out what they need. The secret to success for today's rainmaker is to stay focused on the customer. What does the customer need? What worries keep the customer up at night? What prompts a consumer to become an active customer?

Who are the customers, and which ones are best for reaching your goals?

In many ways, once customers begin the process—to sell or buy a house—they follow roughly the same step-by-step scenario. Of course, some race through the steps faster than others, some hopscotch two steps at a time, but most go from step one to the finish line in a fairly predictable order. What separates one customer from another (and one group of customers from another group) is their special interest. To appeal to customers' needs requires only that a rainmaker's marketing target those special interests.

Your customers' needs depend on whether they are first-time buyers or first-time sellers; whether they are move-up consumers or downsizing consumers; whether the owners will occupy the house or are absentee investors, second-home buyers, or estate heirs; or whether the customers are bilingual or foreign-born. All of these target-customer segments help you define and focus your marketing on the customer's needs.

BEGIN AND END WITH THE CUSTOMER

Customer-centered marketing and services that customers care about are the key to profits. Put yourself in the shoes of Aikos about to appeal to Zeus for rain. Aikos' customer is Zeus. Zeus must be persuaded to make it rain. From experience, Aikos knows how not to appeal to Zeus. He knows Zeus will have no interest if he says, "Aikos is the greatest rainmaker with more rainstorms than anyone else" (volume). He knows Zeus won't respond if he says, "Aikos is the best-looking rainmaker in the land" (personal marketing). He knows Zeus won't care if he says, "Aikos has more rainmakers in his clan than any other family on the island. We're number 1" (company size).

What Zeus *does* care about is his own problems. Mostly, what Zeus worries about is keeping believers coming to him, not that pesky competitor, Poseidon, God of the Sea. For Zeus, the "value-based service" he wants most is help keeping converts out of Poseidon's hands. That's why Aikos says, "My people will worship you, not Poseidon, if you fulfill my request" (customer-centered marketing).

The same formula works for all marketing: Appeal to the self-interest of your customer, help solve your customer's problems, help save your customer time or money and avoid costly mistakes. Be focused on the customer.

HOW THE LITTLE GUY CAN BEAT THE GIANTS EVERY TIME

While the consolidator giants are concentrated on selling diversified services beyond the core brokerage service to customers (a fatal mistake Trout and Ries call "line extension" in *The 22 Immutable Laws of Marketing*), following the **Real Estate Rainmaker** system, you can turn this mistake to your advantage.

Remember, the transaction begins and ends with the customer. Your principal objective is to develop customers for life by focusing on the customer's needs. Happy customers are then cultivated for the referrals they can provide. Once you have a customer on your side, it is always easier to generate high-profit word-of-mouth referrals than to find an entirely new customer from the marketplace of strangers. Repeat business will be icing on the cake. The rainmaker's ultimate challenge is to generate customers by specializing in people, not property, because only the customer is truly valuable.

Simply put, do a better job of building a lifetime relationship based on a customer's needs with personalized high-touch service, and the little guy can beat the consolidator giants to the customer every time. This is because the giant competitors concentrate on mass-market advertising and economies of scale to deliver lowest-cost service, whereas you can focus on the individual needs of a one-to-one customer relationship that values customized service and abundant local knowledge.

Rainmaker Strategy #3: Beat the Profit Squeeze with Productivity

Giving up any part of your commission hurts your bottom line. But the squeeze is on. One solution is to increase revenue. Raising the brokerage rate won't fly with home sellers, so rainmakers need other approaches. These include increasing your average price or selling additional ancillary services to existing customers or by adding on a flat fee.

Some rainmakers charge a flat "transaction fee" (also called a documentation fee, processing and handling fee, administrative and processing fee, regulatory compliance fee), generally between $100 and $395 to sellers or buyers. The fee pays for the services an employee provides to process paperwork and coordinate closing. Another add-on fee in a similar price range we're seeing more agents use is an up-front nonrefundable "listing fee" that stays with the agent even if a listing is canceled, withdrawn, or expires. These add-on fees can help, but the bottom line still is not pretty. Profit—and your net income—is still being squeezed.

Another solution is to cut costs or limit costs by unbundling your commission and negotiating limited service for a reduced fee, similar to Help U Sell's menu approach.

All the above are good, commonsense approaches. But the rainmaker's success strategy takes a fundamentally different approach and goes a step further. For rainmakers, the main solution to "shrinking margins," as the accountants call it, is to increase volume through productivity. In short, do more deals in less time. The name of the game is fitting more customers into the same business day. The result looks like what we see at the doctor's office, where managed health care has shortened patient visits.

Why does it work this way? Productivity. Why is productivity more important than activity? Volume. By assigning less costly tasks to someone else, the rainmaker is able to support an enterprise larger than a one-man band. As Ralph Roberts said in his insightful book, *Walk Like a Giant, Sell Like a Madman:* "If you don't have an assistant, you are one."

Rainmaker Strategy #4: Build a Prospect Pipeline That Eliminates Sales Cycles

One of the most fascinating recent trends in real estate has been the rise of the superagent model. It's been so effective that brokers/owners are now copying the plan as a company model. Before the 1990s, when top producers wanted more, they went out on their own and started their own agency. Today, these same folks have stayed under the broker's umbrella to create a "business within a business."

Financially, this is the best of all worlds. Practitioners build a practice based on service and systems, while the broker is stuck with the expenses of bricks and mortar, technology, and a sales force that could walk at the slightest affront. Super-agents hang their license with a brokerage company as the law requires, but run their own practice autonomously under the company's auspices.

Whether the superagent is an automated solo practitioner or a top producer with a part-time assistant or a two-person team (not uncommonly, a husband and wife team) or a larger group with several assistants, the job functions are consistent. The rainmaker puts in place a Trophy Database and marketing system to run the business. Then, the rainmaker runs the systems. That way, the rainmaker runs the business—the business doesn't run the rainmaker. When volume rises, combined job functions of technology and personal service are separated, and administrative help handles phones, computers, paperwork, and errands. The rainmaker handles the customers.

Behind this model is one central organizing principle: The role of the superagent is simply to close the client. The rainmaker's single primary focus must always be on the customer, on delivering a level of service that exceeds the client's expectations. After all, there must be only one ultimate rainmaker goal: To provide such excellent service that happy customers will tell all their friends.

A BETTER WAY

When you boil real estate sales down to its essentials, there are only three functions: marketing, listing or selling, and processing. Top-producing rainmakers have known this from the beginning. They know their core competence is listing and selling. They know what they are best at: working with a customer face to face, whether prospecting, following up, counseling, evaluating property, presenting an agreement, or negotiating a sale. The bottom line is to be in front of as many people as possible who are ready to buy or sell. Everything else, from marketing details to processing, is a distraction—and should be left to somebody else.

Picture another medical example, this time a dentist. When you call for an appointment, you don't speak to the dentist, you speak to the receptionist. The dentist doesn't greet you and sign you in; that is the assistant's job. The dentist doesn't clean your teeth; the hygienist does that and takes your X-rays. Only when you are "ready" does the dentist come in to look in your mouth and do what dentists do best: fix your teeth. When you're finished, someone else schedules your next visit. Even your computerized bill wasn't prepared by the dentist but by the bookkeeper. The computer also produces your birthday greeting and the reminder of your next appointment.

Only when a rainmaker builds a prospect pipeline and lead management system that maximize referrals and minimize client acquisition costs will the rainmaker eliminate the roller coaster cycles of market and personal sales that devastate lesser producers.

In the superagent business model, the rainmaker must concentrate personally on productive "face time" with the customer, counseling and negotiating, and leave the activity chores to staff and automation technology.

Rainmaker Strategy #5: Develop a Trophy Database

If you don't know where to start, let me share with you the central secret of your financial security. The greatest single rainmaker asset you can build is summed up in two words: Trophy Database.

In today's market, technology has made sophisticated marketing much easier. Armed with a computer database program or contact management software, today's rainmaker can easily maintain a huge collection of past customers and active prospects. This computerized gold mine is your Trophy Database.

Two significant changes have turned "farming" on its head in the new marketplace. First, prospects no longer need to be neighbors. Gone are the days of effective door knocking and block parties. In today's market, the old "sphere of influence" has become a marketing database. Prospects are now scattered all over town. They are simply a list of contacts or prospective contacts in the computer, who hopefully share one common theme: They are likely to buy or sell, or they have friends who are buying or selling soon, and consider you "Their Agent."

The second change is the phenomenal size of the databases today. No longer will 50 or 100 or 200 or 400 contacts support a practice with a goal of more than 25 transactions a year. Today, big numbers produce big results. The farm of yesterday is the agribusiness of today. Marketing is a numbers game, and a Trophy Database is the new math.

A rough formula has emerged. In today's market, rainmakers need a prospect ratio of about 25 to 1. In other words, for 1 transaction you need to market to a database of 25. If you want 10 deals, you need a database of 250. If you want 50 deals, you need about 1,250 in your customer database.

In a market where only 8% of homeowners move every year, for example, your average household turnover ratio is 1 in 12 (8%). Now double that ratio to reflect an imperfect world where a salesperson realistically expects to capture only 50% of the market share of potential prospects. The result is a sobering ratio of database prospects to transactions. To put a finer point to the reality, understand these numbers: In our example, you'll need 24 database households to close one transaction a year (i.e., 1 in 12 prospects move ÷ 50% capture = 24 prospects needed to close 1 transaction).

Insert your own turnover ratio (5%? 7%? 9%?) and capture rate (25%? 50%? 75%?) to calculate your own database-to-transaction ratio. Naturally, these are very rough figures. A higher turnover ratio among your target customers will reduce the ratio. Also, a higher capture rate or market share will further reduce the ratio. But overall, this 25 to 1 ratio works as a benchmark for establishing your own marketing goals and your Trophy Database.

Rainmaker Strategy #6: Attract Handpicked Customers with Direct-Response Marketing

Since the 1920s, a discipline has been perfected that offers a technique for today's rainmaker. That technique is direct-response marketing.

Direct response is a marketing technique designed to generate a direct response from a desired customer by making an appealing offer, often a free premium.

Direct response is the opposite of "image" or institutional advertising that is "ego-centered" or centered on the advertiser, not the customer. A classic image headline is "We're #1." Direct response is also the opposite of personal marketing, that is, centered on the individual placing the ad, not the customer. A typical personal marketing theme is "I'm the GREATEST!"

Instead, direct response requires two principles:

1. Offer something of value . . .
2. . . . that only your target customer would respond to get.

One of my favorite examples is a sweepstakes that has been used by several brokers around the country to generate leads. One "successful" promotion was called "April in Paris" because the prize was a week for two in Paris. All consumers had to do to enter was drop by one of the company's open houses.

Some 7,000 people flocked to the open houses to register. Sellers were impressed. Agents were inundated. Visitors' names, addresses, and phone numbers were amazingly more accurate than usual.

When the promotion was finished, the broker rubbed his hands together over his pile of entry cards. "Oh boy, oh boy, oh boy," he said. "Now I've got hundreds of leads." Wrong. What he had was a pile of travel lovers.

The broker had met the First Rule of Direct Response: Offer something of value. Sure enough, lots of folks loved the idea of a free trip to Paris. But the broker broke the Second Rule of Direct Response: Offer something only your target customer would respond to get. A week in Paris had nothing to do with buying or selling a home. The broker wasted his money because he did not meet both rules of direct response.

Simply by focusing on the customer's needs, you can easily develop offers and premiums that turn your promotions into a stream of true prospects. If the broker in our example had made the prize a "Curb Appeal Home Front Makeover" (what sellers need) or a "New-House to Dream-House Decorating Allowance" (what buyers want), then the company would have had a pile of prospective sellers and buyers, despite no purchase being necessary to enter.

FISH UPSTREAM BY GIVING YOUR ADVERTISING UNIVERSAL APPEAL

When all is said and done, the greatest challenge for a rainmaker is to win the war for the customer by being first to identify the customer and first to build rapport. The secret is to attract self-selecting prospects early in their decision cycle, when they are still information seekers. Marketers call this "fishing upstream" to reach customers *before* the competition. Once prospects have turned into active shoppers and begun to respond to property advertising, often it's too late.

Test this for yourself. Apply the proven rainmaker technique that advertises solutions to problems rather than product descriptions. The reason the technique works so well is because solutions are universal, whereas products (homes for sale) appeal only to a small number of potential shoppers interested in that price or style or location.

Remember our earlier exercise, where you turned to the classified section of your newspaper where houses for sale are listed. Most of the ads were wasted on you because you have no specific interest. Now add this phrase to each of the ads: "Call for Free Report to Avoid the 10 Greatest Home Buyer Mistakes." Things have changed. Presto, all of the ads are appealing. Now there is a reason to call every phone number. The point is a customer-centered offer appeals to ALL prospects with universally needed solutions to their problems. Direct-response marketing allows you to open your intake funnel wider and pour more prospects into your pipeline.

Rainmaker Strategy #7: Use Your Knowledge to Convert Prospects to Customers

When you couple your knowledge with an automated Trophy Database and rainmaker direct-response marketing, you have combined the three tools essential to the *Real Estate Rainmaker* system: knowledge, Trophy Database, and direct marketing.

Your expertise, knowledge, and experience allow you to consult, educate, and advise your new customers. Just as important, these are exactly the qualities past customers appreciate most. Your knowledge is why they say "Thank you" every time they send you a referral. You gave your knowledge, now they are sending you reciprocal referrals in return for a job well done. The *Real Estate Rainmaker* system teaches it is this simple, central, single concept of knowledge that attracts new customers and compels past clients to refer their friends. It is not personal image, not property advertising, not production awards or designations. Your knowledge is one of your greatest business assets.

Knowledge has another magic quality that attracts prospects like bears to honey. Prospects in their early stages—before they become active shoppers working with an agent—are most attracted to a nonthreatening offer of information. Prospects want to be educated and informed to ensure they make a sound decision. That's why customer-focused solutions and consultation are positively perceived as helpful service. It's why "process information" is a more compelling offer early in the customer's buying or selling cycle than product information, which is often negatively perceived as self-serving.

In fact, the more valuable the information you offer, the more reassured prospects are that you sincerely want to help them. This trust opens wide the door to invaluable rapport that wins the customer—and ultimately, a steady stream of referrals from a happy client for life.

Rainmaker Strategy #8: Practice the Three Sales Secrets Successful Salespeople Hide

Ever wonder why prospect follow-up creates a target-rich environment? The following excerpt comes from the eye-opening book *Managing Sales Leads: How to Turn Every Prospect into a Customer* by Bob Donath, Carolyn K. Dixon, Richard A. Crocker, and James W. Obermayer (NTC Business Books, 1996), and is reprinted with permission. The authors are masters of their subject. Bob Donath is a marketing consultant based in White Plains, New York, and the other authors are executives at Inquiry Handling Service, Inc., in San Fernando, California, a company that processes more than two million sales inquiries a year as an outsource service bureau for large corporate clients.

Three Sales Secrets That Successful Salespeople Hide

SECRET #1

The Rule of 45 says that 45% of all leads turn into a sale for someone.

Within one year, 45% of all the leads you receive will turn into a sale for you or your competitor. Of the leads, 22% to 25% will convert within the first six months.

Marketing research studies have proven this for more than 20 years. Nevertheless, only 10% to 15% of top salespeople admit (usually in whispers) that there is a predictable closing ratio for sales leads. This could be because many salespeople are skeptical of marketing research or because the salesperson hides the facts from the green recruit.

Many salespeople know about the Rule of 45 because so many of them say that half of the sales leads they get are not good. They're right—half are no good. But the up side is that half do turn into a sale. It's up to you to determine which half of the sales leads are good, and which half won't be buying.

If you get 50 sales leads a month, there is a potential for you to make 23 sales (within the coming year). If there are 10, you can make four to five sales. If you don't make the sale, someone else will.

Once you know the Rule of 45 and that nearly half of all sales leads turn into a sale for someone, you understand that the someone can be you. But to make the Rule of 45 work for you, you have to know Secret #2.

SECRET #2

Great salespeople follow up every sales lead, until the prospect buys or dies.

Great salespeople don't give up. They call and call until the prospect answers. They visit, write, and follow up until the person says they bought another product or they are no longer in the market.

You must overcome the temptation to believe that only 10 percent of the leads turn into a sale. The reason some salespeople believe this is that they stop following up on most leads after the first 90 days. For them, only 10% may turn into a sale. The fact is, to get your fair share of the sales that can occur in your territory, you have to act on Secret #2.

The salespeople who don't know Secrets #1 and #2 will very often believe that if a lead doesn't turn into a sale within a month or two, they've lost the sale. They dump the lead, and go on to the newer, fresher, most recent inquiries.

Remember, everyone has a different schedule for buying a product. For some, it is a comparatively short time; for others it takes months, a year, or longer. If you get a lead that is a few months old, there is still an 80% chance the buyer hasn't made a decision yet.

When the lead is six months old, there is a 50% chance that the decision is still pending. At nine months, you have a 25% chance to make the sale. Some documented facts:

- 76% of the people who inquire intend to buy.
- 40% of the time the person doesn't approach your competitor.
- More than 50% of the sales leads are not followed up. Some research indicates the number could be as high as 87.5%.

True, as leads age, some begin to fall into the sold category, but the most interesting fact of all is that there is less and less competition for the sale for those prospects who are taking time to make their decisions.

Follow-up for many salespeople is weak initially, and almost non-existent as time goes by. To be in a less and less competitive position, don't give up simply because the person hasn't bought in the first few months. Take courage from the fact that as time goes by, the less disciplined salespeople will stop calling on the prospect.

The person with the discipline to have a follow-up system for their prospects will win more often than they lose. *The odds are always with the salesperson who continues to work the prospect when others give up.*

Which brings us to Secret #3.

SECRET #3

The older the sales lead, the less the competition.

These three secrets seem almost too simple, too easy to be true. Plus, you've probably noticed that if you believe in them, you needn't be the glibbest, slickest salesperson in your outfit. But you do have to be the most persistent.

In organizations where you are overwhelmed with sales leads (more than 30 to 50 a month), you can probably live off the sales leads that convert if you follow up each lead. If you only get 5 to 10 leads a month, then your sales leads can provide the core of your business; referrals, cold calls, and so on, will still be a part of your routine (although a much smaller part than if you had no leads).

Regardless, whether you work directly for a company, or whether you're a dealer or a distributor, if you get sales leads, use the three secrets that the best salespeople in the business hide and you too will be in the top 10% of your sales force.

Once again, here are the three secrets:

1. The Rule of 45 says that 45% of all leads turn into a sale for someone.

2. Great salespeople follow up every sales lead until the prospect buys or dies.

3. The older the sales lead, the less the competition.

Rainmaker Strategy #9: Measure Your Progress by the "Holiday Litmus Test"

The true test of a rainmaker is for you to take time off. Ask yourself: "If I took a holiday, would the business carry on without me?" Often in the beginning, the answer is no, even if the holiday is only one day. Gradually, as you build a system and an organization that carries on while you are gone, you will be able to take a day here and a week there, then a month, then several months throughout the year. Ultimately, you will have a practice that almost runs on autopilot without you—just the kind of practice someone else could step into and take over.

A holiday is the litmus test that exposes the difference between a "job" and a "practice." You work at a job. You work *on* a practice. To get out of town, you must be able to turn off your personal prospect appointments while the marketing and processing continues without you. If you can't take a holiday, then you don't have a practice, you have a job. Behind every rainmaker's valuable six-figure practice is an autopilot marketing and processing system.

HOW TO KEEP CATCHING THE BIG ONES

The challenge for rainmakers is to keep their pipeline full of prospects. To do this, we must systematically pour prospects into the "prospect pipeline" to have customers steadily come out the other end. By the time the customers stick their heads up and say "We're ready!", ideally the prospect pipeline will have conditioned them to be presold on our services.

The *3-Step Rainmaker Lead System* is the pipeline. In fact, this pipeline is a watertight system designed to be a circle, never ending, always moving customers along, forever producing

Figure 2.1
Closed-Loop 3-Step Rainmaker Lead System

3-STEP RAINMAKER LEAD SYSTEM®

referrals and repeat business. Customers are never turned loose. Rainmakers constantly keep in touch through their Trophy Database and keep the customer within their sphere so that they control the customer. The endless *Rainmaker Lead System* is as close as we come in marketing to a perpetual motion machine.

Here are the three simple steps (see Figure 2.1):

1. Create customers with lead generation.
2. Capture customers with prospect follow-up.
3. Keep customers with long-term contact.

COMPLETE LEAD MANAGEMENT

The beauty of the *3-Step Rainmaker Lead System* is its holistic approach and comprehensive treatment of the natural prospect-customer-prospect cycle. By utilizing the circular pipeline of lead generation, prospect follow-up, and long-term contact, the **Real Estate Rainmaker** technique will consistently build your business and grow your practice with an endless stream of prospects. More prospects mean more sales. And getting more prospects begins with lead generation, our next chapter.

RAINMAKER CHAPTER 2 SUMMARY

A Better Way: All You Do Is Close

▶ Rainmaker Strategy #1: Concentrate on Marketing, Sales Will Follow.

▶ Rainmaker Strategy #2: Make Your Relationship with Customers Job One.

▶ Rainmaker Strategy #3: Beat the Profit Squeeze with Productivity.

▶ Rainmaker Strategy #4: Build a Prospect Pipeline That Eliminates Sales Cycles.

▶ Rainmaker Strategy #5: Develop a Trophy Database.

▶ Rainmaker Strategy #6: Attract Handpicked Customers with Direct-Response Marketing.

▶ Rainmaker Strategy #7: Use Your Knowledge to Convert Prospects to Customers.

▶ Rainmaker Strategy #8: Practice the Three Sales Secrets Successful Salespeople Hide.

▶ Rainmaker Strategy #9: Measure Your Progress by the "Holiday Litmus Test."

TWO

STEP 1: CREATE CUSTOMERS WITH LEAD GENERATION

Media Strategies to Win in Any Market

> Half the money I
> spend on advertising
> is wasted,
> and the trouble is
> I don't know
> which half.
>
> John Wanamaker
> (1838–1922),
> Philadelphia
> department store
> magnate

Understanding the Direct-Response Lead Generation System

Consumer-direct marketing is a strategic system, not a tactic, incorporating the disciplines of media, offers, and creative. The success of a direct-response system depends on the 40-40-20 Rule, developed years ago by one of the deans of direct marketing, Ed Mayer. The rule simply recognizes success or failure of a direct-response effort depends 40% on the media, 40% on the offer, and 20% on copy and creative design.

In practice, this immutable law shifts in proportion when more powerful offers or expensive creative are needed to cut through a fog of competitors' commercials or entertainment programming. Yet, the fundamental secret to success for a direct-response lead generation system rests on these three pillars.

Thus, the next three chapters will explore the three strategic sections: media, offers, and creative. Each strategic section includes essential secrets rainmakers must know, as well as some costly mistakes to avoid.

Four Fundamental Truths of Customer-Direct Marketing

Customers come to you. With direct-response marketing, customers come to you instead of your pursuing them with intrusive telemarketing or expensive image advertising or self-focused personal marketing. *They* initiate the response. Their response translates into more qualified leads, higher conversion rates, lower costs, and greater lifetime value for a rainmaker.

You can measure and test. With conventional (traditional) advertising, you never know how successful it is. Direct response, however, deals only in "results." Only direct response allows you to accurately measure your cost per lead, cost per appointment, and cost per closed transaction. You know exactly what works and what doesn't. This fact allows you to get maximum return on every dollar.

You can out-market the competition. While your competition is breaking the bank running property ads and ego advertising— spending two or three times more than you do—you'll be making direct and measurable sales, allowing you to analyze and track your results and spend less on marketing that produces more results.

Direct response boosts your other media. Direct response can stand alone, but one great advantage of direct response is that it's easily inserted into all your marketing to maximize results from all the other media you use. Prospects are far more likely to respond favorably to a mailing, for example, if you've already made them aware of you with other media, such as newspapers, home magazines, the Internet, yard signs, open houses, radio, or cable TV. With its helpful customer focus, direct response sets the tone for all your integrated rainmaker promotions (see Table 3.1). Campaigns can be as simple as a postcard, a message left on voice mail, or a two-line classified ad.

Table 3.1
Five More Reasons Why Direct Response Works for Rainmakers

1. Direct response presells prospects by presenting you as the credible expert.
2. Direct response produces leads from cold market strangers as well as referrals from warm past customers.
3. Direct response allows you to control your schedule, set up appointments when you want, and spend more time with your family.
4. Direct response creates an endless marketing plan for growth in good markets and bad.
5. Direct response builds a pipeline of prospects that want to buy or sell in the future.

Maximize Your Media Pie

Lead generation begins with mass media. Imagine a pie. Your prospects can be identified by the different slices of the media pie they use. Some people respond to direct mail. Another audience slice responds to print advertising, newspapers, and magazines. There is another slice that responds to the radio, TV, and cable. Other people respond to yard signs and outdoor advertising. Still another group—and this group tends to be in the most active home-buying years, between 30 and 45—responds on the Internet.

To maximize your pieces of the pie, you need to be generating leads from as many media slices as possible.

Which media work effectively to generate leads? Just about all of them. The best answer comes from asking recent home sellers, repeat home buyers, and first-time buyers themselves, according to the NAR's study, *Home Buying and Selling Process.* Table 3.2 contains the combined results from two parallel questions: "What advertising media helped you make the first contact with the real estate agent you used?" and "What best describes how you were referred to or came into contact with the real estate agent you selected?"

Table 3.2
What Advertising Media or Referral Source Helped You Make the First Contact with the Real Estate Agent You Used?

Media/Referral Source	Sellers	Repeat Buyers	First-Time Buyers
Advertising/Marketing			
Visited open house and met agent	7%	8%	7%
Personal contact by agent (telephone, etc.)	6	6	3
For sale sign/brochure box	6	6	7
Newspaper ad	5	6	9
Walked into office and agent was on duty	4	4	3
Home magazine/book ad	3	3	4
Met agent through builder's model home	3	2	2
Internet/online/website	2	1	1
Yellow pages ad	1	4	2
Direct mail (newsletter, flyer, letter)	0	1	0
Seminar about home buying/selling	0	0	2
Subtotal	**37%**	**41%**	**40%**
Repeat			
Used agent previously to buy or sell a home	12%	11%	0%
Subtotal	**12%**	**11%**	**0%**
Referral			
Agent is a friend, neighbor, or relative	19%	18%	25%
Referred through my employer/relocation company	9	8	2
Referred by a friend	9	10	17
Referred through another real estate broker	7	7	4
Reputation of real estate agent	6	6	6
Referred through my membership organization	1	1	1
Referred by mortgage lender	0	0	2
Subtotal	**51%**	**50%**	**57%**
TOTAL	**100%**	**102%***	**97%***

*Column does not equal 100 due to rounding.
Source: National Association of REALTORS®

Seven Rainmaker Secrets to Successful Media Strategies

Strategy #1: Develop a Trophy Database

The first commandment behind every successful rainmaker system is the central idea toward which every activity is directed and, ultimately, upon which rests the value of your practice. This critical concept is your Trophy Database.

Prospects will respond by phone, fax, mail, over the Internet, or they may even walk in or attend a seminar you sponsor. However they come to you, you must have a rain barrel, a Trophy Database, to put them into. This is your retirement fund. When somebody buys your business, they're going to buy this rain barrel, your database of future business. Every prospect goes into the database.

As your database grows by leaps and bounds, it will become your most important asset for prospect follow-up and long-term contact, as well as market-stranger lead generation. It will be your single greatest source of target customers and prospects. Build it. Use it. Clean it. Expand it. Invest in it. Treat it for what it is—your biggest bank account in your plan for financial independence.

Your Trophy Database will also become your "downturn insurance policy" in a tough market. No other medium is as efficient at generating qualified leads and referrals and converting prospects. When tough times come, your Trophy Database will allow you to target your marketing like a rifle shot, not waste it on shotgun mass marketing.

Also, direct mail and telemarketing using your database are the most flexible budget economizers. Because the cost of direct marketing relates to the number of pieces you send or calls you make, you are in complete control of your investment. That control allows you to trim or boost your direct marketing expenses. More details on developing your Trophy Database are in Chapter 16.

Strategy #2: Generate a Deluge of Wholesale Leads

In a nutshell, the strategy of wholesale leads means integrating your advertising so every medium boosts response from all other media. In marketing, we call this "cross-media advertising" or "synergy": direct mail, newspapers, magazines, radio/TV, the Internet, signs, word-of-mouth, all work better when they work together. Your goal is to generate more leads than you can handle. Then, work with the best and sell the rest over time, or refer them to other agents as top real estate trainer Pat Zaby suggests.

Because different media attract different prospects, the rainmaker needs to use as many media as possible to generate wholesale leads. Mass media stimulates prospects to act like a lightning bolt in a storm cloud. Some miss the cloud all together; other prospects see it but do nothing about it because no advertising can persuade someone to buy who isn't ready. Your job as rainmaker is to be there like a lightning rod to attract the prospect when the prospect is charged and ready to strike.

Remember, your role is marketwide. Think mass media. Think sophisticated technology. Think more prospects than you can work. Think wholesale leads.

Strategy #3: Capture Calls with Telephone Hotlines

Hotlines or 800-number call-capture systems have been around, but today's technology makes them even more powerful. Hotlines work like this: An ad is placed, say, in a home magazine. The ad contains an ID number. When customers call, they are prompted to enter the ID number on the touch pad and listen to a recording about a property or a free report offer. The technology captures the caller ID as often as possible. (Because 800 and 888 toll-free calls are technically a collect call, caller ID cannot be blocked as can calls to regular numbers.) The number is matched against a database to get the name and address of the number's owner when published, typically successful on 30% to

60% of the numbers. Then you enter the prospect into your *Rainmaker Lead System* for follow-up, ideally after talking to the caller.

You can either rent the technology (activation fee, monthly service fee, and per-minute billing) or you can buy the machine from SoftKlone™ based in Tallahassee, Florida (see Resource Guide under Hotlines). Either way, the technology has several benefits:

- Exposes listings and response offers hands-free, 24 hours a day, 7 days a week. (Sellers love this.)
- Captures caller identification and property/price interests of prospect.
- Tracks advertising results by media and specific advertisements to control costs.
- Impresses prospects with immediate automated response through optional voice mail (messages), fax back (reports, highlight sheets), and pager notification capability.
- Replaces recorded property information with direct response offer script of free report for universal appeal.

Walter Sanford, a top producer in Long Beach, California, and a real estate speaker, teaches this impressive demonstration to listing prospects of a hotline system. Before going on a listing appointment, Sanford's assistant creates a brief property profile sheet and stores it in his call-capture system. During the presentation in front of the sellers, Sanford records a brief voice description of the prospect's house on the system using his cellular flip phone. He then plugs a fax machine into the owner's phone jack and calls the hotline from another extension in the house. Walter punches into the hotline system a fax-on-demand request for a property profile sheet using the seller's phone number connected to his fax machine. No sooner does he hang up than the fax rings and prints the seller's profile sheet. Within moments, Sanford's beeper goes off displaying the homeowner's phone number to demonstrate how his system captures all buyer calls to his listings. He then closes, saying if the sellers would like this technology working for them, all they need to do is sign the listing form. Need a pen?

Using a hotline call-capture system is a proven media strategy for successful rainmakers.

Strategy #4: Turn a Flood of Hits into Live Prospects on the Internet

Few people ever click their mouse and buy a house sight unseen, but they are clicking their mouse to shop for information early in their search. Today, rainmakers are on the Internet with websites and e-mail because it is a basic tool of business, just like the fax and computer. Not being on the Internet puts you out of the loop, like not having a telephone or not getting mail.

In the cyber age, the three commodities of information, knowledge, and wisdom have become salable products. Customers demand information. But the flood of information is so great they are quickly overwhelmed. The opportunity for the rainmaker is to know what information they want most, swamp them with more information than they can manage, then help them sort through it to select the important information for their specific situation.

Trying to deny customers information, like leaving the price or address out of ads, is self-defeating. Withholding information today simply drives customers to competitors who are happy to supply the information. The old fear goes like this: "If we tell customers everything, then they won't need us." The reality is few customers have the time to make themselves so expert in a field they can replace a specialist. All they want is a level of information high enough to make them comfortable making key decisions along the purchase path. Then they can leave the guiding to the guide.

Three fascinating trends on the Internet have emerged from Gooder Group's analysis of over 3,000 prospect inquiries to subscribers through our Leads Online link, which is part of our Rainmaker E-Leads program.

The Internet generates mostly local leads. Most Internet prospects are local, not long distance. When we compared the zip code of the prospect to the zip code of our subscriber, this is what we discovered about Internet prospects:

- 63% live inside the area and are moving inside the area (local move).
- 22% live outside the area and are moving to the area (in-bound relocation, domestic).
- 10% live outside the area and are moving to another area (point-to-point referral opportunity).
- 2% live inside the area and are moving outside the area (out-bound relocation).
- 2% live outside the country and are moving to the area (in-bound relocation, international).
- 1% live outside the country and are moving to another area (point-to-point, international).

Internet prospects have not yet called the competition. Three out of four Internet prospects say they are not working with an agent. This is a tremendous opportunity for rainmakers to use follow-up to convert an early information-seeking prospect into a customer and eliminate the competition. Here are the results to our question, "Are you currently working with a real estate agent?"

- 75% no.
- 25% yes.

Internet prospects, whether owners or renters, are first shopping to buy. Third, we discovered Internet prospects are so early in their information-seeking "search channel" because they are initially looking to see what is out there to buy. Although you might expect homeowners to say they are primarily interested in selling, even owners say they are interested in buying first. In our study, 51% were renters and 49% owners. When asked, "Which of the following are you interested in?" they responded:

- 65% want to buy.
- 15% want to sell.
- 14% want to relocate.
- 6% want to rent.

The Internet is a unique communication media that all rainmakers must add to their mix—or risk missing out on the fast-growing population of Internet prospects. Here are two quick e-marketing checklists, one with Internet and website tips, and one with e-mail tips.

Quick Checklist on How to Make Money with the Internet

☑ Become a student of the Internet. Go online. Visit agent and industry websites. Attend seminars. Talk to other rainmakers. Read. Grow with the Internet as it grows.

☑ Register your own domain (yourname.com). This gives you a permanent Internet address that won't change if you change companies, cities, or Internet service providers. Register your domain online with Internic: www.rs.internic.net/cgi-bin/whois.

☑ Establish your own website. Use the site both for direct response and as your home office on the Internet. Take care to keep the site customer-centered, not ego-oriented. Use the word "you" often and edit all content by the "What's in It for Me?" consumer-interest test. Provide informative content buyers and sellers want and need.

☑ Link your website to as many property portal sites as you can by including your Internet address (Universal Resource Locator or URL) in your property listing information. Your goal is to generate maximum prospect traffic locally, nationwide, even worldwide. Portals include www.REALTOR.com, www.homes.com, www.homeadvisor.com, www.citynet.home-seekers.com, www.homescout.com, www.cyberhomes.com, to name a few.

☑ In your home page title, clearly state Your Company Name/ Your City/State/Country/Real Estate using up to 64 characters including spaces, because all search engines search page titles, whereas some don't use META tags or keywords.

☑ Advertise your Internet address locally on everything from business cards to classifieds to home magazines to direct mail to yard signs, even on your vanity license plates and lapel badge. Your goal is to generate local prospect Internet traffic to your website.

☑ Build your Internet farm e-mail database. Every Trophy Database must include e-mail addresses of contacts, prospects, customers, and referral sources, as well as postal addresses and phone numbers. Use response forms and have an e-mail link on every web page.

☑ Produce virtual tours of your listings and post them on your website. Using a digital camera, plus photo arranging and enhancing software, such as PhotoShare and Picture-Works, create a direct-response reason for prospects to visit your site. Consider giving your buyers the website after the sale to show their friends the new home.

☑ Enrich your website with direct-response content links. Use universal offers that appeal to ALL prospects to maximize response from your site, rather than depicting specific properties that appeal to relatively few prospects. Make the site content rich. Content is what brings people back to the site and makes them recommend it to others.

☑ Launch a follow-up system to qualify and capture virtual e-mail leads and convert them into live prospects for more business.

Allen F. Hainge, a leading technology trainer and Residential Sales Council instructor, believes e-mail is the best and most effective marketing tool the real estate industry has ever seen. Here are his tips for e-mail:

Quick Checklist on How to Make Money with E-Mail

☑ Get e-mail from an ISP. Using an Internet Service Provider (ISP) gives you strongest business features compared to an online service, which is oriented toward personal e-mail. With an ISP, you are less likely to experience problems with attachments, mailboxes, or filters. Plus, you don't lose the flexibility of responding to a prospect on Internet Explorer and Netscape Mail, which increases your confidence anything you send is received by the recipient.

☑ Manage and track your e-mail using mailboxes. By assigning different e-mail addresses or mailboxes to your promotions, you can track your media and sales. Set a separate folder to receive mail, not the "inbox," by using a predefined subject line or a specific e-mailbox such as *buyers@yourdomain.com* or *sellers@yourdomain.com* or transaction *smith's@yourdomain.com*. Count messages for media tracking, then cut and paste messages to save them in the correct client record.

☑ Check your e-mail four times a day, at least. Hainge says the most common comment he receives about e-mail is agents telling him they got the business either because they responded to the prospect right away, or they were the only agents who responded to the prospect at all.

☑ Install an auto responder e-mail system. You will be able to provide WOW! customer service completely hands-off while prospects are still online. Set your e-mail software to send back a generic message within seconds that says, "Thank you for your e-mail. We'll be responding to you shortly."

☑ Structure response forms to match customer record fields. Hire the techie who does your website to create e-mail response forms that organize prospects' data so it easily populates a customer record in your database without having to rekeystroke all the information.

☑ Learn to do attachments. Attachments such as photos, scanned documents, or multimedia presentations created with PhotoShare will add money-making pizzazz to your e-mail.

☑ Use a signature. Create it once, store it, and one click adds it to each message you write. It should have five lines: (1) name and designations; (2) company, city, state; (3) postal address, web address; (4) e-mail address, 800 number, other phone numbers; (5) line of PR stating what services you offer. Include in your signature a direct-response offer and hotlink to your website.

☑ Include only part of the original e-mail message in your reply. Do not forward the whole message or list of previous cc: recipients. Simply cut and paste a line or two of text, just enough to remind recipients of the gist of their previous message.

☑ Learn to use blind carbon copy. When you send messages to a group of people, using blind carbon copy (bcc:) will suppress all the other addresses, which is good for privacy and reader convenience.

Strategy #5: Change Delivery Mix to Test Media

Change the delivery of an offer by mixing the media and the timing of a campaign. For example, one campaign may entail four to six weeks of continuous radio play complemented by direct-response newspaper ads featuring a toll-free 800 number to call. A later campaign could include four to six weeks of full-page home magazine ads complemented by two direct-mail drops in weeks three and six using a reprint of the magazine ad. Experience will show how to best deliver your message to the target prospects. The rainmaker's goal is to seek new ways to reduce delivery cost and increase response.

Strategy #6: Play the Media Markets

During certain seasons, some media are more expensive than others. Before Christmas, TV and radio are more costly because retailer demand bids the cost up; however, during the first three months of the year, broadcast prices are often lower. With print media, lower rates can be earned with extensive use or multiple insertions. This is particularly true with newspapers. When using direct mail, the post office charges 29–44% less for standard presorted bulk mail than for first class. Further automation savings of 45%–58% off are possible if addresses are bar coded and sorted by zip code or carrier route. Taking advantage of any media savings will help reduce costs.

Strategy #7: Use Different Media for Different Objectives

The potential for a direct-response offer is different from one medium to the next. Matching the rainmaker's objectives and the offer to the appropriate medium can significantly increase the offer's results and lower the cost.

- *Direct mail.* Traditionally, mail is the strongest direct-response medium. It is excellent for real estate prospecting because it's easy to target renters and owners, and reply coupons are a natural—plus, it's rejection-free. What makes direct mail the supreme direct-response medium for real estate is the powerful marriage of the essence of the medium and the industry: a home address. There is no more powerful, more direct medium than direct mail for rainmakers. For example, say you want to generate first-time home buyers. Buy a list of non-owner-occupied properties in your area from a list broker such as First American Real Estate Solutions, Database America, DataQuick, or your title company. Bingo. Every renter on the list is a prime prospect. No medium reaches them as directly as direct mail. Another simple starter list is homeowners who hold a garage sale. They are an ideal target to generate listings. Collect the addresses from the newspaper classifieds and mail to the owner.

- *Newspaper.* Coupons and inserts can be very effective. Newspapers reach a wide spectrum of readers, and different sections permit effective targeting of prospects.

- *Magazine.* Coupons, tip-in reply cards, and inserts all are effective ways of reaching prospects. Home magazines are very effective at reaching interested buyers, because prospects seek out the free magazine.

- *Electronic media.* Television is the most expensive but most powerful, reaching huge audiences in an extensive area. Cable TV, with its specifically targeted subscribers, is often a more affordable value. Radio is generally more cost-effective, and mobile phones are fast overcoming the difficulty of getting listeners in their car to respond. One alternative to 60-second ads is to become a business-radio personality and buy your own one- to two-hour infomercial time slot with a talk-show format. The Internet is also electronic, although it is a unique blend of communication tool (like the telephone and fax) and advertising medium (like TV and radio). As the Internet penetrates more households, e-mail has emerged as a direct-response tool, especially for cyber-savvy prospects that prefer e-mail.

- *Outdoor advertising.* Yard signs work well. Don't forget brochure boxes, and always use the reverse side of every highlight sheet to feature response offers and other listings. Billboards are designed primarily for awareness, not direct response.

Costly Media Mistakes to Avoid

Mistake #1: Failing to Integrate All Your Marketing

Response advertising works at many levels, from mass marketing to one-to-one. No single part will produce results as well as a whole, coordinated campaign.

Solution: Plan ahead to coordinate mass media, premiums, follow-up, tracking, and staff training into a single profitable effort.

Mistake #2: Timing Your Offers to Mirror the Market

Response advertising must be valued by prospects to produce results. If a campaign is too late or too far ahead of a market's timing, the resulting response will suffer.

Solution: Schedule campaigns to break about four to six weeks prior to the time you want to begin generating results. Determine the market's peak periods, and advertise several weeks in advance.

Mistake #3: Failing to Test Your Lists

If your advertising isn't getting through to the right people, the greatest offer in the world and the most fabulous creative design won't make it rain prospects.

Solution: If you can afford to test only one thing (media, offer, or creative), test the media. A great direct mail list, for example, will make a good offer better. But a great offer can't help a bad list.

Quick Checklist on Where to Place
Advertising in Direct-Response Media

☑ Replace one or more property ad boxes in a HOME MAGA-ZINE ad with an offer for free reports.

☑ Add a sentence to your CLASSIFIEDS, or run a separate ad: "Buyers Handbooks available, just call." In open house ads: "Stop by for a FREE financing brochure on 17 ways to increase your buying power."

☑ Put COUPONS in farming mailings, local coupon packs, or on door hangers. Postage-paid business reply on the back will increase response.

☑ Include an offer for brochures or handbooks in MAILINGS to your farm areas.

☑ Use SIGNS—billboards, yard sign riders, directional signs— to offer special reports.

☑ Turn the back of every PROPERTY HIGHLIGHT SHEET into a direct-response ad with an offer for a free report or video or invitation to a buyer or seller seminar.

☑ Send a PRESS RELEASE to your local newspaper. A special report available free to consumers is newsworthy. Ask readers to enclose a self-addressed stamped envelope.

☑ Include buyer brochures, *Homebuyers Handbook* or *Relocation Handbook* as a part of your RELOCATION KIT.

☑ Turn FLOOR TIME into opportunity time: *"I'll be out that way tomorrow. Is 2 o'clock a good time to bring by your copy of our Homesellers Handbook?"*

☑ Run RADIO spots with an offer to call for a free report.

☑ Include an offer for brochures or handbooks in your showcase TELEVISION SHOW. Be sure to make your phone number prominent throughout the commercial.

☑ Attract buyers and sellers to SEMINARS by offering free handbooks and brochures as handouts.

☑ Print a certificate on the back of your BUSINESS CARDS: "Save This Card. Good for Free Homebuyers, Homesellers, or Relocation Handbook."

☑ Close appointments for LISTING PRESENTATIONS by offering to drop by with your brochure or handbook for sellers.

☑ Offer Relocation Handbook and relocation services in a LETTER TO NEW LISTINGS to generate buyer leads.

RAINMAKER CHAPTER 3 SUMMARY

Media Strategies to Win in Any Market

► Strategy #1: Develop a Trophy Database.

► Strategy #2: Generate a Deluge of Wholesale Leads.

► Strategy #3: Capture Calls with Telephone Hotlines.

► Strategy #4: Turn a Flood of Hits into Live Prospects on the Internet.

► Strategy #5: Change Delivery Mix to Test Media.

► Strategy #6: Play the Media Markets.

► Strategy #7: Use Different Media for Different Objectives.

Offer Strategies That Attract Prospects Like a Magnet

> Nothing is more profitable than the right offer powerfully stated to the right person at the right time.
>
> Gary Kauffman
> *2,239 Tested Secrets for Direct Marketing Success*

Although they may not know it, real estate professionals have a long tradition of using "response advertising." Traditional property advertising is response advertising. Unfortunately, in today's competitive marketplace, property advertising has as many disadvantages as advantages. This chapter is designed to go beyond traditional response advertising and share some advanced techniques to increase results with more effective consumer-direct marketing offers.

The secret to successful response advertising is to develop an offer that makes the phone ring. Prospects don't care about you as much as they care about how you can help them. They want to know "What's in it for me?" or, as it's abbreviated, WIIFM. The essence of direct response is to show your prospects how your offer will make them richer, smarter, happier when they sell or settle into their new home after using your services.

Nine Rainmaker Strategies to Increase Results with Response Offers

Strategy #1: Handpick the Customers You Want

By picking your response offer, you can pick your customer. Customers call to get a copy of a report that intrigues them. For example, only prospects interested in beach houses want a special report titled "9 Ways to Avoid Getting Burned When You Buy Waterfront Property."

Direct-response offers give you the power to pick your customer by picking your offer. You're in control. Want first-time buyers? Want FSBOs? Want expireds? Want move-up sellers? What about empty-nesters, retirees, or seniors? People divorcing? Second-home buyers? New home buyers? You name it. With direct response, you can easily target only the type of customer you want.

Strategy #2: Focus on the Customer's Problems

The power of direct-response marketing is the power of focusing on the customer, not on yourself or on your production or on your company. What are their problems, worries, fears, concerns? What keeps them up at night? What do customers want? To get the answers, my company, Gooder Group, sponsored several questions on the NAR's national survey of home buying and selling. Table 4.1 summarizes how sellers answered.

Home sellers were even more specific about what services they most wanted from their listing agent. Table 4.2 shows how they answered another Gooder Group–sponsored question.

Home buyers were equally clear what services they most wanted. Table 4.3 shows their responses.

Strategy #3: Translate Your Solutions into Offers

One of the most effective techniques for developing an offer is to listen to what prospects ask when they call you. What is on their

Table 4.1
What Was Your One Biggest Worry before Putting Your Home on the Market for Sale? (Check only one)

Biggest Worries	Sellers
Getting enough money to recover what I put into the house	17%
Hassle of keeping home in constant showcase condition	14
Closing on time to meet my relocation deadline date	11
Selling in time to buy the house I want before it sells to someone else	11
Avoiding the need for temporary housing and a second move	8
Finding an effective, trustworthy real estate agent	7
Accepting contract from buyer whose financing falls through	6
Emotional strain of uprooting and moving all my things	5
Hassle and time involved in fixing up to sell	5
Inspection revealing need for costly repair	5
Physical chore of boxing and moving everything	5
Cost of fix-ups to get ready to sell	2
Coping with trauma my kids will experience in a move	2
TOTAL	**98%***

*Total does not equal 100 due to rounding.
Source: National Association of REALTORS®

Table 4.2
Before You Put Your House on the Market, What Did You Most Want Your Agent to Do for You? (Check only one)

Most Wanted Service	Sellers
Help find a buyer for your house	30%
Help you price it competitively	28
Help sell the house within your time frame	26
Help with negotiations and dealing with buyers	6
Tell you how to fix up your home to help it sell for more	5
Help with paperwork, inspections, and getting ready for settlement	4
Help you see homes available for you to buy	1
TOTAL	**100%**

Source: National Association of REALTORS®

Table 4.3
Before You Bought Your Current Home, What Did You
Most Want Your Agent to Do for You? (Select only one)

Most Wanted Service	Repeat Buyers	First-Time Buyers
Help you find the right house to purchase	62%	60%
Help with paperwork	12	9
Help with price negotiations	11	11
Tell you what comparable homes are selling for	8	5
Tell you how much house you could afford	4	8
Help find and arrange for financing	3	7
TOTAL	100%	100%

Source: National Association of REALTORS®

mind? What do they need? Their question or problem can be re-stated into an offer. In short, listen for their problems, their wants, their fears, their desires, and their interests. Figure out how to solve their problems. Then translate your solution into an offer.

Let's use an out-of-town buyer example. Imagine transferees stepping off the plane and thinking, "It's a jungle out there." Their problem is not knowing the new area. The solution to that problem is information. Your offer may be a relocation kit. It may be an area tour. It may be a special report, like the one prepared by Risa Saltman, an outstanding agent in Orlando, Florida: "20 Things You Better Know about Purchasing in Central Florida." Remember to listen to their problems and translate your solutions into your offers.

Strategy #4: Turn Your Solution into a Premium

Now, take your solution and turn it into something prospects want, something tangible, a "thing" they can get and hold. It could be a kit or brochure or video or seminar or home page. It can also be a service. It can be counseling, an area tour, a broker price opinion, loan preapproval. The only requirement is your premium offer must be something tangible. You must be able to name it in a few words and picture it in ads. Offering prospects an added-value premium is a proven marketing technique. Think how tie-in toys with Happy Meals and surprises in Cracker Jacks spur sales. Prospects respond when the premium captures their interest and motivates them to act.

- Want FSBOs? Make an offer that says, "Selling by owner? Discover six critical legal provisions every purchase contract must have. Call for free report."
- Want first-time buyers? Offer a report, "Money-Saving Secrets for First-Time Buyers."

Another example: King Thompson Realtors, a market leader in Columbus, Ohio, noticed "info only" prospects were calling to get a general sense of prices and available homes in their market. The solution was to copy their television home show on videotape and offer a free copy to prospects (see Figure 4.1).

Perhaps the longest running offer for the marketing department of Long & Foster REALTORS®, one of the nation's largest diversified megabrokerages, is a free offer for a Home Buyers or Home Sellers Guide (see Figure 4.2). The company's agents give out more than 200,000 copies to prospects every year. The booklets are so popular Long & Foster recently translated the 24-page booklets into Spanish. "The Guides are an ideal prospecting tool," says corporte advertising manager Michelle Beaubien Ball. "They're informative, work in any market, and fit easily into an envelope. They also make our office phones ring. We like that."

Seminars Make a Powerful Offer

Seminars are another opportunity. Do it in a big way and put on seminars for all buyers and sellers. Or you can target niche markets, such as first-time buyers, first-time sellers, immigrants (present seminar in their language), folks who are divorcing, seniors, or those buying second homes.

Figure 4.1
King Thompson Home Video Offer

Courtesy of King Thompson, REALTORS®, Columbus, Ohio

Marilynn Cedarstrom, an innovative relocation director for Coldwell Banker Mid-America Group in West Des Moines, Iowa, uses seminars in her corporate calling. Once Cedarstrom gets in the door to service corporate relocations, she also goes after the company's local business by putting on seminars in the lunchroom. She offers the company a choice of:

- FREE "Lunch and Learn" presentations on requested topics.
- FREE first-time home buyer seminars.

Figure 4.2
Long & Foster "Home Buyers and Home Sellers Guide" Offer

FREE
KNOWLEDGE

Call your neighborhood Long & Foster office and ask for your personal copy of our Home Buyers or Home Sellers Guide.

The Guides are full of valuable information about the home buying and selling process in today's market.

Best of all they're FREE.

Courtesy of Long & Foster Corporate Services, Fairfax, Virginia

- FREE counseling for retirees. (For this, she gathers relocation packets from resort areas.)
- FREE market analysis of present property.
- FREE information on new financing and interest rates.
- FREE relocation information on other market areas.

Typically when twenty people attend a "Lunch and Learn" seminar, Cedarstrom generates five to seven leads for the one-hour effort. Clearly, her free-lunch seminars work. Keeping the group small and informal with twenty or fewer is critical, she says, sometimes scheduling two or three seminars in a day plus an afternoon coffee for "come-backs." That way people ask personal financial questions, and Cedarstrom along with a loan officer and an agent are able to present themselves as real people with solid advice and useful information, not salespeople.

Seminars are a natural way to present yourself as "the real estate expert" in your area. Give care to create a nonsales, non-threatening atmosphere, where unbiased experts have attendees' best interests in mind. Bring lots of handouts about yourself, your company, and your services. Remember, the purpose of seminars is lead generation. Hold off the sales pitch for later during follow-up.

Do some planning. Who will come? What's the agenda? Who will present? How do you take the registration? Who does the follow-up? How do you capture the names? You'll need a whole system in place before you run your ads or send invitations. *Tip:* Schedule a first-time buyer seminar to coincide with National Homeownership Week sponsored by the National Association of REALTORS®, often in June. NHW spotlights the value home-ownership brings to the community. Your community seminar can shine in that same spotlight too.

Quick Checklist of Rainmaker Premium Offers

☑ Special free reports.

☑ Booklets.

☑ Videos.

☑ Seminars.

☑ Evaluations/critiques.

☑ Coupons/discounts.

Strategy #5: Make Your Offer Valuable

For an offer to be effective, it must promise prospects a huge self-serving reward. Yet, an offer also must be believable, not out of this world. Not "ZILLIONS of DOLLARS!!!" The successful rainmaker must strike a balance between value and believability.

Save money. First of all, make your offer worth money. Be specific and make it worth thousands or a great saving:

- "Save thousands in interest and taxes."
- "6 little-known ways to cut closing costs."
- "How amazed buyers paid $12,000 less and still got their dream home."

Save time. Another way to make your offer valuable is time. Time is even more valuable than money for some of today's time-short prospects. You've seen them: two-income families faced with selling, buying, moving, two job relocations, and kids dragging their feet.

- "Call for a free report that reveals 27 tips to sell your home in the shortest time."
- "Discover how much house you can buy with one 3-minute phone call."
- "One call does it all."

Avoid problems. You can also save people hassles and help them avoid making costly mistakes. Ask them, "How much would it cost you . . .

- ". . . if you were not able to move?"
- ". . . if you couldn't take on the job?"

- ". . . if you couldn't sell?"
- ". . . if you had to own two houses and pay two mortgages at once?"
- ". . . if you had to make a double move?"
- ". . . if you missed a buyer by overpricing?"

Learn revealed mysteries. For some prospects, discovering insider secrets and becoming savvy consumers is a compelling offer:

- "New report reveals how to avoid the trauma your kids experience when you move."
- "Cool inside tips for home buyers in today's hot real estate market."
- "Discover 12 secrets to a stress-free family move."

Note the editorial, newspaper-style technique used to tell a story in the ad in Figure 4.3 while making a valuable offer. The text-style ad also has the benefit of being inexpensive to prepare and can be sized to fit easily. By the way, the $61,423 savings are achieved by a combination of interest savings from a fifteen-year mortgage compared to a 30-year loan, and tax savings from mortgage interest deductions. Together, they add up to the attention-grabbing figure over 15 years. Thus, a common practice is turned into a powerfully attractive offer to generate home buyer prospects.

Strategy #6: State Your Offer Clearly

Make it big, bold, up front, no small print—absolutely knock 'em over the head by stating your offer clearly. Don't hide it at the bottom. Put it right up at the top. Prospects must see your offer at a glance and understand it. Make sure the copy features a clear benefit to the consumer and tells them "What's in it for me?" Your goal is to own a piece of your prospect's mind. Make your prospects do something. Make them call, write, e-mail, fax, or come by. Your offer must compel them to respond in some

Figure 4.3
Bridgeview Home Owner Saves $61,423

Free Report Available   *Advertisement!*

Bridgeview Homeowner Saves $61,423 In Interest And Taxes... And Gets *Brand New Home!*

This little known <u>three</u> step plan shows homeowners how to save thousands of dollars in interest and taxes... and get a brand new, more spacious home too! Call for a FREE Report that reveals how!

Your Town - Just ask Bridgeview homeowners Bob and Mary Smith, and they'll tell you that all real estate agents are definitely not the same!

As a result of meeting with Gerry Ballinger, the Smith's stand to save $61,423 in interest and taxes that they would have otherwise paid. And, they are also going to be moving into a brand new home in Brentwood Estates as well!

The interesting news is, other Bridgeview homeowners may be able to save a similar amount with the little known advice that the Smith's received. Plus be able to get a brand new home too!

According to Jeff Paul, a local financial planner and CPA, most homeowners are not aware that the current low interest rates and prices of homes, create a unique situation. A situation where some homeowners can not only save thousands in interest and taxes, but also trade up into a new home for the

same payment they are currently paying!

Bridgeview homeowners Bob and Mary Smith recently used this plan to reduce their mortgage interest by over $61,000 over the life of their loan, increased their monthly cashflow by over $426, and were able to move into a new home in Brentwood Estates. A luxury home that would have cost thousands more a few years ago!

Smith, who is an executive with TRW Data Systems, says " What amazes me, is that I didn't think of it myself. After getting a few postcards from Gerry, I decided to give him a call, and I'm sure glad we did!"

With higher taxes on the way, every dollar you save is important. To find out more information about this plan just call the FREE recorded message line below and ask for information to be sent to you in the mail.

Call 1-800-278-9788, 24 Hrs, For Free Recorded Message And Report!

Compliments of ABC Realty. If your property is currently listed with a broker, this is not intended as a solicitation of that listing.

© 1993 Money Making Marketing, Inc., McLean, Virginia

---

way. State your offer in clear, concrete language and you'll be ahead of your competition.

Strategy #7: Limit the Time or Supply of Your Offer

Push prospects to respond now. They can't put it off; they must respond now or risk missing out. If you don't have a cutoff, prospects can put it off. Limit the offer's time or your supply. A never-ending open offer doesn't give the prospect a reason to get off the fence and respond. A deadline creates urgency:

- "Offer ends on this date."
- "Call now while we have some reports left. First come, first served."

- "Seminar seats are limited. Call now while space is still available."

Another benefit of a limited offer is you can let your campaign take a breather for a little while—a month or two—after the deadline. Then, bring the offer back again to a fresh market. An expiration date allows you to return to the offer again and again and again.

Still another bonus from a limited offer is a reminder follow-up. For every contact on your list that does not respond before the expiration date, you can write or call again 10 days before the deadline and say, "Act now, because time is running out. Only 10 days left."

Strategy #8: Everything Must Contain a Response Offer

Everything a rainmaker sends out or advertises must contain a response offer. When you send payments to your accounts payable, insert a response offer. When you mail a letter to a prospect, include a P.S. with a response offer. When you leave a voice mail message, include a response offer, a reason to call you back. When you print highlight sheets for your yard sign brochure boxes, include an offer for a free report. When you print your business cards, include a response offer on the reverse side. When you send an e-mail, include a hyperlink to "Click here to see the latest listings on our website."

All of your marketing, advertising, and prospecting should include response offers.

Strategy #9: Constantly Test Offers

Your best offers—whether they are reports, booklets, services, or videos—will be the result of literally hundreds of tests over the years. Different target prospects will have a different "best" offer. Again, if an offer doesn't produce results within an acceptable time period, it should be eliminated. Fire your worst ad every month.

Test your offers. Reuse good offers, but restructure the presentation. Give it a new headline, add a new twist, try a shorter expiration period. Combine it with another offer (two reports) or update its value. Don't stop using the best offers as long as they work. (Even if you're bored with them, the market isn't.) No response advertising effort should be undertaken without a test of some kind. The simplest form of advertising test is the "split test." This test involves using half the mail or ads for one offer, and the other half for a different offer and then comparing the results.

Test "soft" and "hard" offers. "Soft" offers, such as a free report, appeal to a larger number of prospects early in their decision process that need to be qualified and worked. "Hard" offers, such as a listing appointment or prequalification, result in lower response from people who are already shopping you and the competition. Test both types of offers.

Test your media mix. Compare media effectiveness: direct mail versus brochure boxes, print versus broadcast, newspaper inserts versus freebie home magazines, local radio versus billboards, website classifieds versus newspaper classifieds. If an offer works on radio, try it in direct mail to see if it generates more or less response. The combinations are endless.

Test your timing. Test running your ads continuously versus "pulsing" your ads: the ads run, the ads stop, the ads run, the ads stop. See what works best for you.

Test your season. Measure if your ads work better in the winter or in the spring or in the fall. For open houses, test a weekday versus a weekend, test Super Bowl Sunday versus watching the game yourself. Test it.

Test, test, test. Take to heart a bias for action from Tom Peters, author of *In Search of Excellence,* whose theme is, "You'll never improve until you stop doing what you are doing." Every time an offer is tested and succeeds, the rainmaker adds more profit to the bottom line. Every time you beat your best offer, you make money. Never assume your old ad is the best. Always test it. Always try to beat the champ. Remember, nothing is forever in marketing. Rainmakers always have a "Plan B." They must always have an encore.

Quick Checklists of Prospect Problems in Search of Rainmaker Solutions

Seller Prospect Problems

- ☑ What is my home worth?
- ☑ How do I sell with a broker?
- ☑ What can a broker do that I can't?
- ☑ How can I prepare my home to sell fast?
- ☑ What is the best way to market my home?
- ☑ How do I get ready for an open house?
- ☑ How much net cash will I get from a sale?
- ☑ What are the tax consequences of selling?
- ☑ How can I benefit from buying a more expensive house?
- ☑ How can I convert my home equity into investment cash?
- ☑ How long will it take to sell my home?

Buyer Prospect Problems

- ☑ How much can I afford?
- ☑ What financing is available? And which is best for me?
- ☑ How do I buy a house?
- ☑ Will buying be more cost-effective than renting?
- ☑ Will my take-home pay change if I buy a house?
- ☑ Why does the same house cost more in another location?
- ☑ How do I know if a specific house is a good buy?
- ☑ Can investment property pay off?
- ☑ Is buying a second home a good move?
- ☑ What is the right size down payment?

Relocation Prospect Problems

- ☑ Where can I get information about an area across the country?
- ☑ Whom can I contact for a home-finding area tour?
- ☑ Is there a way to get inexpensive relocation counseling?

☑ Where do I get information on school districts?

☑ How can I be sure to sell my old home in time to buy a new home?

☑ How much will it cost to move my household goods?

☑ What are some tips on coping with the stress of relocation?

☑ How can I compare company relocation benefits with other employers' policies?

☑ How can I sell a job candidate on moving to our area?

☑ How can I keep costs down when moving a group of employees?

Costly Mistakes to Avoid with Your Offers

Mistake #1: Hitting Prospects over the Head with Same 2 × 4

Too much of a good thing can be bad. Even the best offer can become stale with unrelenting promotion. Too many calls to a past client list can leave you with a worked-over, worn-out list.

Solution: "Pulse" the effort, offering a premium quarterly or perhaps twice a year. Once you acquire a prospect, for example, "work" that prospect for some weeks, pause, then repeat the process several weeks later. By pulsing an offer, a rainmaker often can create a better result, and the timely flood of appointments keeps flowing.

Mistake #2: Letting the Offer Do All the Heavy Lifting

Response advertising works better with a high level of public awareness. Every rainmaker must establish the inherent value of the rainmaker's service before people will respond. In real estate, if other things are equal (the same multiple listing service, the same financing, the same basic services), then prospects perceive all sales agents to be interchangeable "commodities." If a rainmaker is unknown or is not perceived as being a knowledgeable, experienced professional who delivers results, then response offers will not be credible.

Solution: Make it clear in your response advertising campaign that you're a knowledgeable real estate expert. Cultivate a general awareness of your expertise by including positive statements of your knowledge and experience as a specific goal in your marketing materials (slogan, business cards, tag line of ads, personal brochure) to precede or accompany any response advertising campaign.

Mistake #3: Aping the Competition's Offer

Response advertising will not work as well if the competition is using the exact same offer.

Solution: Restructure offers from time to time and concentrate on another market niche, or develop a premium the competition doesn't have. But don't avoid an offer just because the competition is using it. Simply recast the offer to give it a different spin to different prospects.

Mistake #4: Sending the Steak before Asking If They Are Hungry

An all-too-common mistake with inexperienced marketers is to send the premium along with the initial mailing. Unfortunately, prospects then no longer have a need to call and say, "Yes, I'm interested. Tell me more."

Solution: Send the sizzle, not the steak. Let the mailpiece describe an offer no true prospect in his or her right mind could live without. That's what lead generation is all about. If you send the information in advance, you remove the tantalizing mystery—and the reason to respond.

Mistake #5: Offering Discounts to Use Your Service

We all know a direct response offer must be valuable. But to whom? A discount to use your service ("Free warranty with listing," or "$250 off closing costs") attracts price-sensitive comparison-shopping bargain hunters. Not the ideal rainmaker customer. The "value" in a discount is really a self-serving tool mostly of value to the salesperson, not to the customer.

Solution: Focus on the customer. When developing a valuable offer, think in terms of making the customer's life richer, easier, happier, and less expensive or more rewarding ("Free Report Reveals the Greatest Mistakes Even Smart Sellers Make"). A truly valuable offer is a solution to a customer's problem, not a discount on your price.

RAINMAKER CHAPTER 4 SUMMARY

Offer Strategies That Attract Prospects Like a Magnet

▶ Strategy #1: Handpick the Customers You Want.

▶ Strategy #2: Focus on the Customer's Problems.

▶ Strategy #3: Translate Your Solutions into Offers.

▶ Strategy #4: Turn Your Solution into a Premium.

▶ Strategy #5: Make Your Offer Valuable.

▶ Strategy #6: State Your Offer Clearly.

▶ Strategy #7: Limit the Time or Supply of Your Offer.

▶ Strategy #8: Everything Must Contain a Response Offer.

▶ Strategy #9: Constantly Test Offers.

5

Creative Strategies to Beat the Competition Every Time

> **A good advertisement is one that sells the product without drawing attention to itself.**
>
> David Ogilvy
> *Ogilvy on Advertising*

Creating an Identity for Your Practice

Rob Fey, an astute marketer in the Baltimore area and author of *The 200 Minute Marketing System,* describes in his book a telling principle of marketing every rainmaker should take to heart. Fey calls it the "best, better, different" principle, or BBD. The first objective of every rainmaker is to be the best. If you are not the best, then you must be better than the competition. If you can't be better, then as a last resort, be different.

Being the best in your market means you are in a class by yourself. No one comes close.

Being better means you're above average: better than most, a leader, but still one among several agents in the area who are all outstanding. Your prospects sense, unfortunately, that they could switch agents and probably not notice a drop in service.

If all else fails, be different. Ideally, being different means being focused on customers, on their needs and worries, on providing a solution to their problems. By providing useful customer-oriented information, such as special reports or services, you'll be different and appreciated. Being different means standing out from the crowd. Being different may not mean your delivery system is the best. It may not even mean your service is better. But if you focus on the customer first—and yourself second—you'll stand out in the customer's mind.

At its least effective, being different simply means a self-centered image: a personal logo, a slick personal brochure, a salon photo or signature accent or clever slogan that is different. Nothing more. Only when your system is fundamentally outstanding and your service is focused on the customer does a rainmaker become the best, not just different.

Confusing Corporate Identity with Personal Identity

When creating a corporate identity, ask yourself, "Could someone else step into this identity easily?" Or would they have to spend big money to make over, or, worse, reinvent the entire brand in a different image? If the buyer of your practice doesn't need to pay for an image makeover, then your buyer will have money to pay you for the corporate identity already complete! To follow through on the *Real Estate Rainmaker* model, you must be able to turn over your corporate identity to a future buyer the same way you turn over tasks to your staff.

Yes, you need an identity. Without question, your name and reputation are invaluable assets. They are your personal identity. But don't confuse your personal identity with your corporate identity. Your corporate identity is the graphic and visual representation of your business. Focus your corporate identity on the customer, not yourself. Focus on answering the consumer's question, What's in it for me (WIIFM)? In fact, the ideal identity accomplishes two goals:

1. Marketing identity designed to attract customers.
2. Sales identity designed to convince customers to use you.

Claude Hopkins is one of the founding fathers of modern advertising. In his pioneering book, *Scientific Advertising,* he detailed the secret behind a powerful business name, a name that is remembered and is transferable to your future practice buyer. "There is great advantage in a name that tells a story," Hopkins wrote in 1923. "The name is usually prominently displayed. To justify the space it occupies, it should aid the advertising. Some such names are almost complete advertisements in themselves."

Here are some identity do's and don'ts for the rainmaker:

- *Do use your system.* Use the word "group" or "team" to describe the customer-focused service: Property Group. Real Estate Group. Dream Team. Home Team. The 5-Star Team (Mary Harker, Keller Williams, Dallas).

- *Do use a slogan.* Reinforce your corporate identity with a customer-centered slogan: "One Call Does It All." "Marketing the American Dream." "Shopping for Good Reasons to Choose an Agent? We Have a Couple" (Bill and Peggy Sloan, RE/MAX, San Diego). "Providing Million Dollar Service in Every Price Range" (Coldwell Banker, Barbara Sue Seal Properties, Portland, Oregon). "Everything We Touch Turns to Sold" (Tony Whalen, Vitale Sunshine Realty, Staten Island, New York). "Over 700 Families Served!" (Dick Mathes, ERA, Mason City, Iowa). "Because Every Move Matters" (Mike Brodie, Keller Williams, Dallas, and Linda Soesbe, McGinnis BH&G, Colorado Springs).

- *Do use a symbol or prop.* Use a symbol or prop as your signature to represent you without words: Sold sign. Telephone. Pet ("Approved by an independent lab," Bill and Peggy Sloan). Doctor's coat (The Real Estate Doctor®, "We make house calls," Jerry and Irene Stoffer, Orlando, Florida). Hat ("The Hat Lady," Sandra Nickel, Montgomery, Alabama, 800-HAT-LADY, sandra@hat-lady.com). Robes and crown ("Condo King," Ft. Meyers, Florida; "Queen of the Top Dollar Sale"). Superman-like diamond ("Super Agent"). Lightning bolt ("Call Me Today and Start

Packing," Larry Bender, Prudential Tucson). Area map ("Your Detroit-Metro Connection"). Doors ("Doors to Your Dreams" logo, "Our mission is to open doors to your real estate dreams," Lyndi Simpson and Joy Simpson-Oke, Long & Foster, Fair Oaks, Virginia). "Satisfaction, and Then Some."

- *Do use your town name.* "First Names in Arlington Real Estate" (Lynne and Harry Lilly, Long & Foster, Arlington, Virginia). "Your Dallas Experts." "West Meadows Neighborhood Specialists." "Selling Peoria One Yard at a Time" (Marilyn Kohn, RE/MAX). *Caution:* Be sure you don't plan to do business outside the town or market. If so, broaden the area: "Your Chicagoland Experts."

- *Don't confuse your "corporate identity" with your personal identity.* No future rainmaker can use your personal name as an identity: "My name is April, but you can call me any month of the year." "My name is Hershey. Call me for a sweet deal." "Dan, the Real Estate Man." "The Real Deal O'Neal." Clyde "Tex" Smith: "Let me rope you a buyer real fast." Holstein, Heifer, Angus: "Remark-A-Bull Service."

- *Don't use your photo as your only identity.* A full-body "action shot" or fashion photo requires you to be the sole deliverer of service seven days a week. It will also require a complete back-to-square-one makeover of all marketing campaigns by a buyer. Certainly, use your head-and-shoulders photo on all materials to help people remember "a name and a face." Use staff photos, too. But don't use your personal image as the corporate image. You'll be sorry when a buyer of your practice discounts the price to compensate for all new marketing materials.

Quick Checklist to Guarantee
Maximum Creative Direct Mail

☑ *Write like you talk.* Letters are a conversation between friends on paper. Use the words you would use on the phone.

Be friendly, warm, colorful. Give your mail "I" appeal by using the first person. Put your high school English teacher out of your mind. Imagine yourself standing in front of a room of prospects telling it like it is. That's what they came to hear. Simple, clear sentences. Be direct.

☑ *Touch the prospect's emotions.* Every rainmaker knows people buy on emotion and justify with reason. Touch their emotions with benefits and you'll be deluged with results. Focus first on prospects' needs, problems, wants, fears, concerns. Then your offer will provide the safety, security, comfort, prestige, or status they want.

☑ *Tell your story and stop.* Make the letter as long as it takes to tell your story. Readers will read long letters if the letter is relevant, compelling, and informative. One page is okay; so are eight.

☑ *Testimonials are your best friend.* Identify them. Include their name and town. No initials. Your "live" testimonials will give your offer the credibility it deserves.

☑ *Don't send junk mail.* Think quality. Use original letterhead. Print the letter rather than photocopying it. Use color. Multiple inserts are a plus. Direct imprint of addresses looks better than labels every time. Internal personalized addressing is even better. Mail yourself a copy. If you're not impressed, your prospects won't be either.

☑ *Plan for a hurried scan reader.* Use boldface subheads, lead-ins, italic, and underline to emphasize your principal points. Give them the full story in the headlines.

☑ *Print big.* Use a typeface large enough for adults of all ages to read. Use it consistently throughout the letter.

☑ *Leave the name inside.* On your envelopes, put only your street address and city, state, and zip in upper left corner. Don't give market strangers a reason not to open the envelope by using your name and real estate company in the return address.

Four Rainmaker Strategies to Increase Creative Results

Strategy #1: Spend 75% of Your Time on the Headline

The headline is the "ad for the ad." Spend most of your time on the headline. The key is emotion. Headlines must make an emotional connection with the consumer's needs or wants or desires or fears.

An effective headline must make a compelling offer, something that actually compels prospects to respond, and must be interesting, intriguing, fascinating, pique the prospect to want to know more. The first self-test of a headline is to read it. Does the headline make you say, "Hmmm. That's interesting," or "Yeah, I'd like to know more about that," or "Wow! That's just what I need." The second test of a headline is to actually test it in a promotion. Don't just write one or two headlines. Write dozens and then pick the best.

Figures 5.1 through 5.4 depict some proven headlines that have been used by successful brokers nationwide featuring Gooder Group reports. First of all, notice how big the headline is compared to the size of the ad. Often, the headline takes up more than half the space to demand attention. Second, notice how the words target the consumer's mind with a reader-centered benefit. Remember, the headline states the problem; your offer is the solution.

Quick Checklist of Tested Direct-Response Headlines

- ☑ Stop Before You Try to Sell Your Home Yourself—Know the Most Costly Mistakes.
- ☑ Your Landlord Says: "Hi, and thanks for paying my mortgage."
- ☑ What You Don't Know Can Cost You When You Buy a Home.
- ☑ You're Selling Your Home. Learn Why the First 5 Minutes Are Crucial.

Figure 5.1
Step-by-Step Secrets to Attract Buyers Like a Magnet

Courtesy of Gooder Group Rainmaker Lead Ads

☑ Do You Know What Your Neighbors Did Last Night?

☑ Avoid the Single Biggest Mistake Most Home Buyers Make.

☑ Free Report Reveals How to Reduce the Trauma Your Kids Experience When You Move.

☑ 28 Questions You Should Ask before You Shop for a Home.

☑ Discover the Secret to Selling Your House in the Shortest Time—And Still Getting Top Dollar.

☑ Don't Fall into the Trap of Losing Your Buyer over Terms.

Figure 5.2
Don't Even Think about Selling Your Home by
Yourself before You Read This . . .

Courtesy of Gooder Group Rainmaker Lead Ads

☑ Learn How to Avoid the Frustration of Keeping Your Move on Your Timetable *Before* You Decide to Sell.

☑ Little-Known "Closing Secret" That Gets Your Buyer to Accept Your Price (seller-paid points).

☑ Four Little-Known Wealth Builders Every First-Time Buyer Should Know.

Strategy #2: Make It Easy to Respond

Prospects respond on impulse. But impulses pass. Don't miss out on a single response because the prospect has to call

Figure 5.3
Want to Save Thousands on Your Taxes?

Courtesy of Gooder Group Rainmaker Lead Ads

directory assistance or search for an envelope and a stamp. Make it easy:

- *Use an 800 number or 24-hour phone number.* Prospects simply pick up the phone. Call-capture hotlines are good examples. A sample headline: "Now buyers and sellers can get information on houses without speaking directly to an agent." Easy. And nonthreatening. Prospects simply get what they need over the phone.

- *Use a reply-mail coupon.* Prospects simply tear off a postage-paid coupon or use the business reply envelope, and pop it in the nearest mailbox.

Figure 5.4
Call Now to Avoid the Single Biggest Marketing
Mistake Most Sellers Make

Courtesy of Gooder Group Rainmaker Lead Ads

- *Use e-mail.* This is especially effective with prospects you have solicited with e-mail or who have responded to you by e-mail. All the prospect must do is click to send a reply. Indeed, the two most powerful direct-response words in cyberspace are "Click here."

- *Use a cutout coupon.* Make it easy to respond to print ads (newspapers, home magazines, newsletters, etc.) by offering a clip-and-use coupon. Be sure to include your address, fax, and phone in the coupon.

- *Use the fax.* Provide the fax form for prospects to simply stuff into a fax machine after checking the right boxes. Note: only about 4% of American households have a fax. Most fax responses and fax-on-demand requests come from prospects at their workplace.

Not only can you make it easy to respond, you can make the initial contact easy. Sample headline: "Find out on the Phone How Much Your Home Is Worth." The service is valuable—especially for the time-short consumer—because prospects just pick up their phone. When they call, you say, *"Yes, you will find out on the phone, it doesn't take a personal appointment. But first I need to find out a few things about you."* You then ask your qualifying questions. Close by saying, *"I can get back to you on the phone after I do a computer analysis and some research. When would be the best time to call you back?"*

Use a tax assessment-to-value ratio or pull quick thumbnail comparables. When you call, use a value range, not a specific price, which requires a more thorough property inspection and gives you a reason to ask for an appointment. You now have two contacts to qualify the prospect. Not only does the headline make it easy to respond, it also appeals to the consumer's mind.

AUTOMATIC RESPONSE TO E-MAIL

Here's a terrific e-marketing tip from my friend, Allen Hainge, founder of CyberStar Seminars based in Springfield, Virginia. Many e-mail software programs, such as Eudora Pro and Microsoft Outlook Express, allow you to automatically e-mail a specific file to a prospect that sends you a message with a prearranged simple code, such as the prospect's last name. That way, when the Smiths send you an e-mail containing their name, your auto-responder program e-mails the Smiths your Activity Report on their home for sale. Totally hands-free. Plus, the Smiths are pleased because they got their report instantly when they wanted it. Cool.

Tip: Include a hyperlink to your website address in your e-mail signature. That way, when prospects open your e-mail, they can easily click on the link and visit your website seamlessly. Another chance to impress!

Strategy #3: Always Ask Qualifying Questions

The first thing you want is every prospects' phone number, "in case we get cut off." Prospects' phone numbers are even more important than their name. Next are the Big 5 questions. Say, *"Before I send you a report, I need to know a little bit more about you,"* or *"Do you mind if I ask you a few questions to match my services to your needs?"*

- When do you want to move?
- Why do you want to move?
- Do you presently own or rent?
- What are you interested in: buying, selling, renting, relocating?
- Are you working with an agent?

These questions are especially useful for reply coupons. We call them "sight qualifiers." At a glance, you know if you have a hot immediate prospect or a warm long-range prospect.

There are many more qualifiers, and you will develop the ones that are best for you. (More on qualifying questions in Chapter 6.) These are some typical questions:

- Home desired: single-family? townhouse? condominium? apartment?
- Price range?
- Available down payment?
- Are you prequalified for a loan?
- Annual household income?

Sometimes, people are reluctant to put dollar figures in a mail-back coupon. But if they didn't fill it out, it allows you to ask the question and qualify them. Say, *"Well, I noticed you didn't check all the boxes. Are you interested in buying or selling or renting or relocating? What price range are you looking for most?"* Qualifying questions help you focus your approach.

Strategy #4: Use a P.S. in Every Letter

After your signature, the postscript is the most read element in your letter. A P.S. is a "call to action." Don't make the mistake of simply repeating the main point of the letter in this super valuable space. Instead, the most effective P.S. presents a new, additional benefit to the reader while making it clear what you want the reader to do. Ask for the order again, offer a bonus, or remind the prospect of the expiration date of the offer. One P.S. is enough. Avoid the temptation of diluting its impact with a P.P.S.

Quick Checklist of Power Postscripts for Letters

Here are sample postscripts from Gooder Group's collection of 203 *Rainmaker Lead Letters* specifically written for direct-response lead generation and follow-up.

☑ P.S. Here I go again. My colleagues say I'm nuts, but I want to offer you my special report, *BUYER'S AGENT: Why Every Home Buyer Needs One.* It's free, too, like my services to buyers. But call today while copies of this popular report are still available!

☑ P.S. As a bonus I'd like to offer you a FREE copy of *SECRETS: Nine Deadly Sins to Avoid When Buying a Home.* This no-nonsense report outlines exactly what you need to know to buy smart—not textbook concepts but street-savvy tips only the school of hard knocks can teach you. Call NOW before they're all gone!

☑ P.S. Please don't put this letter in a drawer for later. You'll run the risk of missing out on your dream house. Once somebody else buys it, you won't get another chance at it for years. Call now. It will only take a moment to ask for your free report and learn how you can save thousands on taxes and interest.

☑ P.S. MORE GOOD NEWS . . . When you call, be sure to request your FREE copy of my special report, *SELLING: How to Avoid the 10 Biggest Selling Mistakes.* This information-packed report will show you how to achieve your selling goal without getting derailed by the same mistakes other sellers make.

☑ P.S. Any real estate transaction can be fraught with pitfalls if you don't know exactly what you're doing. When you're juggling the sale of one home and the purchase of another, the potential dangers multiply. You don't have to go through this obstacle course blind! Call now for your FREE copy of *TRADE UP: Six Inside Strategies to Avoid Trade-Up Mistakes.*

Costly Creative Mistakes to Avoid

Mistake #1: Featuring the Features and Not the Benefits

Direct response ads, like property ads, that discuss only the built-in features—the things your service already comes with—and not the benefits, will not draw maximum response.

Solution: Stress the benefits. Benefits are what the customer gains, what the features do for the customer, a specific outcome. Readers should know right away how you will help them save money, make money, save time, avoid effort, or satisfy curiosity. For example, a free report has a Q&A format with 28 questions. That's a feature. But the answers will save the customers hundreds, even thousands of dollars. That's a benefit. (Headline: "Whether You're Buying or Selling, This Free Report Will Help You Avoid Costly Mistakes.")

Remember, people don't buy "things," they buy what the things will do for them. Benefits affect people's emotions. Emotion attracts response. To turn a feature or advantage into a benefit, ask yourself: "So what?" The answer is the benefit to the prospect. Example: "fireplace" is a feature. So what? "Cozy fireplace" is a benefit. "McLean" is a feature. "Sought-after McLean address" is a benefit. "Four baths" is a feature. "No waiting on school days with four baths" is a benefit.

Mistake #2: Assuming Low Initial Response Is the Last Word

Prospects must see an offer, understand it, and act on it. It may take several exposures to reach a desired prospect and prompt the prospect to take action. If there aren't enough advertisements, the offer results in institutional exposure, not prospect response.

Solution: Change the presentation of the offer to give it enough punch to move prospects to take action.

Mistake #3: Failing to Enclose a Response Device

Prospects should not struggle to do business with you.

Solution: Insert a reply card, coupon, postage-paid envelope, or fax form. If you're using a label, stick it to the reply form. Make it easy for prospects to respond. Repeat your offer, limited time cutoff, or guarantee (if any) on the response form.

Mistake #4: Not Testing with Dress Rehearsals

Spending heavily on an untested idea can waste a lot of money fast.

Solution: Before you roll out the big bucks, send out several test mailings in smaller quantities. Use the results to polish your encore for prime time. This works for lists as well as offers. If you have 10,000 on a list, mail three offers of 1,000 each as a test. Then mail the best offer to the encore 7,000.

Mistake #5: Not Asking Readers to Do Something

What do you want the prospect to do? Call? Drop by? Send the reply card? Visit your website? Pass along your offer to a friend? Make an appointment?

Solution: Be clear about what you want, and make it the focus of the marketing. Don't be shy. Keep it simple. The less a prospect has to think and do, the better. Use an illustration to boost response.

Mistake #6: Not Using the Magic Words

Not pushing the right hot buttons can leave prospects cold.

Solution: Decades of direct-response results have identified a short list of words that are long on results: you, free, save, now/at last, new, today, discover, introducing, announcing, guarantee, easy, limited offer or time, urgent, bargain, last chance, exclusive, improved, revolutionary. It's impossible to use them too much. Every time you write a "we" phrase, change it to a "you" phrase. You'll improve everything you write.

RAINMAKER CHAPTER 5 SUMMARY

Creative Strategies to Beat the Competition Every Time

▶ Strategy #1: Spend 75% of Your Time on the Headline.

▶ Strategy #2: Make It Easy to Respond.

▶ Strategy #3: Always Ask Qualifying Questions.

▶ Strategy #4: Use a P.S. in Every Letter.

STEP 2: CAPTURE CUSTOMERS WITH PROSPECT FOLLOW-UP

Customer Conversion Strategies to Maximize Sales

> If you caught a fish every time you put your line in the water, they would call it catching, not fishing.
>
> Jimmy Buffett
> *A Pirate Looks at Fifty*

Follow-up is where rainmakers make their money. Why? Because sales are mostly closed with follow-up, not lead generation.

Once your lead-generation marketing has attracted predisposed prospects, it's time for the rainmaker to focus on follow-up to convert those prospects into presold customer appointments. One of the first steps to maximize your follow-up is to understand the "prospect pipeline."

When you advertise in the mass media, understand you're working the bottom of the market. Imagine you have two telephone books: the white pages list 50,000 names of everybody in town; a Little Black Book lists 500 names of people who recently have shown interest in real estate. Which phone numbers would you call first? The Little Black Book, of course, because prospects are more valuable than market strangers.

Telephone prospecting points out the difference in quality between market strangers and prospects in the pipeline. Rejection from cold-call market strangers is inevitable. No wonder most salespeople have call reluctance: it's natural. It's also unnecessary. By focusing your calls and other contacts not on market

89

strangers but on interested prospects, you penetrate the top of the market.

But here's where it gets tricky for the average real estate agent. Too many overlook this step or drop the ball or don't know what to do with a lead that isn't ready to buy immediately. If I've heard it once, I've heard it a hundred times: "I just get too busy to follow up. There are only so many calls I can make. I know I should, but how can I be in three places at once?" I'm about to show you.

As prospects steadily move through your prospect pipeline, they are moving through a natural cycle to become a customer. Along the way, a rainmaker educates the prospects, answers their questions, and builds rapport as a trusted consultant, counselor, and advisor rather than a salesperson.

With every contact, the rainmaker must qualify the prospects and requalify the prospects. Like a mother hen, the rainmaker keeps turning all the eggs until they are ready. Some will buy or sell soon; others are just beginning to look and are weeks or months away from being ready. At any time, prospects will signal their readiness by surfacing from the pipeline to schedule an appointment. Sometimes, this happens in the first call. Sometimes, it takes years.

The critical prospect follow-up strategy is to have a system in place that allows the rainmaker to spend precious personal time, not with prospects, but only with active shoppers who have broken the surface and are ready to act. Prospects still in the pipeline are nudged along at their own pace by the system. Sure, every once in a while you'll get a relocation buyer or an open house neighbor who must buy or sell right away. But most often, prospects need to be nurtured, cultivated, incubated, and just plain worked before they are "ready" to sign. That takes follow-up.

Today's Leads Are Tomorrow's Sales

Remember the *Three Sales Secrets That Successful Salespeople Hide* that we read in Chapter 2. The three secrets bear repeating now:

1. The Rule of 45 says that 45% of all leads turn into a sale for someone.

2. Great salespeople follow up every sales lead until the prospect buys or dies.

3. The older the sales lead, the less the competition.

What the executives from Inquiry Handling Service, Inc., have learned about lead management in the general marketplace proves to be even more true in real estate. Look at the numbers.

"Of people who inquire, 76% intend to buy." The Gooder Group's analysis of our Rainmaker Leads Online responses showed it can take many months for prospects to become buyers. When you combine all the real estate prospects who want to move in six months or more, they add up to 44% of all inquiries. Does the competition stay in touch with somebody who contacted them at an open house six months ago? The answer is generally no. Only a **Real Estate Rainmaker** system is equipped to keep in touch with every prospect for as long as it takes. Not following up consistently is probably the single biggest mistake your competition makes. But that's their problem.

"The person doesn't approach your competitor 40% of the time." In real estate, the figures are even more significant. As Gooder Group's question on the NAR survey showed, 63% of sellers and 61% of repeat buyers worked with the first agent they called. They never called a competitor. The prospects are satisfied with the service received; their needs are met. The secret to capturing the maximum number of presold prospects is follow-up.

"More than 50% of sales leads are not followed up." That's your competition's biggest mistake. In contrast, the rainmaker strengthens the relationship with the prospect beginning with the first phone call. Scott Williams, general manager of Phone Pros, a mystery shopping service in Westlake Village, California (800-746-6776), says they've gotten the following miserable results from more than one million undercover conversations with real estate salespeople mostly on duty desk, as reported in the October 1997 *Today's Realtor:*

- 46% of agents didn't ask to schedule an appointment.
- 66% didn't ask the caller for a phone number.
- 74% told callers to sell before shopping for another home.
- 82% didn't ask if the caller's house was already listed.
- 89% were unfamiliar with advertised property if they weren't the listing agent.
- 98% didn't ask when the caller needed to move.

When Phone Pros returns the taped customer calls to real estate professionals for telephone skills training, it's like returning an X-ray of the business. The most common observation is agents tend to be human information booths on the phone, passing on information ad infinitum, rather than giving customers a reason to come in or do business with the agent.

Quick Checklist of Cardinal Rules for Prospect Follow-Up

☑ Focus on strengthening the relationship.

☑ Presell prospects on you and your service with a consistent, trust-building message.

☑ Center all efforts on the customer. Do not be me-centered.

☑ Keep the system simple, so anybody can do it, even when you're not there.

☑ Keep your eyes on the prize: an appointment where all you do is close.

Why the Competition Quits

The second biggest mistake your competition makes boils down to focusing on themselves, not the customer. That is, they wear their "sales" hat from the beginning, trying to convince the prospect they are the greatest. This, however, has the opposite effect of driving prospects away.

Experience shows rainmakers must wear the consultant-advisor-teacher hat to nurture, cultivate, and incubate a prospect by focusing on the prospect's needs. The savvy rainmaker doesn't switch hats to sales UNTIL an appointment is made or requested by the prospect.

It is understandable that the competition quits. It's hard enough to keep track of the guests from last weekend's open house, much less the week before that or the week before that— not to mention 12 weeks ago or 24 weeks back. Nobody can— unless you have a system.

Triple Your Business with Effective Follow-Up

Bob Donath and his colleagues at Inquiry Handling Service show the way for savvy rainmakers to triple their business with effective follow-up. In *Managing Sales Leads,* the authors' research discovered sales are captured throughout the first year after a prospect inquires. On average, 15% of prospects buy in the first 90 days, then 10% buy in the second ninety days, 10% in the third and another 10% buy in the fourth quarter after their initial inquiry. Thus, 45% buy in the first year.

Most real estate salespeople cherry-pick sales from the first quarter only. By the time the second quarter arrives, "old" prospects are long forgotten and displaced with a fresh crop of "new" prospects. The nearly 30 out of 100 prospects who will buy "later" are routinely ignored by the competition. Instead of cherry-picking your share from only the 15 who buy in the first 90 days, rainmakers can triple their business by converting customers from the additional 30 prospects who buy in the second, third, and fourth quarters after inquiry.

Only a **Real Estate Rainmaker** system is equipped to keep in touch with all prospects for as long as it takes. Keep in mind, follow-up to get an appointment is a marketing function, not a sales function.

Jim Clayton, the vice president for marketing at L&A Direct, an award-winning graphics agency in Fairfax, Virginia, is a master of follow-up and shared with me his simple "3B System":

1. *Be prepared and organized.* "When you say you'll call on April 2nd, you *must* keep your promise," Clayton says. "Only a system can keep all your contacts in place."

2. *Be persistent.* "You just have to have the discipline to do it."

3. *Be patient.* "You can't rush them. You just have to be on their radar when they reach the point when they are ready." Wait for the prospect's cycle.

Five Rainmaker Strategies to Effective Prospect Follow-Up

How do you sift the genuine prospects from the pond and not waste time chasing after fruitless wannabes? And how, at the same time, do you convince them you're the only real estate agent they need? Here are five **Real Estate Rainmaker** strategies to effective prospect follow-up designed to take less time and close more transactions.

Strategy #1: Qualify, Qualify, Qualify

At the initial contact, remember the First Commandment of qualifying: Gather information, do not sell. Get information now, not commitment. The initial information you gather must answer one question: Do you want to do business with this prospect?

When prospective buyers call, for example, you'll sense the prospects are ready if they start asking specific questions. A strong need for particular, technical information reflects a prospect's clear problem that you can propose a solution to solve.

When prospective sellers call, for example, ask, *"What do you think your house is worth?"* If it's wildly unrealistic or they have no motivation to sell, you may choose to put them on a mail follow-up plan rather than a personal/phone follow-up plan. Never ignore them completely. At a minimum, add the respondent to your Trophy Database.

Ask qualifying questions. When the inquiry is by phone, ask specific questions to qualify the prospect's resources, desire, authority, need, and timing, then use the information to build a customer profile. You can say things like, *"I need to ask you some short questions before I send out the report. Would that be okay?"*

- *Identification.* Who are you? (Phone numbers, best time to call, name, and address? Own or rent? Year of purchase? Value of current home?) *Tip:* Ask for the all-important phone number before the address. Rather than ask for an appointment, encourage trust by asking the best time to call.

- *Needs.* What are you interested in? (Buying, selling, or both? Renting?)

- *Timetable.* When do you want to move? (1–3 months, 4–6 months, 7–12 months, more than a year?) More ways to ask the critical *when* question: *"How soon must you move?"*; *"When do you plan on moving?"*; *"If you were to move, when would that be?"*; *"How soon will you be able to move if we find the right home?"*; *"If we find the perfect home today, are you in a position to buy it?"* *Tip:* Rank prospects according to their desired move date: "A"/Blue Chip: 1–3 months; "B"/Red Chip: 4–6 months; "C"/White Chip: 7–12 months; "D"/Green Chip: 12 months or more. Then launch a follow-up program that turns up the pace as the prospect nears the move date: 120 or more days to move date = monthly follow-up; 120–60 days to move date = weekly follow-up; 60 or fewer days to move date = 3 times per week follow-up.

- *Location.* Where do you want to move? (Within the area or outside the area?)

- *Motivation.* Why are you interested in moving? (Relocating, upsizing, downsizing, divorce, new construction, new floor plan, etc.?)

- *Competition.* Are you working with an agent? (Yes or no?)

Use "Two Report Choice" technique. Here's a simple one-question technique to easily determine a prospect's timetable. When a prospect calls, say, *"We have two reports. One for homeowners planning to move in less than four months, and one for homeowners moving in more than four months. Which report is right for you?"* If they say less than four months, offer them, for instance, "27 Free and Easy Fix-Ups to Sell Faster for the Best Price." If they say more than four months, offer them "Makeovers: Market-Smart Improvements Every Seller Should Know." For buyers, select two other reports. Presto. You've learned their critical time frame by focusing on their needs.

More qualifying questions. If you are on a roll with a prospect, continue asking questions to complete your customer profile. Some additional qualifiers could include: Home desired: single family, townhouse, condominium, apartment? Price range? Available down payment? Are you prequalified for a loan? Annual household income?

Sight qualifiers. When the inquiry is by mail, ask similar questions on the reply card to be used as "sight qualifiers." With experience, you or your staff can get a good sense if the prospect is truly qualified or really interested. The more cards you see, the sharper your sixth sense will become. Your instinct allows you to call the good ones right away and schedule the not-so-good ones to be called at the end of the day. Questions left blank are natural door openers. Skipped questions are a flag to probe for problems and more information to get inside the customer's mind: *"One reason for my call is I noticed you didn't check some of the boxes. Are you interested primarily in buying or selling or renting or relocating?"*

Handle e-mail inquiries with persistence. When prospects inquire by e-mail, you may have only their e-mail address and no idea where in the world they live or who they are. The solution is to immediately e-mail those prospects a direct-response offer to mail them something that requires their name, address, and phone number. (Yes, it's back to snail mail!) Anonymous e-mail prospects are notorious for guarding their privacy. Keep trying. Persistence is the only answer. Consider including a statement in each follow-up e-mail you send that asks them to confirm they are still interested. If they don't respond, you'll have to make a flip-of-the-coin decision to keep them on your e-mail follow-up (no cost) or eventually delete their e-mail-only record.

Suggest an appointment. Simply by proposing to telequalified prospects that you meet in person goes a long way toward rating their level of interest. If the word "appointment" proves to be a put-off, use the more informal "visit" or offer to "just stop by," implying you won't need to stay long. Ideally, the rainmaker steps into the selling process in person only when marketing follow-up is finished, not before.

Some rainmakers are effectively using lender preapproval as a defining rule before accepting a personal appointment with a prospect. The rainmaker explains that in today's market, a buyer must be preapproved by a lender to have the buyer's offer seriously considered by a seller. Thus, the way the rainmaker does business is to have clients meet with "our" lender first. Point out the initial step can be done over the phone. All the lender will need is the prospect's Social Security number, income, debts, and permission to request an in-file credit report. The lender will then run a credit score and get back to prospects quickly, ideally within the hour, to tell them if a further personal appointment should be made. If the prospects are not ready to speak with your lender, ask how you can best assist them, and gather answers to your qualifying questions.

Use a promotion code. Be sure to use a promotion code, such as a number, on all your follow-up activities. If you prefer a name, use a code name, such as, "Ask for Nancy Henry." Nancy Henry can be a code name. The initial "NH" code identifies the medium, *New Homes* magazine. When prospects ask for Nancy Henry, simply say, *"I'm sorry, Nancy is away from her desk, but I can help you."* Be sure to record the source of business promotion code.

Enter prospects in database. Both the hard and the soft questions go into the computer as you build a Prospect Profile. This profile should be printable as a report. The report goes in the prospect's case file that your assistant hands you on the way to your appointment, or it's given to the buyer's agent or referral agent or when you hand off the prospect to someone else. This profile is critical to being focused on the prospect's needs. The work it takes to capture the information is also what earns you a referral fee. Just a prospect's name and address aren't a qualified lead. Your in-depth Prospect Profile, on the other hand, is going to be an essential tool to close the prospect early.

Strategy #2: Launch Follow-Up Immediately with High-Impact Response Kit

Response kit. Before the phone is cold, send a same-day response kit. Your kit should be complete but not overstuffed. A three-piece kit that includes a cover letter with a call to action P.S., a free report, and a reply card offer is an excellent start. Personalize the printed materials with handwritten notes, highlighter, or sticky notes. Remember, your kit is a "salesperson in print." Its goal is twofold:

- Generate a further response from the prospect.
- Establish a reason for your telephone follow-up.

For example, your P.S. should offer an additional targeted report of interest to that type of prospect (seller, buyer, renter, etc.). If prospects don't respond to that report, when you call, say: *"The reason for my call is to find out if that special report fits your needs."* If they say no, step back and get permission to ask a general qualifying question: *"If you waved a magic wand over your house, what are the three things you would improve?"* Their answer would be your opening for your next follow-up contact to offer even more information, not to demand "Are you ready to buy yet?"

Offer an ironclad, no-questions-asked, best-service guarantee. No-risk guarantees are a powerful tool to stand above the competition and show you are the only agent prospects need. Insert your guarantee in your response kit. The fundamental psychology of a guarantee is to remove the risk or fear of making a mistake. Effective guarantees include "I'll sell your home in 90 days or give you a $500 refund at closing," or "I'll pay for your credit report if my lender doesn't get you the lowest rate available in the market." The result is prospects no longer need to "shop" for an agent. They already have the best deal possible.

Say thank you. Remember, you can't ever say thank you enough. Thank people for calling. Thank them on your voice mail message. Have a supply of thank-you postcards or greeting cards in your drawer stamped and ready for your signature. Open your follow-up letters with "Thank you for contacting us 12 weeks ago." Close your notes with "Thank you for letting me be of service to you."

Jay Jones, owner of the training firm Business Letters Unlimited in Arlington, Texas, and author of the award-winning book *Business Letters That Get Results,* shared these three steps to the perfect thank-you note at a real estate workshop I attended in Orlando, Florida:

1. Honor the deed. Open with how useful, helpful, timely, appreciated their action was to you.
2. Thank them.
3. Close with letting them know they are in good hands.

Strategy #3: Use the F.O.R.D. Method to Build Phone Rapport

After you've collected the "hard" information on a prospect with qualifying questions, the rainmaker begins to add "soft" information. Soft information is gathered best using the F.O.R.D. method developed by Larry Kendall, a respected real estate sales coach with The Group, Inc., in Fort Collins, Colorado, and a Howard Brinton "Star of the Month" in April 1998.

When you climb into a person's world, Kendall says, the doors to that world are labeled F.O.R.D. These are the most important things in their lives and the subjects they want to talk about the most.

F is for Family. Here you find out about the prospects' family, about their spouse, kids, parents, everyone who lives in the household, pets included.

O is for Occupation. What do they do? What are their titles? Where do they work? Is their workplace growing or downsizing or relocating?

R is for Recreation. What do they do when they are not working? What's their favorite recreation? Do they ski, fish, travel, garden, show dogs, collect antiques, have other hobbies? Where did they go on their last vacation?

D is for Dreams. What are their dreams? Particularly, what is their real estate dream? What would they change about their current house? Just as important, what is their dream in life? If they won the lottery, what would they do?

Use the F.O.R.D. method in prospect follow-up and customer service calls to build rapport and generate leads. Here is the 5-step calling process Kendall teaches on how to apply the F.O.R.D. method to a follow-up call. The real power of this process is Step 2 and Step 4. When you take the time to engage prospects or customers in conversation, not only do they feel good because you care about them, but out pop even more sales leads from the things you learn, Kendall says.

1. *Salutation.* Identify yourself: *"Good morning, this is Larry Kendall from The Group real estate company."*

2. *Look for common ground.* Ask about their family or their work or their recreation using the information you learned on the last call: *"Have you been out fly fishing lately?" "Is your daughter's broken arm mending okay?"*

3. *Purpose of your call.* *"The purpose of my call is (state your objective)."*

4. *Return to common ground.* Ask another family, occupation, recreation, or dreams question. Build your prospect's soft information profile.

5. *Close by looking for change.* Spend two to three minutes here. Probe for anything that has changed since you last talked, such as family size, job, golf game, college planning: *"I read where your company is moving. Does that affect you?" "If the house is a little empty now, ever consider moving closer to the golf course?"*

Making calls to prospects you know, rather than wasting time on cold calls to strangers, will produce more business than you can handle, Kendall says. He also points out the F.O.R.D. method works as well for moving a stalled negotiation forward as it does for rapport building and prospecting.

In every conversation, take the opportunity to build rapport. One of the best follow-up professionals I know in real estate is Vicki Rusinak from Rusinak Real Estate, just down the interstate in Colorado Springs. Rusinak told me the soft information on a prospect is critical. When she calls the next month, if she can't say, "The last time I talked to you, your husband was sick. How is he?" the prospect may think she is a telemarketer and hang up. The personal information is especially important in the beginning, when a prospect may not remember Rusinak from the call the month before. If you don't have the soft stuff to jog their memory when you call, they might not even talk to you, Rusinak says.

Strategy #4: Flood Prospects with an Abundance of Information in the Mail

As the top of your prospect pipeline fills with prospects, you'll have to stay in touch with hundreds of people. Some hotline users report getting as many as 45,000 calls a year. How to reach this broad prospect base and sort out the best prospects is the question. The answer is simple: the only practical way to keep in touch with hundreds of people is the mail. Once your mailing system becomes automatic, it can run virtually hands-free. Even when you get busy, the mail still goes out to everyone in your pipeline.

Remember to keep it simple. Mailing to all your prospects in mass once a month or every two weeks is just as effective as mailing a handful of individually printed letters daily. With hundreds of prospects to follow up, the first place to turn for mailers is to commercial publishers such as Gooder Group that provide high-quality, competitively priced newsletters and mailers personalized and ready to mail. As your basic direct-mail follow-up system becomes more established, you can incorporate into the mix one-to-one mailers and personal correspondence for prospects.

First follow-up letter. After you send your response kit on the day of the request, five to seven days later is the ideal time to send your first follow-up letter. If you get no response, send a second letter five to seven days after the first follow-up letter. Figures 6.1 and 6.2 are two excellent letters that I have adapted

---

Figure 6.1
First Follow-Up Letter

Dear (Prospect's Name):

Hello! This is Dan Gooder Richard from Gooder Group, your neighborhood real estate experts, writing to you again. I'm writing to you today because about a week ago, you requested a special copy of my customer awareness report entitled,

"27 Free and Easy Fix-Ups to Sell Your Home Fast."

I didn't hear back from you, and, frankly, I was concerned that you didn't receive your copy. (Did you know the U.S. Postal Service has a 5%–7% nondelivery rate?)

I just wanted to follow up to make sure you received your copy and see if I can be of any assistance to you. Let me explain:

If you're like many homeowners who request my special report, you may be considering getting your house ready to sell, but you're in the *thinking about selling and not sure where to begin* phase. If that describes you, then allow me to offer you a little **FREE** help.

As one of the area's knowledgeable and most experienced real estate professionals, I'd like to offer you a **FREE,** no-obligation Marketability Analysis. You get a chance to talk with a professional about what's on your mind—you can get all your questions answered for free! And, of course, you're *never* pressured or obligated to buy anything.

Plus, this letter will provide you with an additional guarantee: I will sell your home in 90 days or I'll pay you $500 at settlement.

If this sounds good to you, please call my office now at (703) 698-7750 to set up your free, no-obligation Marketability Analysis.

Looking forward to talking to you soon.

Cordially,

Dan Gooder Richard

P.S. If you did not receive your copy of my special report, please call me at (703) 698-7750 and I'll make sure another copy is sent to you right away. If you did receive your copy, I would love to hear your feedback, opinions, and comments on it!

Figure 6.2
Second Follow-Up Letter (If No Response)

Dear (Prospect's Name):

Hello! This is Dan Gooder Richard, your Gooder Group Real Estate neighborhood representative.

I wanted to drop you a line to see how your real estate plans were coming. As you may recall, about two weeks ago I sent you a copy of our special consumer-awareness report entitled:

"27 Free and Easy Fix-Ups to Sell Your Home Fast."

Please remember your **FREE,** no-obligation Marketability Analysis that entitles you to preferred status, plus, our additional guarantee to sell your home in 90 days or we'll pay you $500 at settlement. But I didn't hear back from you.

Perhaps you're not ready to undertake a move right now. Perhaps you're thinking about it for some time in the future. If so, we understand. May I make a suggestion?

When you are ready to talk about planning your move, you'll know how to get your questions answered for free. So please call us for a **FREE,** no-obligation Marketability Analysis. If you'd like to talk about your ideas now, I'd be happy to meet with you and talk.

Our schedule fills up pretty quickly. To make sure you get priority treatment, please call and schedule your **FREE** consultation now. That way, your VIP status is assured.

Just call (703) 698-7750 and ask for me or leave a message for anyone on our team. (Make sure to tell them you have a VIP coupon.)

Cordially,

Dan Gooder Richard

P.S. If you would like our second report for homeowners planning to sell in 6 months or more, *MAKEOVERS: Market-Smart Improvements Every Seller Should Know,* just a give us a call. It's free, too!

---

to real estate with the permission of Long Fence and Home in Riverdale, Maryland, a leading window and siding specialty company in metropolitan Washington, DC, who originally sent me the letters.

Crumpled-letter technique. Ed Hatch, a national speaker and sought-after RS Council instructor, suggests this clever follow-up technique: After mailing the first follow-up letter, wait long enough for the prospect's trash to be picked up. Then print the first letter again, crumple it up, smooth it out, write with pen in the corner, "Please don't throw this away again," and mail the crumpled first letter a second time to the prospect. Hatch says the impression is unforgettable, and often turns a cold follow-up call into a warm sales opportunity.

Eight in eight. Don Hobbs and Greg Herder, co-owners of Hobbs/Herder Advertising, an innovative advertising agency and seminar company in Santa Ana, California, that specializes in real estate personal marketing, have developed this intense direct-mail awareness-building idea. The eight-in-eight approach is to blitz prospects with a different mailing every week for eight weeks. At the end of the eighth week, be sure to call prospects to determine if their needs have changed or been met. Inserts could include a house-hunting map, notepad, recreation schedules, school calendar magnet, school absence telephone numbers, city reference guide, or Gooder Group special reports. The goal is to make an everlasting good impression of top service in a short period of time.

Proof of results. After the first set of response kit and first and second follow-up letters, if you use the eight-in-eight technique or send mail over many months, what do you mail to prospects? Beyond educating prospects, every mail or phone contact should contribute to convincing them to work with you because you've provided proof of your results and evidence of professionalism. Here are ten tested direct-mail follow-ups to choose from:

1. *Use company listings* to mail just listed, just sold, and new neighbor announcements.

2. *Use your own sold listings* to create a four-piece listing series and testimonial postcards. The first card is just listed: "Do You Know What Your Neighbors Did Last Night?" The second is just sold: "We Did It Again!" The third card is a brief testimonial from the seller. Ask sellers to answer in their own words in one sentence: "Why did you select us to market your home?" Add a positive headline over the testimonial, such as "Sold in 8 days" or "The Gold Team

got us full price!" Then, under their words, add a tagline, such as "Another Worry-Free Home Sale by The Gold Team." The fourth card is a new neighbor announcement: "Meet your new neighbors . . . A service of your neighborhood realty experts, *(Your Name)* (703) 698-7750."

3. *Mail "Attaboy" letters.* These endorsement letters are from your professional referral sources, such as your title companies, lawyers, settlement companies, and lenders. Endorsement letters can also come from your broker and assistants. The professional writes a letter to "Dear Prospective Home Buyer or Seller." You make a color photocopy of the letter so the letterhead and signature in blue ink looks original, and you mail it to prospects. These endorsement letters will supply proof that you back up your claims of great service. Encourage your endorsers to write a letter along these lines: "Dear Prospective Home Buyer (or seller): As a (industry) professional, I have the opportunity to work with many real estate agents. In my years of experience, only a few agents consistently provide as high a level of professional service as (your name). Not only does (your name) respond to even the smallest need of every client, but it's a pleasure to work with a professional whose service system is so organized and finely tuned that almost every transaction comes off without a serious hitch. Take my word. You'll be in good hands when you use (your name) to help you with all your real estate needs." Collect a dozen or two dozen letters and bombard a qualified prospect with all the letters in the first thirty days after first contact. Your referral sources will be glad to get the exposure, too. *Tip:* Offer to swap a similar letter from you on your letterhead that your sources can use with *their* prospects.

4. *Send testimonial letters from past clients.* First, make it standard procedure to collect a letter from every client. (Get their signed permission to use the letter for promotional purposes.) Lay the groundwork early. Show them

other client testimonial letters when you first meet. Say that you want to do such a good job for them they'll send you a letter like this after they move. Make it easy: ask your clients to write as they talk, using short sentences and everyday words. Their letter should sound conversational, as if they were talking to a friend. Ask them to explain honestly how your service solved a problem for them or fulfilled a need. A good question to ask them to answer: "What part of our team's service did you find the most helpful?" Again, mail color photocopies to prospects.

Take a tip from Dave Blewett, a top agent in San Carlos, California, and a RE/MAX Hall of Fame and Lifetime Achievement member, who has a photo of himself taken with his sellers holding a "sold" rider or a "I ♥ My RE/MAX REALTOR®" sign. Blewett then assembles nine photos and testimonials into a full-page ad with the headline, "Start Packing! Because . . . When You List Your Home with Dave Blewett, You're Going to Be Moving!" The ad reprint makes a great handout to consumers and referral agents.

5. *Company results.* How have your sales been? Whatever the production, the dollar figure sounds astronomical to consumers. If you've got comparative figures for the prior month or year or for your competition that make you look good, use them. Design a flyer using your desktop publishing software or have your printer design it.

6. *News articles.* Reprint any publicity and mail it to prospects. You'll probably get more direct benefit from the reprints than the original article.

7. *Prepare an annual report.* Big corporations do it; so can you. Prepare an annual report about all the things you did last year, all your staff, all your services, all the families you helped, all the elements of your success. Point out how your customers benefit from your services. Send prospects a copy.

8. *Send market statistics.* This is a classic. One approach is sending the figures for current listings on the market using easy-to-read bar charts that compare the current month to prior months or the same month in a prior year. How many listings are on the market? What is the average price of those listings? The average days on the market for those listings? The average percentage of listing price to sales price? Percentage of listings that sell? Absorption rates? (If homes sold at the current pace, how many months would it take to sell the entire inventory in the MLS: 90 days, 120 days, 180 days? Sellers get a sense of how far in advance of their move date to list with you.) Prospects love market statistics. And statistics present you as the expert.

9. *Mail mortgage rates.* If prospects see in the newspaper the rates for conventional, adjustable, and VA/FHA financing, consider publishing rates on other types of mortgages available. But don't be overly concerned about the basic loan rates, because many folks may not see the newspaper.

10. *Trumpet your enrolled buyers and sellers.* Tell prospects how many buyers and sellers you have currently enrolled in your preferred customer programs. Prove to prospects that you already have buyers for their home and homes for them to buy. (More on preferred customer programs in Chapter 7.)

Everything must contain a response offer and a code. Just like lead generation, every follow-up effort *must* carry a response offer—without fail. Every letter, every postcard, every answering machine message, every newsletter, every just listed or just sold card must have a response offer. Include benefits: what the prospect will save or avoid or reap by calling for the offered item. Make 'em drool. Compel prospects to respond, ideally with a phone call. (You'll discover it's much easier to talk with them when *they* are interested than to catch them at your convenience when you call back.)

Strategy #5: Hook Clients with the Phone Like Hungry Fish

On top of the direct mail base, the **Real Estate Rainmaker** system builds a telephone follow-up system. Time is precious. When a rainmaker becomes busy with buyers and sellers, there's even less time to stay in touch with prospects by phone or in person. That's why your telephone contacts must be targeted and efficient to consume the least amount of time.

Repeat three-peat call system. Many rainmakers discover that one hour a day can be dedicated to making prospect phone calls—your "Hour of Power," as national speaker Bill Barrett calls it. Put off returning your waiting voice mail messages until your follow-up calls are complete. The appointment you set with yourself for prospect follow-up each day is just as important as any listing presentation or buyer appointment you make, Barrett says.

Plan to make calls in two groups of three. Make three calls to new prospects or prospects you have never called. These are prospects you either have met or have a true business reason to call; they are warm calls, not cold calls to strangers. The calls can be simple "Howdy" calls to existing prospects. Next, make three repeat calls to prospects you have called before. I call this your "Repeat Three-Peat Call System" in honor of Michael Jordan's work ethic. This is sacred time. Don't fail the rainmaker gods. If you work 250 days out of the year, you will make 1,500 follow-up calls with this system! You'll be amazed at how your business grows.

Messages are a must. Be prepared to leave messages on answering machines or voice mail. Experienced telemarketers know about 60% of their connected calls reach an answering machine or voice mail, not a human. Have a script at hand to leave a message designed to generate a direct response for a free report. Some rainmakers team with an assistant to make calls. If the assistant gets a live answer, the phone is handed to the rainmaker. If not, here is a voice mail script for an effective assistant:

Hi, this is (Assistant's Name), (Company), (phone number). You were kind enough to stop at our open house at (address) last Sunday and you talked to (Rainmaker) at the time. (Rainmaker) is out of the office and asked me to give you a call to see if we can chat some more about your interest in marketing your property or purchasing. If you'd be kind enough to give me a call, I'd be delighted to speak with you and send you a special report we have that helps homeowners avoid the ten costliest mistakes most sellers make. Thanks again and have a great rest of your day. Again, this is (Assistant's Name) for (Rainmaker), (Company), at (phone number).

What time to call? Among salespeople and telemarketers, no question goes around in more circles than the best time to call. Experience is your best guide. Many believe evenings, 5 to 9 P.M. Monday through Friday are best: "People are home," they say. Others swear by their "Hours of Power" in the mornings 9:15 to 11:15 A.M.: "People will listen in the morning. People you reach don't need two incomes to qualify, or they're retired with equity. Both are good prospects," they say. Still others believe in Saturday morning or Sunday evening: "Folks are relaxing. They're impressed I'm working weekends to get their business, so they think I'll work even harder to keep it," they say. *Tip:* Ask your prospects and customers the best time to call them at home or work.

Generally, you can count on reaching about 45% with your first call, 20% more with a second try, and perhaps an additional 10% on the third try, according to Bob Donath in *Managing Sales Leads.* That means to reach 75 of 100 prospects, you or your assistant will need to make 190 calls (100 + 55 + 35). That's a week's work for a telemarketer, who can handle 35 to 40 prospect dials, conversations, and fulfillments a day. Clearly, to reach everyone, only a robust mailing program will do the job.

Automate your messages. One of the most innovative technologies for prospect follow-up is automated "voice broadcast" messaging services. The technology dials the phone number you've loaded into the service and leaves your prerecorded message only on an answering machine or voice mail. If a person answers the call, the technology simply hangs up. To be effective, the recorded message must include a response offer for a free report or videotape or some call to action. Rainmakers use the service for prospect follow-up, especially to follow up scores of leads from call-capture hotlines.

The voice messaging service also works well for cold lead generation of sellers, buyers, expireds, and FSBOs, as well as advance notice to a database to "watch for" a coming mail piece with a special offer. For long-term contact, voice messaging is a successful way to automate open house invitations and just listed and just sold announcements to past clients. I suggest you close the message with the reminder that referrals are always welcome.

Generally, voice messaging service fees include a one-time activation fee, a charge per minute billed, and a monthly service fee. Prices can vary by volume. (See Resource Guide under Voice Broadcasting.)

RAINMAKER CHAPTER 6 SUMMARY

Customer Conversion Strategies to Maximize Sales

- ▶ Strategy #1: Qualify, Qualify, Qualify.
- ▶ Strategy #2: Launch Follow-Up Immediately with High-Impact Response Kit.
- ▶ Strategy #3: Use the F.O.R.D. Method to Build Phone Rapport.
- ▶ Strategy #4: Flood Prospects with an Abundance of Information in the Mail.
- ▶ Strategy #5: Hook Clients with the Phone Like Hungry Fish.

Shooting Fish in a Barrel

> The closure rate from qualified leads can be two to four times as effective as cold calls.
>
> Bob Stone
> *Successful Direct Marketing Methods*

How do you convert first-stage prospects into second-stage shoppers? How do you nudge a fence-sitter into action? What carrot will compel a truly motivated prospect to step forward out of the prospect pipeline and become a client?

One of the most effective techniques is to create a menu of services for a Preferred Customer Program. Basically, buyer or seller prospects that enroll in your program will receive special services reserved for program members only—but first, they must qualify as ready shoppers. The service is intense, and, frankly, you can't provide the level of service to anyone who isn't ready to buy or sell *now*. Only "qualified" customers can be accepted.

Some prospects sign up at the first contact. Others need to be sold on the benefits of the preferred services during your prospect follow-up campaign, and will sign up when they are ready to be serious. The secret to the Preferred Customer Program solution is that it's designed to be an offer truly motivated prospects can't refuse—and that is exactly the kind of customers the **Real Estate Rainmaker** system wants to capture.

Convert Prospects into Shoppers with a Preferred Customer Program

Give your preferred customer program an impressive name. Call it Qualified Buyer Program, Red Carpet Club, Certified Seller Program, Home Finders Service, Buyers Advantage, Gold Club (Platinum, Silver, or Diamond Club, or use your company color), Winner's Circle, Educated Consumer Program, Customer Care Service, Premiere Privileges, Insiders Club. National real estate speaker Walter Sanford calls it his VIP Club or Perks Club. Once prospects are enrolled, they receive special services, such as personal attention from the rainmaker, available only to qualified preferred customers.

Start enrollment right over the phone. To enroll in your Preferred Customer Program, prospects are first required to be qualified by your lender over the phone (10–03 loan application, in-file credit score) and contacted within an hour to tell the prospects if they should make a personal appointment with the lender. If needed, prospects will be instructed what to bring into the office for a loan application. In addition, to qualify, prospects must have a private session with you, or at least with your assistant or buyer's agent, either in your office for buyers or in their home for sellers, to submit their application and personal financial information. The application is their customer profile information and their personal statistics. Naturally, if these requirements turn into a listing presentation or buyer qualification appointment, that's okay too!

Promote the number of enrollees. Say today, you have 24 buyers who are enrolled in your Preferred Customer Program. Tell your prospective sellers you've got 24 buyers in your buyer pool who are looking for houses right now: *"If you list tonight, we can sell your house promptly, because we have the buyers."* Take advantage of your enrollment to attract even more prospects.

Personal enrollment package. Assemble an impressive enrollment package prospects receive when they are accepted. This package is essentially a prequalification kit for buyers or a prelisting kit for sellers. Have a picture taken of the kit and use it in your program flyer or brochure where you describe the benefits of your Preferred Customer Program. Here are some effective items to include in the enrollment package, which is designed to weigh a ton and impress the soon-to-be-shopper prospect:

- Rainmaker mission statement.
- Testimonial letters.
- Ancillary services or recommended suppliers.
- Affiliated professionals (and their exclusive discounts).
- Open House Guest Pass (once a buyer's agency agreement is signed). Prospects can show the pass to open house agents indicating prospects that are exclusively represented by you as their buyer's agent and all calls should be directed to you.
- Steps in the process of buying or selling a house.
- Steps in loan financing process and information about closing escrow/settlement.
- MLS abbreviations decoded to enable prospects to read property profile sheets.
- Information brochures and special reports on specific topics.
- Area maps with subdivision or neighborhood names.
- A list of documents the prospect should sign or gather before appointment.
- Video on buying a home or pricing and fixing up a home to sell.
- List of satisfied past customers from prior two years.

Seven Sure-Fire Preferred Customer Services

Strategy #1: Personal Shopper Program

One of the most successful agents in the country, Zac Pasmanick, a top producer with RE/MAX Greater Atlanta-Intown, uses a "personal shopper program" very effectively. In a nutshell,

---

Figure 7.1
Zac Pasmanick's Personal Shopper Program

You've heard of the Home Shopping Network. But how about the Home Shopping Experts?

That's right—your very own personal shopper to help you find your new home, and seal the deal before it gets away. Don't let your dream home slip into the hands of another buyer, because you didn't have proper representation or because you found out about the listing too late. Get the edge you need. You need a tough negotiator who has the finesse to handle a complicated real estate transaction. You need a fast-acting, skilled professional with a trained eye and attention to detail. You need a home shopping expert. Where can you find one? You're in luck. Zac's Dream Team of buyer's agents can't wait to help you find the perfect home. Call today to schedule a hassle-free consultation with your home shopping expert from the zac team.

404.874.SOLD

Courtesy of Zac Pasmanick, RE/MAX Greater Atlanta–Intown

Pasmanick assigns the prospect to one of his buyer's agents, and the buyer's agent completely services the needs of the prospect. Pasmanick's program is best explained in his own words. Figure 7.1 is the ad copy he uses to promote the program.

Strategy #2: Personal Home Buyer Hot List

This is a property search and notification service that is either manual or automated. Using prospects' property search requirements, you mail, fax, or e-mail buyer prospects a Hot List daily or weekly or monthly, including a thumbnail description of each new listing that matches. (If sellers don't have a home fax machine, lend them an inexpensive one until they move. For buyers, provide a pager, cell phone, or e-mail account. Guess who they will be talking about to their friends!) The preferred customers benefit by getting a jump on new-on-the-market properties before the properties are advertised or held open. Only your preferred customers get this advantage. You can do the MLS search manually or use a software program to provide the service automatically by printed report, fax, or e-mail. That way, you don't lift a finger. The computer does it all for you.

One automatic software is called SOAR MLS™. Once you enter a prospect's criteria, SOAR MLS automatically dials your MLS searches, and then prints (you must stuff the window envelopes) or faxes or e-mails MLS information for all your prospects every day, week, or month as you select. Send buyer prospects a new list of properties. Send prospective sellers an updated Competitive Market Analysis. Send active listings an updated CMA to encourage price reductions. SOAR MLS charges a one-time activation and a monthly service fee, and service is available in select metropolitan MLS markets. (See Resource Guide under Technology Tools.)

Coldwell Banker has a similar, award-winning system linked to its website, called Personal Retriever. The NAR's website (www.REALTOR.com) offers a similar e-mail notification under its Personal Planner function. Microsoft Home Advisor's (www .homeadvisor.com) comparable service is called Home Tracker. Windermere Real Estate, based in Seattle, calls its property e-mail notification service The Personalized Home Search. Windermere features a hyperlink in every e-mail for the prospect to click and return easily to Windermere's website for full listing information.

For the rainmaker, these hands-off Internet-based search services for property listings are an ideal prospect follow-up offer to exchange for a registered prospect's personal information and property criteria, such as location, price range, number of bedrooms and baths, and so on. The system automatically sends prospects an e-mail with information on matched listings.

After a drive-by, the prospect calls you to say, "I'm interested in 123 Oak Street." You say, "How did you learn about it?" They say, "You sent me an e-mail." "Of course! Would you like to see it inside? My pleasure, but first tell me who I'm talking to. Terrific.

Would this afternoon be convenient?" Perhaps your assistant or a buyer's agent takes the opportunity to gather additional qualifying information missing from the prospect's profile and makes an appointment. "Great. Meet me at my office at 1 o'clock. It's my pleasure."

Notice how more information, not less—such as address, price, down payment, and monthly payment—raises the quality of the prospect call from a low-quality info-only "ad call" to a high-quality appointment-getting "sign call." That's the power of information today. By providing full information, rainmakers can change the prospect's often negative perception of a real estate agent as a predator into the positive perception of a valuable service provider.

A similar property notification service using voice mail, called DirectConnect, won "best new idea" when it was demonstrated at the sixth annual Great Idea Conference in October 1998 by broker/owner and designer Ralph Leino of Preferred Carlson, REALTORS®, in Kalamazoo, Michigan. The system searches the local MLS for new listings, back-on-market listings, price reductions, and other changes in the MLS and leaves an appropriate voice-mail message on a daily basis in the personal mailbox of enrolled buyers whose requirements match those of the new listings. The buyer calls into their DirectConnect mailbox to get their property messages. To enroll in DirectConnect, a prospect must have signed a buyer's agent agreement and have loan preapproval before a personal mailbox is assigned. The primary difference the company has experienced with DirectConnect, Leino says, is that the service gets buyer's agency agreements signed like crazy. The voice message includes property address and price. Preferred Carlson wants customers to drive by the properties; the voice message even tells the customer what sign to look for. That way, people can shop the way they like to shop, anonymously, says Leino. With DirectConnect, Preferred Carlson's agents can work scores of buyers at once. When a customer wants to find out more or inspect a property, the customer simply forwards the property message to their buyer's agent.

Strategy #3: First-Time Buyer Hot List

This is a specialty Hot List for properties attractive to low-down-payment, below-market, first-time buyer prospects. These properties are "bargains" or "values." Prospects who have expressed an interest are sent a list of handyman specials, REOs, relocation management third-party listings, foreclosures, divorce or estate sales, distressed properties, or condominiums, whatever suits their price range or specific needs. Properties might also be selected from the rainmaker's database of clients who may be selling soon (future listings no one else has). Plus, preferred buyers can choose from your expireds database (off-the-market-sellers motivated to sell). All these Hot List properties, as well as your proven negotiating skills, can deliver preferred clients a nice savings that is a greater average percentage discount than the market standard listing-price-to-sales-price discount. Be sure to track your success, and promote it to first-stage prospects.

Strategy #4: Personal Price Hotline

Enrolled customers can call your team with the address of any properties for sale they pass when they drive through neighborhoods that appeal to them. The rainmaker's office gives them the prices over the phone, or faxes, e-mails, or mails a complete MLS profile of that property if they prefer. Preferred customers benefit from the convenience of one information source they know they can trust.

Strategy #5: Personal Open House Tour

For preferred customers under a buyer's agreement, the rainmaker prepares a personal self-guided open house tour. The night before or in the morning, the rainmaker's office faxes, e-mails a map, or customers pick one up with the property locations, directions, and a profile sheet for each house held open by your company that day.

A high-tech variation of the Personal Open House Tour is a private virtual tour on the customer's own personal website you have prepared. A web page is created just for the prospect with his or her "private access password." The site is a virtual tour of houses that fit the prospect's search criteria. Software such as PhotoShare can do the tour beautifully with music, voice-over, and professional transitions. Also, PictureWorks software can prepare a home tour specifically designed for a web page. (See Resource Guide.) Whatever your clients want to see (and you have the time to input) is available in the privacy of their home on their own time. Later, after the prospect has become a customer under agreement, this same private access website can be used to maintain an online listing activity report for sellers or update a client's settlement status. Walter Sanford, a real estate speaker from Long Beach, California, maintains the customer's personal website forever, and posts "points" the past client earns through referrals and repeat business. These points will translate later into commission discounts off their next transaction.

Strategy #6: Personal Comparable Alert for Sellers

You can give preferred seller prospects a Competition Alert. The rainmaker sends them notice of new comparables that have just come on the market. Because these comparables are now on the market, the competing properties may affect the prospect's soon-to-be-decided asking price, terms, and fix-up plans. A notification can be sent by e-mail, fax, or mail. A variation is simply to send enrolled homeowner prospects a weekly "just sold" report on area sales.

Strategy #7: Preferred Property Program for Sellers

This program for sellers sets standards for a *property*, not a prospect, to be "accepted" as a Preferred Property. The seller is educated during the follow-up phase, then enrolled at a prelisting presentation. The property—before it goes on the market— must be certified as passing the 8-Step Preferred Property criteria to earn a special sign rider as a "Blue Ribbon" preferred property (give it your own name to tie in with your rainmaker practice). Criteria might include preparations the prospective seller must complete before the property is accepted:

1. *Curb appeal.* First impression is perfect. Landscaping, front of house, door, hardware, windows, walk, and driveway, everything in magazine showcase condition.

2. *Market value price.* Within 5% of fair market value.

3. *Appraisal.* Seller pays for professional appraisal because buyers won't accept an agent's or seller's opinion of value. Thus, higher offers result. Or seller can market "below appraisal" for fast sale.

4. *Home inspection.* Seller does repairs after inspection but before going on market and saves money because buyers typically ask for more expensive replacement than repair.

5. *Warranty.* Buyer is assured against unexpected expenses and seller's liability is reduced.

6. *Pest inspection.* Preferred before the listing period begins so that any problems can be corrected.

7. *Cosmetic improvements.* These items are more than elbow grease, but less than a remodel. They might include fresh paint, new floor coverings, and professional cleaning to pass a room-by-room "white glove" inspection.

8. *Property display.* A collection of documents that merchandises the property to prospective buyers, such as subdivision plat, property survey, history of utility costs, garden and plant map, floor plans, warranties, owner's manuals, chronology of improvements with project costs—in short, a "home book."

A Final Tip

At any one moment, a rainmaker has scores of prospects in the pipeline all at different stages in the process. Nudge them constantly along the pipeline to your mutual goal: buying or selling a home.

After the prospect has signed a listing or buyer agreement, continue your follow-up to lay the groundwork for referrals during the sales process. Tell your clients that if you're not available, the client can always reach your team for answers and information. One of the first postagreement calls should be a welcome call from a team assistant: *"(Rainmaker) asked me to call to give you my direct number and to tell you it's my pleasure to help you personally in any way I can. Call me anytime."*

After all, the customers don't care whom they talk to, they just want service. And remember, extend membership in your Preferred Customer Program to all your past customers as a value-added benefit. This is only one of the secrets to referral generation, as you'll learn in Part Four.

RAINMAKER CHAPTER 7 SUMMARY

Shooting Fish in a Barrel

▶ Strategy #1: Personal Shopper Program.

▶ Strategy #2: Personal Home Buyer Hot List.

▶ Strategy #3: First-Time Buyer Hot List.

▶ Strategy #4: Personal Price Hotline.

▶ Strategy #5: Personal Open House Tour.

▶ Strategy #6: Personal Comparable Alert for Sellers.

▶ Strategy #7: Preferred Property Program for Sellers.

FOUR

STEP 3: KEEP CUSTOMERS WITH LONG-TERM CONTACT

Customer Retention Strategies for Optimum Profits

> The most important order you ever get from a customer is the second order.
>
> Maxwell Sackheim
> *Maxwell Sackheim's Complete Guide to Successful Direct Response Marketing*

Long-term contact is the most profitable part of the **Real Estate Rainmaker** system, and the reasons are simple. The lifetime value of a customer is geometrically greater than a one-time deal. Second, word-of-mouth referrals generate business at the lowest cost of acquisition (your biggest marketing expense!). Thus, you earn the highest profit.

If prospect follow-up is where the money is made, then long-term contact is where the profits are made. Perpetual referrals multiply the value of lifetime customers, reduce expenses, maximize profits, and offer unlimited opportunities to cross-sell and up-sell.

Exhaustive market research and customer buying studies show it costs five to ten times more to get a new customer than to keep an old one—across all industries. Why? Because you spend less to generate a loyal referral prospect who is "presold" on your expertise and is easier to work with than a more expensive uncommitted advertising-generated new lead. It's the difference between a slam dunk and a midcourt last-second Hail-Mary shot in basketball. Referrals are slam dunks.

123

True rainmakers ultimately aren't after the single deal, they're after the referrals. Dedicate yourself to acting long-term with the customer's best interests in mind, not just the current deal. Think of your customers as an annuity that pays you referrals year after year. Once you make it your intention to loyalize every customer you acquire, the money will flow.

Many people think referrals are free. Wrong! Word-of-mouth advertising is the cumulative effect of all your advertising in newspapers, home magazines, direct mail, Internet, signs, open houses, prospecting calls, and, in short, the lifelong net sum of all your advertising and marketing activities. Although a successful rainmaker gradually will be able to reduce lead generation expenses to create market-stranger prospects, that lead generation expense will always be significant as long as the rainmaker wants to grow the practice. The cost of cultivating word-of-mouth referrals, on the other hand, will always be a fraction of the cost of lead generation.

Two signs of a practice in decline are referrals accounting for 90% or more of the business, or 10% or less. Too many referrals is incestuous. Without a steady stream of fresh new customers, eventually every customer database ages. Contacts move or die off or simply age into an inactive cohort of friends and family that is not in a home-buying phase, leaving the referral-dependent practitioner without a practice. Too few referrals is ruinous. With the first market downturn, advertising-addicted agents spend their way out of business, leaving behind a fat and happy collection of advertising sales reps.

Understanding New Customers versus Lifetime Customers

Remember the distinction between *market share* and *lifetime customer value* you learned in Chapter 2. Market share refers to your percentage of the pie of all market transactions in one year. These are one-time transactions. Their value is a straightforward multiplication of units times average commission dollar. (The only way to make the market dramatically larger is by adding ancillary businesses in a one-stop-shopping approach. Only then can you sell more to these one-time customers, such as mortgage loans, warranties, homeowners and title insurance, closing services, home improvements, travel packages, hotels, rental cars. One-stop shopping is the reason giant consolidators and diversified megabrokerages salivate over one-time real estate customers, not the value of the single sale.)

Yet, these one-time customers—even the ones who buy ancillary purchases—are worth a lot more over their customer lifetime in referrals and repeat business. Picture a tube of toothpaste: one tube costs very little, but a lifetime supply of toothpaste is worth a lot. The *real* profits in real estate rise from a single-minded focus on the lifetime value of a customer. Simply put, there are two types of customers: one-time deals and lifetime customers. Obviously, lifetime customers have the greatest income value for a rainmaker.

Follow the Example of FedEx

In marketing, we call targeting the lifetime customer a customer-value strategy, as opposed to a transaction-value focus. A good example is Federal Express. In the mid-1990s, FedEx shifted its marketing from a product-oriented strategy to a customer-oriented strategy. Although FedEx invested $50 million-plus to build a database of over four million customers, the strategy was simple.

First, they gathered customer information in two ways. They collected detailed demographic information about their individual company customers by offering a coupon or FedEx premium in exchange for basic company information, such as a company's industry, revenue, and number of employees. Also, FedEx assembled a transaction history of each customer's shipping habits, such as domestic or international, letters or boxes, use of automated airbills or paper airbills, package weight, and frequency.

Next, FedEx analyzed the demographic characteristics of its top 20% best customers who spent the most on shipping with FedEx. The analysis produced a profile of a "most valuable customer."

FedEx then matched the profile against its full customer database to identify *high-potential* customers whom FedEx would expect to be shipping more frequently and at heavier weight, but weren't. Armed with this list of targeted customers, FedEx mailed specific promotions and service education pieces that applied directly to these high-potential customers.

The results were a 400% to 500% improved return on marketing investment, according to FedEx's manager of global distribution marketing/U.S. international marketing, as reported in *Business Marketing,* March 1997.

The **Real Estate Rainmaker** system follows FedEx's example. By simply tracking the value of a customer—measured by the number of transactions a customer caused, either direct deals or referrals—at a minimum, you'll develop a list of most-valued customers who deserve a greater investment to cultivate. If the old saying is correct, *80% of your referral business will come from 20% of your customers.* Then, take it a step further: Identify characteristics of these best customers, such as years in house, customer's age, house price, house style, location, and type of loan, loan amount, and interest rate. Now focus more attention on the other high-potential customers in your Trophy Database who you would expect similarly to become most-valued customers. You, too, could enjoy the success of customer-value marketing, the same as FedEx.

Minimize New Customer Acquisition Costs

The other reason lifetime customers are so profitable is they cost less to acquire. Here is how the cost of acquisition compares for new customers and lifetime customers.

The figures might look like this, using our 800 telephone hotline example. Let's assume that from 720 total annual prospects generated by the hotline (60 per month), you closed only 1 in 72 prospects (1.4%) for 10 transactions. Your gross commission income (GCI) from 10 closings was $20,000 at, say, $2,000 per closing. Calculate the cost of acquiring a customer (see Table 8.1).

Table 8.1
800 Telephone Hotline Strategy

$20,000	Gross commission income ($2,000 × 10)
−12,364	Marketing cost of strategy (Acquisition cost)*
= 7,636	Net income
÷ 10	New customers
= 763	Net value per new customer

* See Figure 14.7 for breakdown of costs.

Maximize Lifetime Customer Value

Let's assume you stay in touch by mail with all 10 customers *every month* for 10 years. The cost of the long-term contact strategy is 50¢ per monthly mailer plus a $3 annual calendar. That adds up to $9 a year per client, or $90 a decade per client, which requires $900 for the entire 10-client 10-year marketing cost of this strategy. After 10 years, let's say, either every customer sent you one referral that closed or returned to use you again one time for a total of 10 deals. Calculate the lifetime value of the customer (see Table 8.2).

The calculation in Table 8.1 tells you the relative value of landing a new customer. The calculation in Table 8.2 shows you how profitable it is to keep an old customer for life. In our example, the 10-year lifetime value is almost three times the one-time value of a new customer. One of the cardinal rules for the **Real Estate Rainmaker** system is to constantly work to minimize your cost of acquisition of new customers. Another cardinal rule is to focus much greater marketing effort on long-term

Table 8.2
Monthly Client Contact Strategy

$20,000	Gross commission income ($2,000 × 10)
− 900	Marketing cost of strategy (Acquisition cost)
=19,100	Net income
÷ 10	Lifetime customers
= 1,910	Net value per lifetime customer

contacts—and also on active prospects in the pipeline—to guarantee you capture the maximum number of customers.

Imagine in our example how incredibly profitable your lifetime customers will be if they send you not one referral in 10 years, but one referral *every year* for 10 years! Your same $90 per customer direct-mail investment over the decade—plus some priceless telephone follow-up—explodes from $1,910 to $19,100 in net income per customer. Just 10 lifetime customers sending you one referral a year over 10 years would yield $191,100 in sales! Now the figures are getting interesting. Imagine if you had 100 lifetime customers—or 1,000!

Dedicate yourself to the **Real Estate Rainmaker** system and lifetime customers will put you on the road to financial independence.

Knowing What Works Makes Getting More Easy

Where do referrals come from? Do sellers, repeat buyers, or first-time buyers tend to depend on referrals more than others? Once again, let's turn to the NAR survey of buying and selling that asked what advertising media or referral source helped consumers make the first contact with the real estate agent they used. The answer is more than half of all business comes from word of mouth (see Figure 8.1).

Four Secrets to Perfect Customer Care (and More Word-of-Mouth Referrals)

Although it sounds simple, a systematic program of referral generation takes as much planning and implementation as any good marketing plan. There are four fundamental secrets to success.

Secret #1: Deliver great service. It all starts—and ends—here. The rainmaker first must provide service so good all clients tell their friends. But don't assume clients don't have anything

Figure 8.1
Understanding How Different Prospects Find an
Agent with Word-of-Mouth Referrals

SELLERS

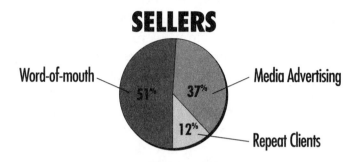

Word-of-mouth — 51%   37% — Media Advertising

12% — Repeat Clients

REPEAT BUYERS

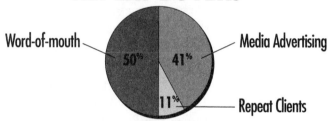

Word-of-mouth — 50%   41% — Media Advertising

11% — Repeat Clients

FIRST-TIME BUYERS

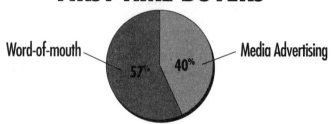

Word-of-mouth — 57%   40% — Media Advertising

	Sellers	Repeat Buyers	First-Time Buyers
Word of mouth (referrals)	51%	50%	57%
Media advertising	37	41	40
Repeat clients	12	11	0

*Percentages do not equal 100% due to rounding.

Source: National Association of REALTORS®

better to talk about than your terrific service. That's where the next three steps come in.

Secret #2: Maintain long-term contact. During the critical active service period from listing or buyer's agreement to closing, make sure to collect detailed personal information about your clients similar in many ways to what your lender requires—and enter it in your customer profile Trophy Database. Gather details such as children's names and birth dates, pets' names, life goals, hobbies, and a special cause, then round out the items you first learned from using your F.O.R.D. rapport-building technique when they were prospects. For the personal touch, after closing, drop off a book by their favorite author or contribute to their favorite charity. You'll be remembered. Stay in touch primarily by mail, but calls and personal visits are a plus. When your client list gets too big to see everyone in person regularly, it may be time for a client appreciation event.

Secret #3: Educate customers about referrals. Teaching prospects about the importance of referrals is your critical mission. One of the biggest mistakes most agents make in regard to referrals is never telling their customers how important referrals are. Everything helps, from being as subtle as mentioning to a client how you helped another client who was referred to you by so-and-so, to publishing your source-of-business pie chart and highlighting how important referrals are to you, to using slogans that say it directly, such as "People who know us recommend us," or "The most talked about name in real estate," or "Do a friend a favor. Give them my name," or "Neighbors helping neighbors achieve their dream." In short, educate clients about how important referrals are to you.

Caution: Never pay a bounty for a referral. That is, don't offer to pay a customer for a referral. Besides the possibility of running afoul of Real Estate Settlement Procedures Act (RESPA) rules or state laws that prohibit sharing a brokerage fee with an unlicensed person, a bounty makes a referral suspect. The referral source is then giving the referral for the wrong reason—personal gain—rather than to help the referral prospect. One of the best ways we've seen to trump the bounty dilemma is to *reinforce* the referral by giving your referral sources a valuable coupon or certificate *they* can give to their friend, who in turn can redeem it when the friend does business with you. All the referred prospect has to do to collect is contact you. There is nothing "in it" for the referral source. An evaluation, a critique, a free report, or donation to a charity of their choice at closing, all of these work well.

Secret #4: Ask for the referral. If you don't ask for the business, somebody else will. In your newsletters, in every letter, in your advertising, ask for the referral business. Don't be shy. Ask *"Who do you know who is moving?"* or *"Who do you know who has questions for a real estate professional?"*

Quick Checklist on How to Ask for a Referral the Right Way

☑ Larry Bender, a top professional with Prudential in Tucson, Arizona, drops by his client's new house the day after move-in to present a large wind chime. ("Every time the wind blows, they think of me," says Bender.) Then he uses a script something like this: *"There you are with your big watermelon smile. You're so happy your ears are about to burst, because you've got a new home. But I'm sad. Why? Because I've lost you as a client. Now you need to help me find another client like you to boost MY spirits."* Bender then tells them about referrals and how important they are to his business and asks who they know that is planning to move. When they do come through with a referral, he sends them a bottle of champagne personalized with his own private label as a thank you.

☑ At the end of taking the loan application, Bill Sparkman, a leading mortgage lender sales and marketing trainer based in San Diego, asks the customer, *"Before I leave, I'll need the name of your tax accountant."* *"Why?"* the client asks. *"Because now we both share the same client,"* Sparkman says. *"I'll be sending your accountant your HUD-1 Settlement Statement form because he'll need it to do your taxes."* Later, Sparkman calls the accountant and says, *"The reason for my call is we now share the same clients, Mr. and Mrs. Homebuyer. And I wanted to ask you if you're accepting new clients, too. I meet many new home buyers who don't have an accountant. What type of client would you like me to refer to you?"*

☑ In their definitive book, *How to Get Clients,* Jeff and Marc Slutsky suggest you never ask a question that is as easily answered by "no" as by "yes," such as *"Do you know anybody who is planning to move?"* Instead, ask for a *name,* not a yes or no answer: *"Who do you know?"* or *"Who do you know in your (church, neighborhood, office, etc.) who is thinking about buying or selling?"*

☑ The Slutskys also recommend you qualify the names given by the customer to get a better idea of the potential new prospects and their relationships to the referral source. Ask *"Why do you recommend this person?"; "May I use your name?";* or *"Is there any reason I shouldn't mention your name?"* It's always good to be sure. Beyond a name, you must, of course, get their phone number and address if possible: *"What is the best way to get in touch with them? Do you have their number?"* Knowing the best time to reach them, at home or the office, is a big plus, too.

☑ The Slutskys then suggest this close: *"I really appreciate these referrals and I promise I'll contact them right away. Thank you!"* or *"Thank you for the referral. The more referrals I get, the less time I have to spend cold-calling and prospecting. That means I've got more time to devote to my customers. Thank you again."* Of course, if no one comes immediately to mind, say, *"If you think of someone, please call me with their name."*

Nine Rainmaker Strategies to Maximize Long-Term Contact Referrals

But who do you stay in touch with? There are nine essential *Real Estate Rainmaker* strategies for a complete long-term contact program. These nine strategies are grouped in two broad referral categories: consumers and business-to-business. In the beginning, rainmakers usually focus on only one or two word-of-mouth advertising strategies. A mature rainmaker practice will pursue all nine strategies simultaneously.

Consumer Word-of-Mouth Advertising

STRATEGY #1: FOCUS ON LONG-TERM PROSPECTS

Most prospects that inquire about buying or selling require months (even years) of follow-up before they are ready to be active shoppers. A long lead time is especially common with Internet leads, new construction, corporate relocation group moves, and retirement markets. Treat these *pipeline prospects* as your first best referral source, even though they aren't "past customers" because they have not yet actually worked with you on a closed transaction. Share with long-term prospects—and with active clients during the transaction—that referrals let you do a better job for them. After all, if you're not distracted by the grind of constant cold-calling to drum up new customers, you can give them the full attention they deserve. Prospects and active shoppers almost always know other people in the same circumstances as themselves.

Your personal *friends and family* are also in this long-term prospect group. They may never have done a deal with you, but they know you and they are an excellent source of referrals. You can even add to your long-term contact list your other sphere-of-influence contacts once you feel they know you enough to remember your name. Include past-life acquaintances you knew before you began your real estate career. Put them into your referral program. *For-sale-by-owners* are another consumer referral source who are often willing to trade some home sale marketing assistance for the names of active buyers who visit their house but decide not to buy it.

STRATEGY #2: STAY IN TOUCH
WITH PAST CUSTOMERS

Customers are people you have done a transaction with in the past. In the business, we call prospecting to retain past customers *after marketing* or *relationship marketing* or *retention market-ing*. Mail your direct past clients a newsletter at least 12 times a year, and call them at least three times or even more if you can. Ask for referrals. This strategy will prove to be the most prof-itable thing you do if you're not doing it now.

Don't limit yourself only to your direct customers. One inno-vative idea is to consider the *property* your past client, too. Build a database of past properties selectable by address using in-depth MLS data to capture complete information in detail about the past listing. After all, you were the broker that last listed the house the prospects live in—and you should be the only broker they turn to when they want to sell. You can initiate the relationship immediately after the closing with a call: *"As the listing agent, I know more about the property than anyone but the sellers. Do you have any questions I can help with?"* Then stay in touch. One effective technique is using a personalized photo calendar from Kinko's featuring a picture of their new house on the calendar.

Next, add to the database the *sellers* who moved across town after selling their house to your buyer client. If anyone has proven he or she can produce a buyer for a seller's property, it's you. Stay in touch.

Now add the *prospects* you worked with but who, for what-ever reason, never closed the transaction, such as fall-through buyers and withdrawn sellers. This is especially important if the transaction fell apart and was left on a sour note. Repairing or at least neutralizing negative past customers is as valuable as cul-tivating past clients who are raving fans.

As you see, for a successful rainmaker, *past customers* has a much broader meaning than simply the obvious usual suspects.

STRATEGY #3: DEVELOP A CUSTOMER WIN-BACK CAMPAIGN FOR ORPHANS

One of the biggest untapped opportunities to jump-start your **Real Estate Rainmaker** system is right in your own office: a customer win-back program for orphaned customers. Orphaned customers are past customers of agents no longer with your company; often they are neglected and abandoned customers. Make it your mission to rescue them. Go to those old dusty file cabinets that hold the ancient case folders. Pay some temps, pay some techies, convert the file cabinet into living names and addresses, and work the customers as past clients of your company. Concentrate your marketing first on orphans who have owned their house between three and seven years; they are most likely to move again soon. Never, ever, abandon them again. Remember, your customers are someone else's prospects unless you win them back.

One of the best agents in Columbia, South Carolina, Ray Covington Jr., did just that. Covington teamed with Hollie Davis, a top loan officer and division vice president with CTX Mortgage Company, to share costs and computerize hundreds of old transactions. Covington and Davis spent more than a year and about $2,000 in temps and techies to organize all his old case files, put them in labeled file drawers, then enter them into a computer database.

Every possible bit of information was recovered, including property address, client's name, home phone, work phone, forwarding address if different and spouse's name and work phone. Covington recorded whether the customer was the seller or buyer in the transaction, the date of purchase, and the sales price. Other fields captured the name of the lender, title company, and listing and selling agents. When you do this, be sure to include the old agent's internal company accounting ID number to cross-match against the list of current colleagues still with the company. Complete information on noncompany co-brokers should also be stored.

After Covington and Davis compiled a rough database, they wisely cleaned the list by mailing first-class to every customer name and deleting the names of returned undeliverables after three unsuccessful phone attempts. "I made extreme extra efforts to get prior customer's addresses from Return Service Requested," says Davis. "I made numerous phone calls and even went so far as to track them down in bars. Ray would just mention someone's name and I made sure they were added to the database." End result: 600 past company customers still living in town. Covington then launched a monthly newsletter campaign to work this list by mail and shared the addressing tasks and costs with Davis. Within 24 months, Covington more than doubled his personal production from $5 million to $12 million, largely due to additional repeat and referral business from the 600 names alone; business that could have gone to competitors if they hadn't installed an orphan win-back program.

Business-to-Business Word-of-Mouth Advertising

STRATEGY #4: DEVELOP PARTNERSHIPS WITH NEW HOME BUILDERS

New home builders understand all too well that three out of four buyers buy resale, and that resale agents are a hugely significant source of new home buyers. Also, real estate professionals know builders have more leads from their model homes than can buy the homes they build. (The National Association of Home Builders reports an average sale-to-model-home-visitor ratio of only 3 out of 100, or 3%.) Include builders in your business-to-business referral network.

Quick Checklist to Develop Relationships with New Home Builders

LeRoy Houser, a master business coach in Chesterfield, Virginia, and a sought-after new home sales instructor for the Residential Sales Council, says he has listed more builder property in his career by simply showing builders' homes to his buyers than any other way. Here are seven secrets to cultivating builder business from Houser's extensive experience:

☑ Identify builders you want to represent. Focus on small builders who build fewer than 20 houses a year. Unlike large builders, small builders often need real estate agents' services.

☑ Launch an excellent direct-mail program to builders that contacts them no fewer than 16 times a year. Continuity and frequency are key.

☑ Exhibit your technology savvy to builders who are tuned into technology. Use e-mail and an electronic newsletter and have a website.

☑ Show builders' homes to your buyers. Leave your business card. Builders come to know you, especially after you're involved in the negotiation of a sale or two.

☑ Develop relationships with other agents who represent builders. Small builders often have one lot here, another lot there, and other lots across town. Multiple locations require builders to work with multiple real estate agents. Typically, builders ask the agents they work with already to recommend new agents.

☑ Focus on expired new home listings on the MLS. Contact builders who have expired listings. You'll probably find a builder who is open to a new agent.

☑ Work the residual traffic that did not buy the builder's property. Not all builders are the same. Some are territorial, some are not. Builders typically don't care if you work the extra visitors as long as their new homes are being represented and sold in a timely manner. Come to an understanding with the builder up front.

STRATEGY #5: CULTIVATE BIRD DOGS

Some rainmakers refer to this personal network group as their "Tip Club" or "Lunch Bunch" or "Board of Advisors." Because these professionals typically work in fields related to real estate, their noses are to the ground, already sniffing deals and relocations both local and long distance, and they can alert the rainmaker. As a group, these professionals can provide a "one-stop-shopping" experience for your clients. Transaction-related professionals include lenders, appraisers, title companies, title insurers, escrow/settlement services and attorneys, even warranty providers, home inspectors, pest inspectors, and surveyors. As a professional courtesy, a rainmaker reciprocates by sending the Bird Dogs new business in their industry.

Building your mutual referral network of other professionals is easy but takes time. The approach is straightforward: Call them to explain many of your customers ask you for referrals to particular professionals like your Bird Dogs. Customers ask you to recommend lawyers for probate, foreclosure, divorces, settlements. They ask for insurance agents for homeowners insurance, car, health, life, umbrella. Still other customers are seeking bargains in foreclosures and REO property for sale by banks who in turn need new customers for their other banking services.

Ask your Bird Dog professionals what type of customers they want, what type of customer is perfect for their specialty or growth strategy. Then stay in touch with your monthly newsletter. Remind them you want the reciprocal relationship to grow and you look forward to exchanging referral business with them.

Don't forget *nontransaction-related professionals* who are in a position to hear about expansions, group moves, new hires, and transfers. The primary group includes nonreal estate attorneys, accountants, truck rental companies, executive recruiters, employment agencies, moving companies, Chamber of Commerce and/or Economic Development Authority officials, commercial leasing managers, hotel managers, temporary housing managers, and state teacher accreditation managers. A secondary nontransaction-related group includes developers, space planners, office furniture sellers and renters, telephone system sellers and long-distance carriers, corporate travel agents, politicians, journalists, and advertising salespeople. Both groups can be easily cultivated with direct mail and regular telephone contact once the initial contact is made. Always ask what kind of prospects they are looking for now, and let them know what type of clients you are trying to generate.

STRATEGY #6: SCRATCH A FEW SUPPLIERS' BACKS

Another business-to-business referral group is suppliers. These contacts provide home services—everything homeowners need for improving, restoring, or maintaining their homes. No need for exclusivity. Suppliers will be happy to be included on a short list of three or so recommended specialists, compared to the crowd of competitors they face in the Yellow Pages. Examples include architects, cleaning services, estate liquidators, floor and carpet installers, gutter cleaners, heating and A/C repair services, home security suppliers, landscapers, lawn and garden services, locksmiths, painters, plumbers, property managers, remodelers, roofers, swimming pool services, telephone installers, tree services, utilities, and window treatment suppliers. *Tip:* Have your assistant insert an envelope stuffer asking for referrals in every check you send to your suppliers. Turn the payment into a business generator.

Ask your preferred suppliers to give you coupons that open house visitors can redeem for discounts—the same offers they use in coupon packs such as Val-Pak, Super Coups, Money Mailer, and United Coupon. The suppliers get increased traffic to their business; rainmakers provide value-added reward for open house guests. A win-win-win for you, the suppliers, and the prospects—and it doesn't cost you a penny! Several popular ideas that work well are discounts on rekeying or replacing all the locks, extra keys at settlement, a tax consultation, or a safety consultation for new purchasers.

Successful rainmakers and some brokerages have begun to prescreen household service providers and charge them a program fee to refer past customers to their service. Another variation is to refer prospects to suppliers who pay for ads in a rainmaker's newsletter or magazine. This "concierge service" concept not only pays for itself, but also is an effective way to stay in touch and provide a service to past customers who otherwise might not contact a real estate agent for years. One concierge service provided by Coldwell Banker Southern California with one manager, three coordinators, and support staff offers over 150 services, including some of the above, plus valet parking service, shelf/closet lining, limousine service, graffiti removal, and feng shui consultants (the Asian art of the alignment of property and good fortune). The most popular services are the handyman service, gardening/landscaping services, and maid service. Coldwell Banker has rolled out this model nationwide for all of its affiliates.

The idea of one-stop shopping, where the real estate professional is the gatekeeper who can arrange any service for home buying and homeownership, has taken hold. For example, Century 21 has created a model called Century 21 Preferred Alliance Programs for its brokers to follow. The model is designed to guide brokers through the most effective ways to tie in these consumer services to their brokerage business and increase profitability.

STRATEGY #7: WEAVE AN OUT-OF-TOWN BROKER NETWORK

Perhaps the oldest referral source is out-of-town brokers and agents. Largely, this strategy generates long-distance nationwide relocation referrals, but rainmakers in large metropolitan areas also cultivate local cross-town referrals (see Strategy #8). Network examples include relocation networks (RELO) and franchise affiliates (Coldwell Banker, Prudential, Century 21, ERA, Realty World, RE/MAX, etc.). NAR designation groups are another natural network, for instance, the Residential Sales Council (GRI, CRS, CIPS) or ABR (buyer's representation), CRP (relocation), CCIM (commercial) or SRES (seniors) and the Women's Council of REALTORS® (WCR).

Successful rainmakers attend conferences, conventions, and meetings in their specialty to meet and greet agents from outside their area. Because these broker-to-broker and out-of-town agent sources tend to stay in the business for years, a targeted long-term contact program pays exceptional dividends from repeat referrals. Think big or think small, but collect out-of-town contacts in your database and stay in touch. On all your correspondence, whet their self-interest. Like Mary Harker, a superagent with Keller Williams in Dallas, indicate how much you paid in referrals in the prior year with a postscript such as "We paid out over $300,000 in referral fees last year. Be a part of our referral network." *Tip:* Perhaps one of the fastest growing techniques to maintain contact with hundreds of out-of-town agents is a regular broadcast e-mail message to stay in touch. Rainmakers have discovered that it's typically much easier to assemble e-mail addresses for business professionals than for consumers because more professionals have an e-mail address and want it well-known.

STRATEGY #8: DON'T FORGET CROSS-TOWN REFERRALS

Another super source of referrals is agents practicing just outside your immediate territory or outside your specialty (residential versus commercial, or resale versus new construction). This may be the next town or the next county or even across town. According to the NAR study, 22% of sellers and 20% of repeat buyers who bought another house moved more than 14 miles but less than 50 miles away from their old house (see Table 8.3). In many cases, that short distance takes the client into a new town and perhaps beyond your service area, but not so far away as to be a long-distance relocation.

Cultivating a select group of reciprocity agents who can service your sellers as buyers in their neighboring territory, and vice versa, will be a lucrative source of referral fees as well as new business. In areas such as New England, where the market is a patchwork of small towns where local REALTOR® boards draw de facto territories, you could cultivate referral sources beyond your territory that aren't many miles away. Offer to help them when they are in your area; provide a lock box or conference room or copier if they need to do business. Give it away and you get it back many times over.

Table 8.3
Local Territories Can Share Customers

Number of Miles Moved	Sellers	Repeat Buyers
Less than 13 miles	48%	51%
14–25 miles	13	11
25–50 miles	9	9
Over 50 miles	30	29

Source: National Association of REALTORS®

STRATEGY #9: TARGET INACTIVE REFERRAL AGENTS

Successful rainmakers keep a sharp eye out for this small but lu-crative referral source. Many agents who are no longer active in the business or are part-time or who simply don't want to han-dle certain types of customers can be cultivated for referrals. Another profitable target is agents who have moved out of the area, but who still stay in contact with past clients and their old local sphere. You might consider a written referral agreement that retains the right to market to prospects after the first re-ferred transaction without owing a subsequent referral fee, just to be sure there is no misunderstanding. One way to generate cross-town referrals is an ad and headline like this: "Call now for a free referral to the best agent in *(city)*." Then pass along these prospects to a select agent in that city (while you service the outbound client's local needs).

RAINMAKER CHAPTER 8 SUMMARY

Customer Retention Strategies for Optimum Profits

▶ Strategy #1: Focus on Long-Term Prospects.

▶ Strategy #2: Stay in Touch with Past Customers.

▶ Strategy #3: Develop a Customer Win-Back Campaign for Orphans.

▶ Strategy #4: Develop Partnerships with New Home Builders.

▶ Strategy #5: Cultivate Bird Dogs.

▶ Strategy #6: Scratch a Few Suppliers' Backs.

▶ Strategy #7: Weave an Out-of-Town Broker Network.

▶ Strategy #8: Don't Forget Cross-Town Referrals.

▶ Strategy #9: Target Inactive Referral Agents.

9

Creating a Perpetual Referral Machine

> **Eighty percent of repeat business comes from 20 percent of your customers.**
>
> Bob Stone
> *Direct Marketing Success Stories*

Whether the target of your marketing is a past client, a sphere-of-influence contact, a prospect with a long lead time, or a professional referral source, long-term contact requires a system to work effectively. Sometimes, rainmakers even get calls from customers they don't remember. Yet the prospect thinks the rainmaker is virtually a personal friend. That's when you know your long-term contact is working.

The power of long-term contact is taking advantage of what marketers call the "multiplier effect." Everybody knows people. Some researchers even quantify the number to be about 20 people on average. That means everybody has about 20 friends, relatives, neighbors, and co-workers who are their close personal circle, their own pond of prospects. When prospects spread the word of a successful experience—a movie, a restaurant, a new car, a new house—they tell people in their circle. In fact, the larger the ticket item, the more they show it off to others.

Thus, long-term contact with a relatively small number of prospects actually leverages your reach to many more people. That is the multiplier effect. It is why successful rainmakers carefully cultivate their past clients and sphere and long-range prospects to reach the "friends and family" networks every prospect has.

Think of long-term contact as the last connection in your prospect pipeline that steadily pours fresh customers back into your lead generating funnel—beginning the perpetual cycle again like a recirculating pump.

Four Rainmaker Strategies to Cultivate Endless Referrals

Strategy #1: Get in Touch and Stay in Touch with Your Base

People who know you must know what you do. Long-term contact is the key to your profitability. A consumer research study showed that after two years, almost three out of four buyers couldn't remember the name of the agent who helped them buy their home. After three and a half years, more than half the buyers couldn't even remember the company's name. The NAR reports only 11% of repeat buyers and 12% of sellers returned to use the same agent they worked with before!

The solution is common sense. Simply stay in touch at least 15 times a year. Mail them a newsletter 12 times a year. Call them at least 3 times a year. Send them small, memorable gifts. As all parents and behavior psychologists know, behavior that is rewarded is repeated. Don't love 'em and leave 'em. Give your practice a "before" and "after" test: Add up on average how much you spend in time and money on a customer before and after settlement. Rainmakers know the after-market investment should be significant to reflect the substantial proportion of business that comes from referrals—which varies between 50%

and 57%—because the greatest customer value is *after* the initial transaction.

Strategy #2: Make Referrals Your Life

There are more ways to generate referrals than there are pebbles on a beach. Here are several. Take them and run with them. Then constantly stay on the lookout for more good ideas to add to your **Real Estate Rainmaker** bag of tricks.

Envelope stuffer. One of the simplest ways to ask for referrals comes from Gladys Blum, a top Prudential agent in Salem, Oregon. Blum's technique is an envelope stuffer she prints three-up on letter-size paper, then cuts into three stuffers (see Figure 9.1). The referral stuffer goes into every envelope she sends. The purpose of the stuffer is to ask for referrals. Its headline: "It's easy to refer your friends, co-workers, and family members to Gladys Blum. Call us. Fax us. E-mail us. Write us."

Here's the information Blum wants contacts to have ready when they refer a prospect:

- **Who?** What is prospect's name and address?
- **What?** Is prospect buying, selling, or both?
- **Where?** Is prospect moving within or outside the area?
- **When?** How soon does prospect need to buy, sell, or both?
- **Why?** Is prospect relocating, upsizing, or downsizing?

Blum's simple envelope stuffer educates her contacts to have complete information in hand when they call her with a referral. "The more you get out, the more it pays off," Blum says, "even if it's with the payment of a bill. Maybe they are speaking to a neighbor or having dinner with a friend who needs to sell. The stuffer creates instant recall, and it's very inexpensive."

Five-step thank-you series. Nothing reinforces desired behavior like a thank you. One effective approach is to write a series of five thank-you notes. The five-time program is mailed to referral

---

Figure 9.1
Gladys Blum's Referral Stuffer

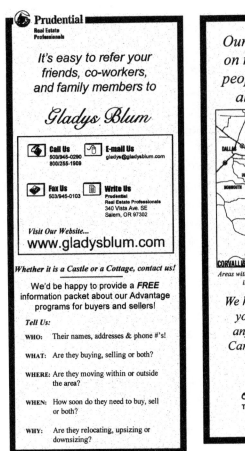

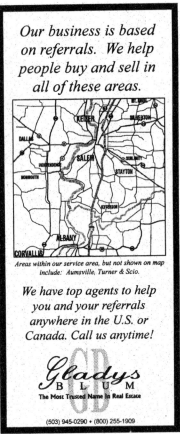

Courtesy of Gladys Blum, Prudential Real Estate Professionals, Salem, Oregon

---

sources to mark each stage of the transaction and keep them informed of their friend's progress:

Step 1: Initial referral ("Thank you for the referral. I talked with them today.").

Step 2: Appointment or enrolled in Preferred Customer Program ("Thanks again for the referral.").

Step 3: Agreement signed either listing agreement or buyer's representation ("Good news. We have a new client. Thanks again.").

Step 4: Contract to purchase accepted ("At last, moving day is in sight. Thanks."),

Step 5: Settlement/escrow ("Congratulations! Thank you! Thank you!").

The lasting impression left with the referral source is the terrific service you have provided their friend, relative, or co-worker. Not to mention getting *five* thank you notes for one referral. As long as state law or RESPA rules permit, consider putting in a progressively larger gift with each thank you, such as movie theater tickets or video rental coupon or telephone calling card or a $50 to $100 gift certificate after closing.

Caution: Once you start sending gifts, don't stop. If you stop, prospects think you no longer value their referrals as much as before—or worse, that you don't value them at all.

Turn your business card into a referral machine. K.C. Butler is a RE/MAX superstar in the Denver area whose rainmaker slogan is "Your Real Estate Resource" and whose e-mail address is kcbutler@thehometeam.com. Butler does just about everything right, including this referral builder idea on the back of all his business cards that he learned from Tony DiCello:

*The highest compliment
my clients can give is the referral of
their friends, family, and
business associates.*

Thank you for your trust,

K.C. Butler

Another technique comes from Joe Klock's refreshing *Sales Tips Newsletter #8* (joeklock@aol.com; www.joeklock.com). In it, Klock writes, "In 1974, I introduced to one of England's most prominent Estate Agency (real estate agency) firms a 'revolutionary' business-building concept, which we called the 'Seven-Second Solicitation.' Entirely foreign to them, the technique was (and is) about the oldest prospecting idea in sales: asking for business. It took the 'seven-second' title from the approximate time it takes to hand a business card to someone and say, 'Will you do me a favor? I'd like you to keep my card; whenever you meet anyone interested in buying or selling a home anywhere, please ask them to call me.' They quickly found that asking for referrals is the easiest and least expensive way to drum up business—bar none."

Here is another idea sent into Pat Zaby's terrific e-mail newsletter, *Real Estate Focus*, at PREP Software in Carrollton, Texas, by RE/MAX agent Joe Atnip of McKinney, Texas. Atnip suggests turning the back of your business card into a pocket-size "marketing card" to print:

- Condensed profile of an active listing with house photo for the sellers to give to friends, neighbors, and co-workers.
- Open house or price reduction notices for seller distribution.
- Buyer representation notice, such as "Representing John & Susie Anderson. Please direct inquiries to number on my business card." Prospects are instructed to present card at open houses and builder models.
- Just listed: "Our home is for sale. Please help us find a buyer." Include address, price, short description of property, and Internet address for a "virtual tour" on your website.

Change of address. All buyers and sellers need to change their address. A consistent system can turn this universal customer need into a flood of referrals using these simple **Real Estate Rainmaker** techniques. Here are four proven approaches:

1. *At the listing presentation.* Ask for the names and addresses of closest friends of sellers to send an announcement of their home for sale as part of your Fast Sale Program. The sellers can also relax after the move because

your team will take the chore of address change off their minds by sending out change-of-address postcards at your expense. Mention you can also take care of business addresses if they give you a list of their magazines, organizations, and so on.

2. *Address labels.* Prior to closing, order or print new forwarding address stickers for your customers. Make up separate labels with the kids' names. Then surprise them at closing with a set of lick-and-stick or peel-and-stick address labels. These can be ordered from several sources, or printed from software using Avery labels.

3. *Postcards.* Two weeks before closing, ask buyers for their "holiday card" list of 30 to 50 local friends to whom they want to send a change-of-address notice. Enter names in your Trophy Database. Print four-up postcards featuring a photo or rendering of their new home, especially if it was your listing. On one side, print a headline, such as "Our New Home." On the other side in postal format, print both old and new addresses, accompanied by a message in small type: "Bought (or Sold) Through *(Rainmaker's team)* of *(Company), (phone),*" or "This service provided by our real estate agent, *(Your Name), (Company), (phone).*" Mail postcards to your seller's list of local friends. Keep names on disk for future prospecting. A variation: Use the blank side of your business card. Text: "Our new address as of *(date)* is: Name, address, phone." Give clients 50 cards laser-printed on an $8\frac{1}{2}'' \times 11''$ microperf sheet from Office Depot or Paper Direct.

4. *Prepaid services.* The post office will forward mail for one year without charge, and a number of private companies offer change-of-address service that makes life easier. For information on post office services (change of household address, vehicle and voter registration, tax forms mailed), visit their website at www.usps.gov/moversnet. Change My Address (www.changemyaddress.com) is a fee service featured on the NAR's website. Another fee service is

AddressCentral (www.movecentral.com) of Before You Move, Inc., located in Boston. Compare prices.

5. *After closing.* For your buyers, offer to send a multimedia photo slide show of their home via e-mail to special friends in the area and out of state using PhotoShare software. Pat Wattam, a top agent with C.J. Brown REALTORS® in Baton Rouge, Louisiana, and an Allen F. Hainge Cyber-Star™, offered this tip in Hainge's excellent online *Real Estate Technology News & Views* newsletter. "My buyers were thrilled," Wattam reports. "I had one couple even do the initial voice on the screen to say hi to their friends and introduce their new home. They thought the idea was fabulous because all their friends had asked them to describe their new home. Another couple asked me to come over in about a month when all their new furniture had arrived and take the photos. What a perfect time to drop by and build my referral base!" writes Wattam. (See Resource Guide under Technology Tools.)

Strategy #3: Closing Gifts That Keep on Giving Referrals

Closing gifts have long been a successful technique to encourage customer loyalty. Prepaid phone cards, flowers, chocolate, plants, wine, pound cake, and cookies are excellent "consumables," especially when delivered and shared with family, friends, or office mates. Another effective approach is giving items that keep on giving because clients save them. Below are some tested closing gifts that have "shelf life" and give the added benefit of continued referrals long after they arrive.

Magazine subscription. One of the most appreciated and easiest items you can give is a magazine subscription. *National Geographic, Home, Practical Homeowner, Gardening, Today's Homeowner,* and *Remodeling* are welcome, or a magazine that fits the interests of your contact. Any appropriate magazine works. The magazine often sends a letter or card to you or directly to the contact announcing the gift subscription and who is sending it. For less than $2 a month, every month, 12 times a year, your best customers get a reminder of you—without your lifting a finger. Presto: customers for life.

Calendar. Calendars are a tried and true classic because they are useful and are saved. Stan Crockett of Melco Marketing, one of the premier calendar providers, has seen from experience how customers of his real estate agent customers come to depend on and expect to receive a practical, memorable calendar for their refrigerator every year. For your core list of past customers, invest in something extra special. But don't fail to put everybody you know on your mailing list and keep them on the list until you read their obituary.

Smoke detector. This technique comes from James Pugliese, Jim Pugliese Seminars, Albany, New York, and was reported in *Today's Realtor,* January 1998. He suggests giving a battery-operated smoke detector to new buyers. Not only will you be protecting their house and family, but you also have a built-in reason to send a replacement battery every year as a stay-in-touch mailing.

Warranty. Some national warranty providers, such as American Home Shield, send the agents of record a card each time a client makes a claim on their warranty coverage. Because the warranty has paid for fixing the problem, this is a terrific opportunity for you to follow up to chat with past customers and ask for referrals—especially if you arranged for the seller to pay for the buyer's warranty.

Home book. This is an album about the home. Assemble the initial album for new buyers, and encourage them to leave it with the home whenever they move again. Some of the things to include or encourage the owners to contribute include:

- Names and phone numbers of people who service the property: plumber, heating/AC, electrician, handyman, yard service, appliance repair, painter, housekeeper.
- Appliance warranties and owner's manuals.
- Floor plans.

- Pictures of every room before and after a step-by-step reno- vation project.
- Pictures of yard and garden in bloom with map of land- scaping naming specific trees and shrubs.
- Community lifestyle: churches, schools, shopping, trails, transportation, parks.
- Your resume and contact information.

Legal documents. A variation of the home book idea is a binder of valuable papers where clients can assemble important home documents. *The Homeowner's Portfolio*™ is a high-quality binder available from Magnets USA in Roanoke, Virginia. Also, Planner Systems in Redmond, Washington, offers *The Homeowner's Records Portfolio,* a handsome binder for documents. Both com- panies offer quantity discounts. Pocket dividers include:

- HUD Settlement Statement (for taxes).
- Homeowners insurance policy.
- Loan note.
- Deed of trust with recordation stamps.
- Maps, plats, surveys (useful for refinancing).
- Seller disclosure form.
- Inclusions and exclusions (conveyances).
- Homeowners association/condo association bylaws.
- Appraisal document.
- Information on selling a house.
- Your resume and contact information.

Phone directory. Assemble and publish a subdivision phone di- rectory, athletic boosters club membership directory, aerobics class list, or golf club roster. Volunteer to prepare the address and phone directory for any group with which you're involved. Con- sider including spouse's and kids' names and e-mail addresses whenever appropriate. Most important: Be sure to get permission of every family before putting their name in a directory.

More gift ideas. Key ring holder, tool kit, mailbox, sketch of home, photo cup or clock, bookmark, area street map book. (See Resource Guide under Closing Gifts.)

Strategy #4: Don't Settle for the Cream When You Can Own the Whole Dairy

Successful rainmakers know that for the first year after purchase, buyers are one of their best sources of referrals. Because the new house and buying it were such a watershed, buyers can't stop talking about the experience as fond memories crowd out the soon-forgotten stress. Start your long-term contact campaign by generating a positive buzz. Send a pizza or bucket of chicken late in the afternoon of move-in day.

After-closing follow-up. Then launch a six-call contact system where your assistant phones new purchasers 3, 10, 30, 60, 180, and 365 days after settlement. Simply ask if their needs have been met and if there is anything you can help with. The calls are an excellent opportunity for your assistant to ask for a short customer satisfaction survey. This is also an ideal time to unveil your own referral service of approved home service suppliers. Offer to refer your clients to a trusted source of service if they have a specific need. After all, the suppliers live by referrals, too.

After-closing follow-up is one of the biggest, most important ideas to grow your business today, but the most often neglected, says Bill Barrett, a leading national speaker. Associates do okay on prospecting, Barrett believes. They do okay on presentations and okay on servicing. But the fourth, and most crucial action, is the one many agents do the worst job on: Follow-up after closing. "What separates the average agent from the top associates today is having a system for past client follow-up," he adds.

When agents come back into the office after a closing, they often have a folder full of signed papers. Too often, they turn it over to the secretary or office manager and walk away from that transaction, says Barrett. Instead—and Barrett is convinced that this is one of the hottest new ideas out there—they should turn on their computer and input multiple contact dates for that client. Not just the next date, but an entire action plan for contact.

Some of the most common phone call dates Barrett recommends are: two weeks after closing, six months after closing, one year after closing, birthdays, wedding anniversary, and other client-appropriate occasions.

Past client personal website. Walter Sanford, a well-known speaker and one of the most innovative real estate practitioners in the country, assigns a special access area on his website to past clients. VIP clients are invited to visit and check on the status of their commission discounts earned for referrals and other activities. Sanford also posts on his website additional services specifically offered to past customers. Some of the services that keep bringing back customers and referrals, he says, include photocopier and fax machine use, rental property analysis, referrals to contractors, evaluation of a purchase contract anywhere in the country, free CMA, marketing plans, and free analysis of refinancing. More VIP services include referrals to lenders, analysis of cost-versus-value for improvements, how to increase income from a rental property, referral to top-quality real estate brokers anywhere, closing cost estimator, and net cash proceeds analysis. Many of Sanford's proven systems are available for purchase (see Resource Guide under Speakers and Trainers).

New Years and escrow anniversary. Staying in touch with a seven-year monthly letter program with prewritten letters on disk such as the industry-leading *LetterWriter Plus* by nationally known speaker Dave Beson out of Minneapolis is an excellent referral builder.

Here are several more tricks of referral veterans. At settlement, make two photocopies of the settlement statement, and then in January, mail them to the new buyer *and* the former seller with a note: "Hope all goes well in your new home. Here is a copy of your settlement statement I know you will need to prepare your taxes this year." Be sure to enclose your referral stuffer. Also consider a short report on tax breaks for homeowners, such as Gooder Group's bestseller *Taxes: How They Affect Your Home*. For a buyer, another insert that works is an assessment tax printout. If the tax assessment is higher than the sales price, offer information on how to appeal for an assessment reduction in your area.

Send a note on the date of their escrow or settlement anniversary: "On this date last year, we helped you move. We can help you again when you're ready. Please call."

Two days *before* a contact's wedding anniversary, call the husband to congratulate him. He will be forever grateful and remember you always—perhaps even better than he remembers his anniversary!

Another effective occasion is a postcard two times a year announcing daylight savings time: "Spring forward. Fall back." Advise customers to change the clocks on the correct date. Don't forget birthday cards, open house invitations, and just listed and just sold announcements. These are all great opportunities to systematically stay in touch.

Bonus idea. "Yes, Virginia, there is such a thing as a free lunch. Lunch with your real estate professional. Get a free market update and value of your home. This ticket is redeemable for a free breakfast or lunch. P.S. Tell your friends to call when they need real estate services and I'll buy their lunch, too."

Client appreciation event. Client events are a powerful tool for rainmakers who have collected hundreds of past customers. The event has also become a useful transition tool to stay in touch with your contact base when you change companies or the old company changes names.

Maxine Gellens, a top agent with Prudential California, San Diego, rents the Del Mar Racetrack once a year for a day. Of the 300 sellers and buyers typically invited, about 150 to 160 show up, she says. Everyone has a good time. You could also throw a subdivision barbecue, newcomer potluck, go to a ball game, rent a movie theater, or host a community flea market sale.

Mike Brodie, a stellar agent with Keller Williams in Dallas and a national speaker, tells about his annual golf tournament.

Everyone who buys, sells, or refers a transaction is invited. About 80 to 100 people are invited and 30 to 40 show up. A photographer takes everyone's picture on the first tee, which is later sent to the client framed. Golf towels with Brodie's logo are given to all the clients. Afterward, there are prizes and a short speech by Brodie. "The reason you're here is you either bought, sold, or referred a customer to me this past year," he says. "This is an annual event. So if you want to play next year . . ." Everyone laughs—and gets the point.

Professionals appreciation event. Once a year, perhaps in spring or fall, preferably not during the year-end holiday hubbub, host an appreciation event for your professional network. Invite them all. Ask your staff to select vendors for special recognition awards that reflect the number of referrals they've sent you. Be creative. The more awards, the better. Prizes can be modest. Print a program listing all the invitees and award winners with their organizations to reinforce who you work with and why: referrals. Open with a networking icebreaker where they swap business cards to give *them* a chance to network. Have fun! Some award ideas:

- Supplier of the Year (overall most closed referral volume).
- Most Referrals Award (units).
- Shortest Referral-to-Close Award (toy rabbit prize).
- Longest Follow-Up-to-Close Award (toy turtle prize).
- #1 Lender Award, #1 Agent Award, #1 Attorney Award, #1 Accountant Award, etc. (You get the idea: one for every profession or group.)
- Largest Single Referral Transaction Award.

Costly Long-Term Contact Mistakes to Avoid

Staying in touch with contacts sounds so simple. Perhaps that's part of the problem. As with lead generation and prospect follow-up, there are some disastrous mistakes that experience shows you can avoid with the **Real Estate Rainmaker** system.

Mistake #1: Treating All Your Long-Term Contact Activities the Same

Lumping all your contact activities into one large category like "referrals" and never knowing what pays off and what doesn't in cold, hard dollars and cents is a costly mistake.

Solution: Bill Sparkman, one of the top sales and marketing trainers for the lending industry, suggests this solution: Treat each referral source or marketing activity or customer group as a profit center. Track how much you invest and how much you get in return from each specific source, activity, or group. Each center must show a profit: more in, less out. Focus on net, not gross. Any profit center that isn't profitable needs attention—or ultimately should be abandoned. Do something else, something new, even something outrageous.

Mistake #2: Trying to Sell Real Estate to a Satisfied Customer

Constantly making "Sell Now!" and "Buy Now!" real estate offers to folks who are satisfied with their house can fall on deaf ears for years.

Solution: Treat your homeowner as a homeowner. Rather than sending solicitations for selling or buying, concentrate on providing unexpected homeowner services. Focus on messages that offer helpful advice for homeowners, such as reports on taxes, cost-versus-value improvement tips, home safety, refinancing, market-smart renovations, how to eliminate private mortgage insurance (PMI), landscaping do's and don'ts. These homeowner-related "refrigerator tips" (worth keeping on the refrigerator) keep your name in their mind when someone asks them to recommend a real estate agent.

Win the War for Control of the Customer

Remember, the fundamental *Real Estate Rainmaker* principle is *control the customer and you'll control the market.* Your Trophy Database and, more important, your relationship to your customers are your greatest business assets. These take years to cultivate and are worth serious money—especially when another rainmaker will pay you to transfer your book of business to his or her practice.

Maintaining control of your customers costs money. Exactly how much money and exactly how to spend it best are the themes of Part Five. See you there.

RAINMAKER CHAPTER 9 SUMMARY

Creating a Perpetual Referral Machine

- ▶ Strategy #1: Get in Touch and Stay in Touch with Your Base.
- ▶ Strategy #2: Make Referrals Your Life.
- ▶ Strategy #3: Closing Gifts That Keep on Giving Referrals.
- ▶ Strategy #4: Don't Settle for the Cream When You Can Own the Whole Dairy.

~~~~~~~~~~

FIVE

WRITING A MARKETING PLAN IN SIX EASY MORNINGS

Morning #1: Benchmarks

It costs five times as much to acquire a new customer as it does to keep an existing one happy and continually buying from you.

Old marketing adage

Writing a marketing plan is easy. It's also fun. What makes it fun is seeing your own practice emerge on paper, tidy, specific, concrete, and focused on a better bottom line. By the end of six easy mornings, rainmakers are often amazed at how good they feel. At last, they have a plan, a road map, a clear aim fixed on where they want to go in the next year. They see it, taste it, and are raring to get started.

What makes a *Real Estate Rainmaker* marketing plan so exhilarating? The fact that it makes life easier. Day to day, minute by minute, big and small decisions are suddenly easy. You will be able to catch—or release—unexpected marketing opportunities as they rise up during the year. Those thunderbolts, like "Wow, maybe that's a good idea—should I or shouldn't I?" With your *Real Estate Rainmaker* marketing plan, you won't be distracted by off-target tangents. Either the opportunity fits into your plan, and you grab it—or it doesn't fit the plan, and in a blink you say, "No thanks," then turn back to the task at hand. Period. End of decision. You'll be amazed.

161

Keeping It Simple

A word of caution at the beginning: Don't make this complicated. There will be plenty of time later to tweak and refine and perfect your marketing plan. In the years to come, your level of detail will grow; your numbers will become more precise.

Avoid complexity this week. Keep it simple. My recommendation is to have only one page of notes for each of the six mornings. In the end, your *Real Estate Rainmaker* marketing plan will be about six pages long, in addition to the worksheets. That's all. If you have more pages than that, you're probably getting too detailed. Keep your eye on the Big Picture. Keep it short.

Another tip: Stay home. Don't try to do your planning in the office. There are too many distractions. Peace and quiet will be your greatest allies this week to reflect, define objectives, focus on customers, run the numbers, and assemble your *Real Estate Rainmaker* marketing plan. Give yourself permission to do it right.

Here are the six easy mornings:

Morning #1: Benchmarks

Morning #2: Objectives

Morning #3: Customers

Morning #4: Strategies

Morning #5: Budget

Morning #6: Case Studies

On the seventh morning, thou shalt rest. Let the power of your plan sink in—then hit the deck running next week and you won't ever look back. Guaranteed.

On your mark. Get set. Go!

This morning, you will put on paper a summary of your marketing in the past 12 months. It can be any 12 months, but most agents prefer to use the calendar year because their bookkeeping and tax figures match that period. Also, the natural cycle of real estate generally fits between January and December. Some agents use October through September as the activity period. This calendar allows them to develop "next year's plan" during the last quarter of the year in anticipation of the new calendar year.

Feel free to insert your own categories into the worksheets, or expand categories with subcategories to fit your situation. But keep it simple this morning. This is a warm-up for the creative thinking that will come later.

Starting with What You Did Last Year

This morning's three Benchmark Worksheets give you a snapshot of where your marketing and your practice stand today. Every year you will expand these worksheets with another year of figures. (If you have figures from previous years, put them aside for now, but add them this afternoon if you easily can: 4th Year Previous, 3rd Year Previous, 2nd Year Previous).

The year-to-year trends and areas needing attention will be obvious. Concentrate on your weaknesses. Your strengths will take care of themselves. Also, this benchmark exercise recorded year after year will become an invaluable activity history for the buyer of your practice when it comes time for that buyer to step into your shoes (after you've cashed in or cashed out and moved on).

Start with a Benchmark Worksheet for your production (Figure 10.1).

Learning about a Marketing Expenses Benchmark

Only direct marketing expenses should be included on this worksheet (Figure 10.2). First, a word of insight. Use the

---

Figure 10.1
Production Benchmark Worksheet

The best place to start is to answer the question: What did you do last year? Answer these benchmark questions:

What was my gross commission income (GCI)?	$___	
What was my rate of profit? (income – expenses)	$___	(___%)
How many total transaction sides did I have?	___	
How many listing sides?	___	(___%)
How many buyer sides?	___	(___%)
From my total transactions:		
How many dual transactions?	___	(___%)
(two sides with same client)		
How many single transactions?	___	(___%)
From my sold listing transactions:		
How many were my buyers?	___	(___%)
How many were co-op buyers?	___	(___%)
What is my average transaction sales price?	$___	
What is my average commission?	$___	
What was my share of all transactions in my area?	___%	
What were the sources of my transactions?		
Advertising/Prospecting (direct response)	___	(___%)
Repeat (previous client)	___	(___%)
Referrals (relocation/company/brokers/builders/		
agents/affiliates' network/friends/neighbors/		
relatives/suppliers/etc.)	___	(___%)
TOTAL	___	(100%)
How many names do I have in my database?		
How many market strangers? ("suspects")	___	
How many active prospects? (inquiries)	___	
How many sphere contacts? (met them)	___	
How many past clients?	___	
TOTAL DATABASE NAMES	___	

Figure 10.2
Marketing Expenses Benchmark Worksheet

Complete the following questions:

Summary

What total did I invest in marketing last year? $_____

What percent of income went to marketing?   (___%)

What was my marketing cost per transaction? $_____

Lead Generation: Advertising to "Market Strangers"

What mass media did I use to generate leads?

   Advertising:

      Direct mail (standard/bulk) $_____ (___%)

      Print (newspapers/magazines/yellow pages) $_____ (___%)

      Electronic (radio/TV/cable/Internet) $_____ (___%)

      Outdoor (billboards, not yard signs) $_____ (___%)

   Public Relations:

      Publicity (publicist/postage) $_____ (___%)

      Events (trade show/seminars/home fairs) $_____ (___%)

      _____ $_____ (___%)

   Subtotal $_____ (___%)

**Prospect Follow-Up: Lead Management of
"Active Prospects"**

What minimedia did I use for prospect follow-up?

   Inquiry Fulfillment (reports/videos/kits/personal
     brochure/gifts/prizes) $_____ (___%)

   Direct Mail

      First class (one-to-one personal) $_____ (___%)

      Standard/bulk (mass mailings) $_____ (___%)

   Telephone

      Inbound (phone hotline) $_____ (___%)

      Outbound (telemarketer) $_____ (___%)

   Meals & Entertainment (deductible) $_____ (___%)

      _____ $_____ (___%)

   Subtotal $_____ (___%)

(Continued)

Figure 10.2 (Continued)

Long-Term Contact: Relationship Marketing to "People You Know"

What nonmedia did I use for long-term contact?

Fulfillment Materials (specialties/gifts)	$_____	(_____%)
Direct Mail		
First class (one-to-one personal)	$_____	(_____%)
Standard/bulk (mass mailings)	$_____	(_____%)
Client follow-up service	$_____	(_____%)
Telephone		
Outbound (telemarketer)	$_____	(_____%)
Promotional Event (party/client event)	$_____	(_____%)
Meals & Entertainment (deductible)	$_____	(_____%)
_____	$_____	(_____%)
Subtotal	$_____	(_____%)

Marketing Employee Expenses

Wages	$_____	(_____%)
Payroll Tax Expense	$_____	(_____%)
Health Insurance	$_____	(_____%)
Employee Benefits (retirement/perks)	$_____	(_____%)
_____	$_____	(_____%)
Subtotal	$_____	(_____%)
TOTAL MARKETING EXPENSES	$_____	(100%)

---

accountant's principle: An up-front capital investment is not a marketing expense; only the using of that capital investment is a marketing expense. Imagine two partners working shifts: One works days, the other evenings; they share the equipment (capital investment), but they each consume their own specific supplies (marketing expense).

An addressing machine, for example, is a capital expense, but the newsletters you send through the machine are a marketing expense. Another example: Your yard signs and brochure boxes are "tools of your trade" and a capital expense, but the property flyers that go into the brochure boxes are a marketing expense. Still another example: A general assistant who does a little of everything around the office is an employee expense, but a marketing coordinator who spends most of the time on marketing duties is a marketing expense. Here are some more specific examples.

Lead Generation Expenses

Advertising to "market strangers": Production (creative preparation); space (print media); time (broadcast); printing, postage, and mailing services (direct mail); billboard rental (outdoor); monthly access and ISP website host fees (Internet); booth rental (trade show); referral commissions (in lieu of advertising).

Prospect Follow-Up Expenses

Lead management of "active prospects": Production (creative preparation); reports, videos, cassettes, relocation kits, personal brochure (inquiry fulfillment materials); printing, postage (first-class and standard/bulk direct mail); telephone hotline toll-free number and long-distance telephone (inbound and outbound phone, beyond General and Administrative); wine, flowers, cookies (prospect gifts); meals and entertainment.

Long-Term Contact Expenses

Relationship marketing to "people you know": Printing, postage (first-class and standard/bulk direct mail); production (creative preparation); specialties (calendars, magnets, etc.); subscriptions, movie tickets, cookies, gift certificates (referral thank-you's and closing gifts); newcomer party, client event (promotional expense); meals and entertainment.

Be sure *not* to include these other expenses as marketing expenses:

- *General and administrative* (G&A) office expenses, such as office supplies (business cards, stationery, envelopes, printer cartridges, software), repairs, equipment (purchase or lease of printer, copier, phones, fax, addressing equipment, furniture, lock boxes), software, franchise fees, telephone lines and long distance, car expenses, utilities, insurance, rent.

- *Professional expenses,* such as travel, subscriptions, educational seminars, licenses, dues, interest, bank service charges, accounting, legal, technology support.
- *Nonmarketing employee expenses,* such as wages, payroll tax expense, health insurance, employee benefits.

UNDERSTANDING THE PAIN-IN-THE-NECK RATIO

Use the "pain-in-the-neck" ratio. If splitting up (allocating) an arbitrary percentage of an expense among several marketing categories is a pain in the neck (⅕ here, ⅕ there, ⅗ over there . . .), don't bother. Assign only the direct expenses to a single, easily allocated category.

You buy, say, a $500 supply of direct-response reports, and feature them in every ad in three different mass media, and in several follow-up mailers, as well as in handouts at a past client event. It's a pain in the neck to allocate a fraction of the expense of the reports to each step or campaign. Simply put the $500 reports expense into one place: prospect follow-up, fulfillment materials. Keep it simple.

The only exception is a huge expense that could skew all your numbers badly if it weren't allocated, such as postage for a large mass mailing that goes to all three steps: lead generation, prospect follow-up, long-term contact. In that instance, make the effort to split the large expense among steps as appropriate.

Now you're ready to complete the Marketing Expenses Benchmark Worksheet (Figure 10.2).

Tracking Your Prospecting Activities

After a Break

An advanced optional aspect of your Benchmarks morning is tracking your activity numbers and ratios, not dollars. After all, marketing and sales are a numbers game. One of the best real estate trainers, Mike Ferry, taught this technique in one of his presentations. His entire system of building a business is well worth looking into. (See Resource Guide under Speakers and Trainers.)

To be able to predict and duplicate your performance, Ferry says, you need to know your ratios and numbers. You need to keep records. Specifically, he suggests you create a record keeping system that tracks these activities:

Attempts: Marketing activities such as telephone calls dialed, direct mail pieces sent, doors knocked, answering machine messages left.

Contacts: Successful outreach attempt; person answered phone or door.

Leads: Direct contact with a prospect; sign call, ad call, returned bounce-back card, referral.

Appointments: Personal presentation face-to-face with prospect.

Contracts: Signed listing agreement, buyer's representation, purchase contract.

Closings: Settled transactions, commission paid.

When you chart these activity numbers from attempts to closings, you will notice relationships or ratios:

- How many attempts does it take to make a contact?
- How many contacts to generate a lead?
- How many leads to land an appointment?
- How many appointments to close a contract?
- How many contracts to settle a paid transaction?

These figures are your activity ratios, which give you valuable benchmarks for improvement.

Let me show you a simplified example. If every step required two efforts, then, working backward:

- To get 1 closing, 2 contracts are needed.
- To get 2 contracts, 4 appointments needed.
- To get 4 appointments, 8 leads needed.
- To get 8 leads, 16 contacts needed.
- To get 16 contacts, 32 attempts needed.
- Thus, to get 1 closing, 32 attempts are needed on average.

That is your ratio of attempts to closings: 32 to 1. If you want one more closing this year, you will need (on average) 32 more attempts.

Keeping track of the numbers lets you shape your objectives, strategies, and budget down the road in future years. Also, it makes it easy to spot any high ratio weaknesses that need attention.

Completing a Benchmark Worksheet for Your Prospecting Activities

Figure 10.3 asks some typical benchmark questions. Again, feel free to add your own, but don't delete the categories where you answer "zero." Those are revealing opportunities for improvement.

For example, one client of mine said he couldn't calculate referrals-per-past-client. Why not? He didn't keep new addresses of past clients and didn't know how many there were. Hello! That's what I call a goose-egg flag—and a terrific opportunity. Build a Trophy Database of all your clients and contacts. If you can't track your activity numbers because you aren't keeping records, you're probably missing a chance to work smarter, not harder.

As you can see, tracking activity requires a sophisticated recording system. My advice is to select some of the most important ratios for your practice and track those rather than every number under the sun. You're a rainmaker, after all, not a bean counter.

Figure 10.3
Prospecting Activity Benchmark Worksheet

In the past 12 months:

Lead Generation Activity

How many pieces of mail sent last year? _____

  How many pieces standard/bulk mail? _____

  How many pieces sent first-class? _____

  How many e-mails? _____

How many open houses did I hold? _____

  How many open house visitors registered? _____

How many property ads did I run? _____

Lead Generation Results

How many total prospect inquiries did I generate?

  How many ad calls? _____

  How many sign calls? _____

  How many direct mail calls/replies? _____

  How many walk-ins? (opens/duty desk) _____

  How many word-of-mouth referrals? _____

  How many website/e-mail inquiries? _____

  Other? (Add category if significant) _____

  Unknown source? _____

    Total Inquiries _____

Prospect Follow-Up Activity

How many attempts were made at follow-up?

  How many phone calls? _____

  How many pieces mailed? _____

  How many e-mails sent? _____

  How many faxes sent? _____

  How many personal visits? _____

    Total Follow-Up _____

Prospect Follow-Up Results

How many appointments did I have? _____

How many contracts did I get signed? _____

How many closed transactions did I have? _____

(Continued)

Figure 10.3 (Continued)

Long-Term Contact Activity

How many contacts were attempted?

How many phone calls? ———

How many pieces mailed? (bulk/first class) ———

How many e-mails sent? ———

How many faxes sent? ———

How many personal visits? ———

Total Long-Term ———

Long-Term Contact Results

How many referrals-per-client (database) did I get?

How many referrals did I get? ———

How many clients/contacts did I have? ———

What was my referrals-per-client ratio? ———
(referrals received ÷ database names)

Tip: To make record keeping easier, PREP Software features a number of outstanding tools in their financial module, including Prospecting Goals & Budgets, Prospecting Estimator, and Production Analysis. Also check out Top Producer's Income & Expense Tracker tools. (See Resource Guide under Database Software.)

An all-too-common discovery is that your marketing activity is almost completely directed toward lead generation and is directed very little toward prospect follow-up or long-term customer contact. If so, fix it. Rebalance your efforts to give more activity to the neglected steps. The ideal is to have lead generation working in the background, almost on autopilot using mass media. Let the ***Real Estate Rainmaker*** system build its own momentum and put your renewed personal attention into follow-up and customer contact.

Typically, a balanced attack will give your marketing a whole different look of working smarter, not harder—which is reflected directly in a better bottom line and more money in your pocket at the end of the day.

That's enough for now. I'll see you back here tomorrow morning. Go sell somebody something!

RAINMAKER CHAPTER 10 SUMMARY

Morning #1: Benchmarks

▶ Starting with What You Did Last Year.

▶ Production Benchmark.

▶ Learning about a Marketing Expenses Benchmark.

▶ Understanding the Pain-in-the-Neck Ratio.

▶ Marketing Expenses Benchmark.

▶ Tracking Your Prospecting Activities.

▶ Completing a Benchmark Worksheet for Your Prospecting Activities.

▶ Prospecting Activity Benchmark.

Morning #2: Objectives

> If you have to swallow a frog, don't look at it too long. If you have to swallow more than one, swallow the biggest one first.
>
> Danny Cox, national speaker and F.R.O.G. (Frequent Reacher Of Goals)

Warming Up

Good morning!

Before you jump into writing your objectives, we're going to take a moment with some warm-up "Who am I?" questions to think about the ways you want to improve your business. Think of the big picture, not details. What do you like most about your business? What do you dislike? What is your greatest strength? Your greatest weakness? In a moment, you will jot a few thoughts down. You may even make a two-column list for comparison if that is helpful: strengths versus weaknesses, likes versus dislikes.

One of my favorite planning questions is "If I went out of business right now, what would my clients miss most?" The answer is what I call your "core competency." In a nutshell, it's what you do best, and probably better than your competition.

Being best means giving such incredible service that your customers will tell everybody they know about you. Try this script on your next prospect. Share with them your personal goal: *My*

175

*goal is to give you such incredibly good service, you will tell
everybody you know about me. We both win. You get great service. I get a lifetime client whose referrals are worth many times
more business than a one-time transaction.* The transformation
in your prospect's attitude—not to mention your own—will be
amazing!

Another of my favorite questions for objectives planning:
Imagine you are a prospective buyer of your business standing
across the street looking at your business from the outside. If
you were to buy that business, "What is the single biggest first
thing you as the new owner would change to improve the business?" ("Get the owner out of the way of success" is an acceptable observation!) Put another way: "How would a large
company solve your marketing problems?"

How to plan to be the best, how to build on your core competency—and get help on the weaknesses and dislikes—that will
be the focus of this morning. After all, as the old proverb says,
"If you don't have a destination, you'll never know when you
get there."

Now, answer the warm-up questions in Figures 11.1 and 11.2.

Crafting Your *Real Estate Rainmaker* Mission Statement

Even more fundamental than being best, better than, or different from your competition is an original question: "Why did you
decide to go into real estate in the first place?" Now, in 50 words
or fewer, using your "Who Am I?" and Marketing Profile worksheets as a guide, recapture your inspiration by answering:
"Why am I in business?"; "Why do I provide the services I do?";
"Why these customers?"; "What principles do I live by?" Your
answers will become the creed you will use to lead your practice
and your staff to new heights.

Jack Cotton, a leading broker in Oysterville, Massachusetts,
on Cape Cod since 1974 who specializes in luxury waterfront
properties, developed two mission statements. One is for his

Figure 11.1
"Who Am I?" Worksheet

Complete the following warm-up "Who am I?" questions:

What are the things I like most about real estate?

1. _____
2. _____
3. _____

What are the things I dislike most about real estate?

1. _____
2. _____
3. _____

What are the three things I do best for my real estate customers? (strengths)

1. _____
2. _____
3. _____

What are the three things I do worst for my real estate customers? (weaknesses)

1. _____
2. _____
3. _____

How would I define *success* if I looked back a year from now and itemized my three biggest accomplishments?

1. _____
2. _____
3. _____

What is the single greatest barrier standing in the way of growing my practice? (staff, time, money, market area, knowledge, technology, etc.)

1. _____

As an outsider, what is the single biggest thing I would change to improve the business?

1. _____

What would I do if I weren't doing real estate?

Figure 11.2
Marketing Profile Worksheet

What basic type of customer do you want to increase? (check one)

☐ Sellers   ☐ Both (Desired split: ＿＿% sellers; ＿＿% buyers)
☐ Buyers

What three customer segments offer the greatest potential to grow your practice? (Examples of sellers: expired seller, for-sale-by-owner seller, first-time seller, cross-town trade-up seller, outbound relocation seller, empty nester/senior, investor, builder, heir/estate seller, government- or bank-owned institutional seller, divorcing seller, etc.) More specifically, describe each of your three best potential customers in five words or fewer.

1. ＿＿＿＿＿＿＿＿＿＿＿＿＿＿＿＿＿＿＿＿＿＿＿＿＿

2. ＿＿＿＿＿＿＿＿＿＿＿＿＿＿＿＿＿＿＿＿＿＿＿＿＿

3. ＿＿＿＿＿＿＿＿＿＿＿＿＿＿＿＿＿＿＿＿＿＿＿＿＿

Which of the following gives you the toughest marketing problem? (check one)

☐ Generating leads
☐ Prospect follow-up
☐ Long-term contact

What was the most successful marketing activity you ever did?

What are the primary sources of your prospects? (Check all that apply.)

☐ Referrals	☐ Property advertising	☐ Geographic farm
☐ Open houses	☐ Sign calls	☐ Investors
☐ FSBOs	☐ Expireds	☐ Repeat customers
☐ Relocation	☐ REOs/banks	☐ Affinity marketing
☐ Hotline	☐ Internet	☐ Walk-ins
☐ Seminars	☐ Advertising specialties	☐ Yellow pages
☐ Builder models	☐ Publicity	☐ ＿＿＿＿＿
☐ Radio/TV/cable	☐ Sphere of influence	☐ ＿＿＿＿＿

Rank your top five sources of business last year. Use transactions or dollar volume. If you use both, make two lists.

1. ＿＿＿＿＿＿＿＿＿＿＿＿＿＿＿＿＿＿＿＿＿＿＿＿＿

2. ＿＿＿＿＿＿＿＿＿＿＿＿＿＿＿＿＿＿＿＿＿＿＿＿＿

3. ＿＿＿＿＿＿＿＿＿＿＿＿＿＿＿＿＿＿＿＿＿＿＿＿＿

4. ＿＿＿＿＿＿＿＿＿＿＿＿＿＿＿＿＿＿＿＿＿＿＿＿＿

5. ＿＿＿＿＿＿＿＿＿＿＿＿＿＿＿＿＿＿＿＿＿＿＿＿＿

team and one is his personal statement. Cotton says he doesn't want to be the biggest brokerage in his market, just the best:

TEAM STATEMENT

WE, the members of the **Cotton Real Estate** team, declare our strong support of one another as individuals and as part of the team.

WE are committed to ongoing community involvement and working toward the preservation of our special environment.

WE believe in high ethics and trust, and that each team member's customer or client comes first.

WE will continue to treat one another as part of this unique family.

PERSONAL STATEMENT

MY pledge is to continue to be at the leading edge of the real estate profession. I will keep abreast of and, indeed, initiate many of the improvements in service, education, and professional standards that will shape the industry into the twenty-first century. Providing only the best possible service to my clients, customers, and associates will ensure our mutual success.

Your turn: What is *your* mission statement (Figure 11.3)?

Exploring Your Objectives

Good warm-up. Now, let's get down to business. Objectives are your guidelines to success. They are measurable and quantifiable, unlike goals, which are general. Also, be careful not to confuse objectives with strategies. We'll work on strategies during Morning #4. An objective is an overall big idea that helps you shape specific strategies to accomplish the general goal.

For example, your objective may be to increase your average sales price. Your strategy is to close more listings and sales from high-end neighborhoods you haven't penetrated in the past, thus giving yourself a raise. On the other hand, an alternative strategy

Figure 11.3
Mission Statement Worksheet

could be to no longer work with first-time buyers who buy low-price starter homes, and instead target only move-up buyers to raise your average sales price. Naturally, your objective and strategy are closely linked, yet distinctly separate. Your objectives will guide your development of strategies and even the targeted direct-response offers you select for your advertising.

Learning the Four Tests of an Objective

An objective must meet four standards:

1. *An objective must have a date.* Give yourself a deadline, such as the end of the year or your business anniversary or an "X" date. Use an actual date, not an elusive "six months from now."

2. *An objective must be specific.* Select an exact amount, such as a dollar amount, percentage, a unit number, a specific market area.

3. *An objective must be written.* If you don't write it down, you can't refer to it, and worse, if you're like me, you'll forget it, especially the objectives that are not reached.

4. *An objective must be realistic.* This isn't blue sky, such as triple your business every six months forever. Even if you do it once, unrealistic objectives are not sustainable. Building a systematic organization behind the objective, so you can do it again next year, is critical. As top RE/MAX agent Craig Proctor in Toronto says, "It must be duplicatable." You don't want to drop the ball in sales or service after marketing generates more leads than you can handle. Keep your feet on the ground, and your eyes on the prize—taking your practice to the next level, however you define it.

Understanding Where to Start

Without question, the best place to start is to improve what you are already doing. Do something you are doing now in a better way. Leverage your current activity. Specifically, ask yourself what are the current benchmarks you want to improve:

- Overall production volume (units and/or dollars)?
- Average price per transaction?
- Market share?

- Geographic penetration?
- Ratio of buyers to sellers?
- Ratio of resale to new construction?
- Ratio of local to long-distance moves?
- Number/percent of referrals from past customers?
- Number/percent of customers who provide referrals (advocates)?
- Number/percent of repeat customers (used your services previously)?
- Increase the number of inquiries or appointments over a specific period?
- Achieve better ratios of responses converted into appointments or presentations into signed listings?

Exactly what are you shooting to improve?

After a Break

If you've thought carefully about your personal marketing objectives and worked out the specifics, you're ready to complete the next worksheet (Figure 11.4).

Ranking Your Personal *Real Estate Rainmaker* Marketing Objectives

Now, go back and rate the "payoff" of your objectives.

First, ask yourself: "If I reached this objective, what would be the likely payoff in my bottom line?" Then, to the left of each objective you completed or wrote yourself, write the letter *B* (Big payoff), *S* (Some payoff) or *L* (Little payoff) in the margin.

Again, keep it simple. Don't get sidetracked with calculations or "analysis paralysis." You might want to ask your partner or staff or spouse to rate the objectives, too, for outside perspective. Then average the ratings.

Figure 11.4
Marketing Objectives Worksheet

Here are several objectives that could guide your marketing. Remember to challenge yourself, but be realistic. Select the objectives you want and fill in the blanks or write your own.

General Business

1. Increase my total sales $_____ million by December 31, ____.
2. Increase my Gross Commission Income (GCI) $_____ by end of year (EOY) _____.
3. Increase my GCI by ____% by _____ (date).
4. Increase my market share from ____% now to ____% by _____.
5. Increase my annual closed listing units (purchases?) from _____ now to _____ by _____.
6. Change my mix of listings and sales from ____% listings/____% sales to ____% listings/____% sales by _____.
7. Increase my average sales price to $_____ by _____.
8. Increase my average commission to $_____ by _____.
9. Increase my overall profitability from ____% to ____% by end of year (EOY) _____.
10. _____
    _____ .

Lead Generation

1. Generate _____ prospect leads from _____ area/subdivision by EOY _____.
2. Generate _____ inquiries from sellers with properties priced above $_____ by _____.
3. Get my name in print in _____ separate stories through publicity during the period January 1, _____ through December 31, _____.
4. Increase my database of contacts from _____ names to _____ names by EOY_____.
5. Increase my e-mail address book of contacts from _____ addresses to _____ addresses by _____.
6. Increase visitors to my open houses by ____%, from _____ total for the year to _____ total for the year by December 31, _____.
7. Generate _____ listing leads from my direct-mail campaign to expireds between _____ _____ and _____ _____, a two-year period.
8. Increase the total number of mass mailing pieces distributed during calendar year _____ by ____% to a total of _____ (quantity).
9. Reduce my percent of total marketing expenses for lead generation from current ____% to ____% by EOY _____.
10. _____
    _____ .

(Continued)

Figure 11.4 (Continued)

Prospect Follow-Up

1. Increase the total "active prospect" inquiries for year by ____% from _____ (quantity) last year to _____ this year.

2. Improve my conversion ratio of _____ leads to get _____ appointments from ____% to ____% (_____ leads: _____ appointments) by EOY _____.

3. Increase total number of direct-mail follow-up pieces mailed to active prospects in the previous twelve-month period from _____ to _____ (quantity) by _____.

4. Increase the annual total number of prospects enrolled in my Preferred Customer Program by ____% by EOY _____.

5. Increase total number of buyer prospects enrolled in my "Virtual Tour" automatic e-mail notification of new MLS listings for next 12-month period by ____%.

6. Increase my percent of total marketing expenses invested in prospect follow-up from current ____% to ____% for the next year.

7. _____
   _____ .

Long-Term Contact

1. Increase number of mass mail pieces to long-term contacts and past customers from _____ pieces to _____ monthly by December 31, ____.

2. Increase my network of affiliated professionals ("Tip Club") from _____ to _____ referral sources by EOY _____.

3. Increase number of referrals from past customers only from _____ in calendar year (CY) _____ to _____ in CY _____.

4. Increase number of referrals received from all spheres (friends, neighbors, relatives, contacts, and networks) from _____ in previous CY to _____ in CY _____.

5. Increase number of closed transactions from repeat customers from _____ in CY _____ to _____ in CY _____.

6. Increase number of contacts in database who are within "ripple rings" of my past customers (Strategy: ask sellers for change-of-address list of their friends, relatives, neighbors, co-workers) by ____% to _____ names by EOY _____.

7. Double annual dollar amount invested in long-term contact from $_____ in _____ to $_____ in _____ .

8. _____
   _____ .

Now, rank in order the top three objectives in each of the four categories—the top three with the biggest payoffs—and write them on your personal *Real Estate Rainmaker* Marketing Objectives Summary (Figure 11.5).

Call it a day for now. The lunch bell has sounded. Put your notes away and sleep on them. Tomorrow, you will learn how to target customers. To create marketing that is focused on what the consumer wants to know and hear, you first have to know more about the customer.

Figure 11.5
Marketing Objectives Summary

General Business

1. _____

2. _____

3. _____

Lead Generation

1. _____

2. _____

3. _____

Prospect Follow-Up

1. _____

2. _____

3. _____

Long-Term Contact

1. _____

2. _____

3. _____

RAINMAKER CHAPTER 11 SUMMARY

Morning #2: Objectives

▶ Warming Up.

▶ "Who Am I?" Worksheet.

▶ Marketing Profile Worksheet.

▶ Crafting Your *Real Estate Rainmaker* Mission Statement.

▶ Exploring Your Objectives.

▶ Learning the Four Tests of an Objective.

▶ Understanding Where to Start.

▶ Marketing Objectives Worksheet.

▶ Ranking Your Personal *Real Estate Rainmaker* Marketing Objectives.

▶ Marketing Objectives Summary.

12

Morning #3: Customers

> If you want to be a
> great fisherman,
> you have to think
> like a fish.
>
> Al Ries & Jack Trout,
> *Bottom Up Marketing*

The first two sessions were focused inwardly on you. Although it can be soul searching, usually, talking about ourselves and our businesses is one of the things we do best. The problem is keeping it short, not keeping the conversation going.

Today, we're going to be outwardly focused on customers and competitors.

In the "olden days" before buyer representation, we called sellers "clients" and we called buyers "customers." Now, both sellers and buyers are both clients and customers. To make it simple, I will call them all "customers."

There are two other reasons behind being customer-focused. First, customers are moving targets: they constantly move up a ladder of value to you. Your job is to nudge them continually higher to the next level. To read more, get the excellent book *Up the Loyalty Ladder* by Murray Raphel and Neil Raphel (Harper-Business, 1995), or attend a "Main Event Seminar" by Joe Stumpf or a "Turning Point Seminar" by Brian Buffini. Here is the Raphels' description of the loyalty ladder:

1. *Prospects:* People who may be interested in buying from you.

2. *Shoppers:* People who visit your business at least once.

3. *Customers:* People who purchase one or more products or services from your business.

4. *Clients:* People who regularly purchase your products or services.

5. *Advocates:* People who tell anyone who will listen how great your business is.

Applying the Raphels' loyalty ladder to your *3-Step Rainmaker Lead System* is easy. For rainmakers, lead generation is doing everything it takes to turn a "suspect" (market stranger) into a prospect (inquiry). Prospect follow-up is what it takes to convert a prospect into a shopper and then into a customer. Long-term contact is the stage where the rainmaker turns the one-time customer into a lifetime referral source (customer to client to advocate).

The second principle behind being customer-focused is that buyers and sellers are not two homogeneous lumps of consumers. They are not all alike. Customers are like mixed nuts in a can; each nut is a different size and condition, yet there are only so many different types and flavors. Home buyers and sellers fall into groups, too, just like mixed nuts can be grouped by nut type. (I love this example!)

Empty a can of mixed nuts on the table and divide them into groups by nut type. You'll discover, as Andy Rooney did on *60 Minutes*, there is a predictable percentage of peanuts (largest group, least expensive), cashews, almonds, brazils, filberts, and pecans (smallest group, most expensive). If you emptied a whole case of mixed nut cans, you still would get the same proportion of nut types. Statistically speaking, on your table, you would have a nut case.

As a marketing guy, I call these nut groups "customer segments." Although the market may be all buyers or sellers, within the market are many subgroups or segments. Each of these customer segments has its own set of characteristics. (Household and neighborhood characteristics are called *demographics,* and attitudinal characteristics are called *psychographics.*) Whatever characteristics are used, the group's character is reflected in a specific set of worries and problems for that customer segment. What keeps one group up at night is very different from what gives another group the cold sweats about moving. Remember, we talked about finding solutions and shaping irresistible offers for these customers' problems in Chapters 3 to 5.

Your first task this morning is to select the particular customer segment(s) you want to target with your marketing.

Targeting the Customer Segments You Want

Big Picture: Buyers? Sellers? Both? Residential or commercial? Resale or new construction or land? Customers moving locally or long distance? Specific geographic neighborhoods or subdivisions? Price range? House style: single family, condo, second home?

Exactly what are your target customer groups?

Sharper Focus: The next step is to identify target prospects within the Big Picture. First-time buyers, move-up buyers, downsizing buyers, relocation buyers, new home buyers, investor buyers? Do you want first-time sellers, trade-up sellers, empty-nester sellers, relocation sellers, senior sellers, REO/third-party sellers? Do you want to concentrate on referrals from past customers (1+ years), active prospects, current clients (pending closings), recent clients (within 1 year), broker and agent referrals, referrals from transaction service providers such as lenders, title companies, attorneys, or sphere-of-influence contacts, professional "tip club" network, nontransaction-related homeowner service suppliers?

Exactly how do you want to grow your business?

Step One

As a warm-up exercise this morning, on the checklists in Figures 12.1 to 12.3, mark the first column for customer groups

Figure 12.1
Target Customers: Buyer Checklist

Buyer Group	Present Customers?	Target Customers?	Rank B, S, or L*
First-time buyer			
Apartment renter	☐	☐	———
Condo/co-op renter	☐	☐	———
House renter	☐	☐	———
Sell-to-buy repeat buyer	☐	☐	———
Inbound relocation buyer	☐	☐	———
Sweat-equity fix-up buyer	☐	☐	———
New construction			
New home buyer	☐	☐	———
Lot/land buyer	☐	☐	———
Second-home buyer			
Personal use	☐	☐	———
Income producing	☐	☐	———
Divorce buyer	☐	☐	———
Investor buyer			
Single family houses	☐	☐	———
Condo/co-op	☐	☐	———
1–4 unit building	☐	☐	———
5+ unit building	☐	☐	———
Other			
————————————	☐	☐	———
————————————	☐	☐	———
————————————	☐	☐	———
————————————	☐	☐	———

*Big payoff, Some payoff, Little payoff

that are your *present customers*. Skip the groups that are not present customers. If you had at least one transaction from a type of customer in the past year, go ahead and check the group as a present client. As your objectives guide you, do all three checklists for buyers, sellers, and referrals, or only buyers or only sellers or only referrals as suits your plan.

Figure 12.2
Target Customers: Seller Checklist

Seller Group	Present Customers?	Target Customers?	Rank B, S, or L*
First-time seller			
Condo/co-op seller	☐	☐	────
House seller	☐	☐	────
Sell-to-buy			
Trade-up seller	☐	☐	────
Downsizing seller	☐	☐	────
FSBO seller	☐	☐	────
Expired seller	☐	☐	────
Outbound relocation seller	☐	☐	────
New home builder	☐	☐	────
Lot/land seller	☐	☐	────
Second-home seller			
Personal use	☐	☐	────
Income producing	☐	☐	────
Divorce seller	☐	☐	────
Estate seller	☐	☐	────
REO seller	☐	☐	────
Investor seller			
Single family houses	☐	☐	────
Condo/co-op	☐	☐	────
1–4 unit building	☐	☐	────
5+ units building	☐	☐	────
Other			
_____	☐	☐	────
_____	☐	☐	────
_____	☐	☐	────
_____	☐	☐	────

*Big payoff, Some payoff, Little payoff

Figure 12.3
Target Customers: Referral Checklist

Referral Source	Present Customers?	Target Customers?	Rank B, S, or L*
Business-to-Business			
Broker-to-broker			
Relocation network	☐	☐	——
Direct agent contact	☐	☐	——
Company ancillaries	☐	☐	——
Referral associates	☐	☐	——
Professionals (transaction-related)			
Lenders	☐	☐	——
Title companies	☐	☐	——
Insurance agents	☐	☐	——
Attorneys	☐	☐	——
Appraisers	☐	☐	——
Inspectors	☐	☐	——
Surveyors	☐	☐	——
Corporate/HR directors	☐	☐	——
Other			
_____	☐	☐	——
_____	☐	☐	——
Suppliers (homeowner services)			
Architects	☐	☐	——
Cleaning services	☐	☐	——
Estate liquidators	☐	☐	——
Floors & carpets	☐	☐	——
Gutters	☐	☐	——
Heating & A/C	☐	☐	——
Landscapers	☐	☐	——
Painters	☐	☐	——
Plumbers	☐	☐	——
Property managers	☐	☐	——
Remodelers	☐	☐	——
Roofers	☐	☐	——
Swimming pool service	☐	☐	——
Telephone service	☐	☐	——
Tree service	☐	☐	——
Utilities	☐	☐	——
Window treatments	☐	☐	——

Figure 12.3 (Continued)

Referral Source	Present Customers?	Target Customers?	Rank B, S, or L*
Other			
_____	☐	☐	___
_____	☐	☐	___
Consumers			
Current client (before closing)	☐	☐	___
Recent client (within 1 year)	☐	☐	___
Past client (1+ years)	☐	☐	___
Neighbor/relative/friend	☐	☐	___
Sphere of influence	☐	☐	___
Geographic farm	☐	☐	___
Other			
_____	☐	☐	___
_____	☐	☐	___
_____	☐	☐	___
_____	☐	☐	___

* Big payoff, Some payoff, Little payoff

Step Two

Check the target customers you *want* to take more *new customer* business from. Remember to be realistic. If you check most of them, that's okay; we'll be allocating a strategy to each group and a portion of the budget later. You can prune the choices later if need be. Be optimistic now, but don't let your eyes be bigger than your stomach.

Step Three

The critical third step is to rank these target groups according to your judgment as to their potential business payoff. Payoff must also be tied to your objectives from yesterday's session. Ask yourself, "How much payoff toward my objectives can I expect from this group?" *B* is a Big payoff, *S* is Some payoff, *L* is Little payoff.

As you eyeball the payoff of each group, think in terms of both an initial transaction *and* lifetime value, including referrals and repeat business. Again, keep it simple. Go with your first intuition, don't bog down with an extensive analysis of the numbers.

Step Four

Finally, recopy onto three short lists the Big payoff buyer, seller, and referral groups you've selected (Figure 12.4). Congratulations! You just selected your top-priority target groups. We'll keep the other groups in reserve for now, with an eye toward future growth in the years ahead.

After a Break

For those who want to probe deeper into the profiles of customers, there is a rich vein of thinking and research available. Rainmakers who tend toward the analytical love this part. And it pays off. The more you can define a consumer's needs and wants, the easier it is to attract them into your Prospect Pipeline. Ultimately, they will also show up on your bottom line.

Here is an advanced exercise in profile by motivation. What prompts these customer groups to enter the real estate market? What pushes a seller to sell? What turns a suspect buyer into an active shopper? *Motivation.* Typically, it is a life event. The more you can identify those motivating life events, the greater your success from targeted marketing. Not to mention you'll spend less on advertising because you won't pay for as many wasted messages.

As direct marketers say, "Junk mail is only the mail that doesn't get opened." By correctly targeting your audience, you

---

Figure 12.4
Target Customers Summary

Target Buyers

1. _____

2. _____

3. _____

_____

_____

Target Sellers

1. _____

2. _____

3. _____

_____

_____

Target Referral Sources

1. _____

2. _____

3. _____

_____

_____

will greatly reduce your costs and increase your profits. That's why this advanced exercise pays off double.

Who are your target customers? What are their average age, education, sex, marital status, and other demographic characteristics? What motivates them? What are their psychographics (preferences, interests, lifestyle)? This information helps the rainmaker pinpoint specific target prospects and design specific promotions that achieve maximum results.

Understanding What Motivates Your Target Customers

Based on the problems, fears, concerns, worries, and needs of your target customers, you can shape solutions that can be turned into specific premiums and incentive programs. Then those solutions will be the offers featured in your marketing.

Why not ask them? Go to the tax records and call any one hundred purchasers who bought a house in the prior year. Go to the MLS and call any one hundred homeowners whose house is for sale right now. Do your own customer research.

For questionnaire ideas, study the survey of 10,000 buyers and sellers nationwide regularly completed by the National Association of REALTORS®. Here is one question that goes to the heart of customers' motivations—and the results—from the NAR's 67-question survey, *Home Buying and Selling Process.*

Question: **"What is the primary reason that *most* prompted you to make a housing change?"** (Select one)

☐ More space because of marriage or growing family.

☐ More space for home business.

☐ Larger home for investment, tax deduction, or upscale neighborhood.

☐ To own a home of my own, not rent.

☐ Newly constructed home.

☐ Less space (children left, divorce, death).

☐ To move after retirement.

☐ To move for a change in climate.

☐ To move because of health/age (too much yard, stairs, allergies).

☐ To move because of job relocation or new job in another area.

☐ To be closer to job, schools, relatives.

☐ To move because of decline of previous neighborhood.

☐ To buy a second home.

☐ Other _____

Table 12.1 contains the survey results. Compare your local market results with these national averages. Some motivations will be similar; others will vary from the average. If you spot a customer group's answer that is significantly skewed from the norm, it could be an invaluable insight to be turned into amazingly effective target marketing. Use your knowledge of the variations that stand out from the averages as an advantage over your competition.

One of my clients in Salt Lake City noticed, for example, there were lots of divorces in her area. She related well to these sellers and buyers because she had been through the same ordeal. First, she helped them sell the family home, this top producer told me. If you can stay friends with both of them, more often than not, you can keep them as clients and help each spouse buy another place.

Table 12.1
What Is the Primary Reason That Most Prompted You to Make a Housing Change?

NAR Survey Results	First-Time Buyers	Repeat Buyers	All Buyers
Own home of my own, not rent	11%	72%	37%
More space: marriage or growing family	19	13	16
Corporate relocation, new job in other area	22	5	15
Investment, deduction, better neighborhood	10	5	8
Closer to job, schools, relatives	8	1	5
Less space: children left, divorce, death	7	0	4
Decline of neighborhood	5	1	3
Retirement	3	1	2
Change in climate	3	0	2
Health/age (yard, stairs, allergies)	3	0	2
More space: home business	1	0	1
Newly constructed home	2	0	1
Second home	1	0	1

Source: National Association of REALTORS®

Within a year or so of being single, they would remarry. The agent would share with the newly engaged couple what many psychologists recommend: that a fresh start deserves a fresh place, that buying a new place together is best, not moving into one of their old houses. That made sense to them, and often the agent would pick up two more listings and a purchase. She says she has been doing this for so long, now she has started to help their kids buy. In one case, the kids are getting divorced, too. It's an incredible money tree, she adds. All growing out of one divorce listing!

Studying Your Competition

After Another Break

You probably have a pretty good idea who your competition is. Test yourself. On one hand, count the names of the top five producing agents in your market area (note their company if it comes right to mind).

That handful of top agents may account for a significant market share. But taken as a whole, *all* the agents combined in your area control the entire "pie of business." Generally, the number of units in this market pie doesn't change dramatically from year to year. The dollar value of the pie may change somewhat with inflation or deflation of home prices. The **Real Estate Rainmaker** system helps you get a bigger slice of the pie. To do that, you must eat somebody else's pie for lunch.

How? The first step is to know your competition. Studying your competition will pay off in several ways.

First, make an e-mail and fax list of the 20 best agents in your market. Include agents who repeatedly show up as cobrokers with buyers for your listings. Every time you take a new listing, get a price reduction, or hold an open house, e-mail or fax them all a notice. They probably have a buyer that's a match for your listing or a property perfect for your buyer. Also, some will return the favor, and your clients will benefit from the advance notice. You'll immediately increase production.

Second, by studying your competitors, you will gather good marketing ideas and competitive practices (discounts, transaction/documentation fees, nonrefundable up-front listing fee, guarantees, warranties, mobile offices, teams, etc.) to be added to your arsenal.

Third, you'll be the first to spot opportunities, such as retiring agents, abandoned "farm" areas, and fragmented markets where no single agent dominates.

Fourth, by staying abreast of the best splits and benefits paid by competitors' companies, if the day should come when you decide to change brokers, you'll know where to go.

The fifth payoff comes from cultivating like-minded cooperative competitors whose practice you might acquire—or who some day might buy your practice.

ASSEMBLING FILES ON YOUR COMPETITORS

Information in the dossier you collect on competitors might include:

- Names, addresses, phone and fax numbers, e-mail of competitors.
- Geographic coverage.
- Approximate share of market (MLS statistics).
- Advertising methods and budgets.
- Competitive practices: Discounts? Guarantees? Warranties?
- Services rendered and their specialties.

If you've made it this far, you're probably so jazzed on caffeine your afternoon will be a blockbuster success. Put your **Real Estate Rainmaker** marketing plan aside for now and go out into the real world to breathe some fresh air. I'll meet you back here tomorrow morning to explore marketing strategies and specific action plans.

RAINMAKER CHAPTER 12 SUMMARY

Morning #3: Customers

▶ Targeting the Customer Segments You Want.

▶ Target Customers: Buyer Checklist.

▶ Target Customers: Seller Checklist.

▶ Target Customers: Referral Checklist.

▶ Target Customers Summary.

▶ Understanding What Motivates Your Target Customers.

▶ Asking: "What Most Prompted You to Make a Housing Change?"

▶ Studying Your Competition.

▶ Assembling Files on Your Competitors.

13

Morning #4: Strategies

> **Discovering why things flop teaches us more than success does.**
>
> Drayton Bird
> *Commonsense*
> *Direct Marketing*

This is the fun part. You've got your sights clearly set on your current business and your future objectives, and you have a solid understanding of the customers you want to target. Now it's time to detail systematic strategies—a literal "Do List" of specific action plans—to reach your objectives and surpass them!

Here you will put into practice what you learned in Chapters 3 to 9 on lead generation, prospect follow-up, and long-term contact as you develop the specific offers and media choices and systems to flesh out the fishbone outline of your strategies.

This morning, you will do the strategic thinking that will drive your action plans in the months ahead.

Knowing the Difference between Objectives and Strategies

Keep in mind the difference between an objective and a strategy: an objective is a goal, a strategy is a plan. For illustration, here is one objective, followed by six separate strategies to reach the same goal. Your job is to select the most promising strategies and put them into action.

Objective: Increase Average Sales Price 20% by the End of Next Year

Scenario: Current average transaction price: $150,000 based on 20 transactions. Goal: $180,000 average price ($150,000 + 20% = $180,000 average price). To reach this goal requires closing 5 of 20 transaction sides (listings or sales) at $270,000 to raise the average price of all 20 transactions to $180,000—and give you a 20% raise doing the same work. (For simplicity, I've assumed all 20 sides are exactly $150,000 each, although we know they will vary.)

UPSCALE SELLER STRATEGY

Identify properties worth $270,000 or more, either house by house or by market area, and target those specific homeowners with a special "Upscale Property" home selling program.

TRADE-UP BUYER STRATEGY

Identify prospective home buyers whose current property is two-thirds of the $270,000 target price, because move-up buyers tend to buy a home 50% higher in price (i.e., $270,000 × .67 = $180,000 or $180,000 + 50% = $270,000), and generate leads for your "Trade-Up Buyer" representation service. *Tip:* Prospective buyers will come from the buyer groups you identified with research: growing families, executive relocations, remarriages (larger blended families), job promotions that can be identified from newspaper announcements and public records.

EXPIRED/FSBO STRATEGY

Target owners of expired and FSBO properties whose property value is within the objective target range of $270,000 or more.

REFERRAL STRATEGY

Generate referrals of prospective sellers in the $270,000+ price range by cultivating current customers, sphere-of-influence contacts, past customers, and your professionals referral network (especially loan officers) whose property or client contacts are in the $270,000+ price range.

CORPORATE RELOCATION STRATEGY

Generate corporate relocation prospects of executive families who tend to buy higher-end homes by targeting top-level executives with a complimentary *Wall Street Journal* and bagel with coffee delivered to their office four mornings a year.

BUILDER STRATEGY

Arrange with builders of new homes priced above $405,000 (50% greater than $270,000) to obtain names of model home visitors who first must sell their $270,000 old house to buy that builder's new home. *Tip:* If a referral fee is appropriate, suggest a fee roughly in line with your allocated marketing budget percentage, such as 10% or 15% or 20%. In effect, you will simply be paying the builder to prospect for you. That is worth the same percentage you would pay out of pocket to do it yourself. If you count the value of lifetime referrals, naturally, the initial sale is worth a great deal more to you, perhaps 25% or 30% or 35%.

Obviously, there are any number of ways to make the same cloud rain. Where do the strategic ideas come from? One of the most effective approaches to develop strategies is brainstorming. Simply generate a list of alternatives. Don't hold back: off the wall is good. Every idea is acceptable at the brainstorming stage; you will evaluate the strategies later. We'll get started in a minute, after learning how to evaluate and score competing strategic ideas.

Using the Five Tests for Strategy Selection

Clearly, you can't do it all—at least, not all at once. You must pick the best strategies from the list of alternatives and treat them like a squirrel with some nuts. Take them home. Work with them. Put the plans in place. Evaluate the results. Polish your technique. Keep improving. Then do more of the best ideas and replace the duds with a different strategy next year and the year after.

To help rank your ideas, put your alternatives to these five Strategy Selection Tests:

1. *Is the strategy doable?* You must realistically be able to accomplish the tasks the strategy requires. You must have the time, the staff, the budget, and the talent to do it. For example, every strategy must be assigned to a person who is responsible to carry it out, but developing a systematic follow-up campaign without having a marketing assistant to do it may not be a doable strategy. Another example: Calling on top executives at large companies is a good idea, but if your market area doesn't have large companies, it is not a doable idea.

2. *Is the strategy tied to your objective?* Ask yourself if successful results would help you reach your objective. Does the strategy target your "big payoff" customer group? Will the strategy, for example, generate higher-price sellers and buyers, or just more average transactions?

3. *Is the strategy based on market research?* In our example, are there higher-priced homes in your area? Are there enough to increase your transaction mix? Have you been in the business long enough to have a referral base of past clients and contacts large enough to generate the needed referrals? Are corporations moving in top executives or mostly doing local new hires? Are there new homes in that price range in your area? Are public records or mailing lists available? If your research doesn't indicate a ready market, then you're better off not trying to dig gold from an iron mine.

4. *Is the strategy within your budget?* There needs to be marketing money available to accomplish the strategy. Does

the budget allow two or three strategic plans this year, but not all six of the best alternatives? Again, be realistic.

5. *Is the strategy measurable?* When you sit down at the end of your marketing period to review, you must be able to identify results and monitor, measure, and evaluate the strategy. Simply ask yourself what system would be needed to flag the transaction as generated by that strategy, such as a response code, and whether you can tabulate that source of business at the end of the marketing period. After all, an untrackable strategy is an unrepeatable strategy. And if you can't duplicate a success, you're condemned to always be reinventing the wheel.

Brainstorming Solutions to Problem Objectives

After a Break

Grab your summary of objectives from Morning #2 (Figure 11.5). Using your General Business objectives and three objectives from each of the three **Real Estate Rainmaker** steps—lead generation, prospect follow-up, and long-term contact—write each #1 objective at the top of a blank sheet of lined paper. You'll have four pages.

Now, brainstorm all the strategies you can imagine to reach each objective. Don't worry about being neat. Let the creative juices flow. Pull together every nugget of marketing gold you can summon from experience, from seminars, from observing the competition, from other industries, from your own imagination. The more ideas, the better.

Brainstorming with others is the most fun, because two, three, or four heads are better than one. Pull in your spouse, your partner, your staff, your coaching club, colleagues in other markets you meet at conventions, other professionals in your local referral network. Use big tablets of newsprint on easels or erasable marker boards or a large 25″ × 30.5″ Post-it® self-sticking easel pad made by 3M if there is a large enough group.

Table 13.1
Strategy Scoring and Ranking

Strategy	Doable?	Objective?	Research?	Budget?	Measurable?	Total
Upscale seller	4	5	3	3	5	20
Trade-up buyer	3	4	5	3	4	19
Expired/FSBO	5	5	3	4	5	22
Referral	3	4	3	3	3	16
Relocation	2	4	3	3	3	15
Builder	5	5	4	4	5	23

No put-downs allowed. All ideas are acceptable. Go until you fade. When you have plumbed all the ideas you have, you will know it. Silence will fall over the group. That's when it's time to recopy the strategies legibly. Take a break.

When you come back, score the action plans against your five Strategy Selection Tests. Doable? Tied to objective? Based on research? Within budget? Measurable? For each strategy, score

Table 13.2
Big Payoff Action Plans and Overall Rank

Strategy	Total	Payoff	Overall Rank
Builder	23	Big	1
Expired/FSBO	22	Big	2
Upscale seller	20	Big	3
Trade-up buyer	19	Some	4
Referral	16	Some	5
Corporate relocation	15	Little	6

each test between 1 and 5 points (5 being highest); 25 is a perfect strategy score. Note the total score for each strategy.

Next, rate the strategies according to their potential payoff: big payoff, some payoff, little payoff. Avoid quibbling. Go for the biggest payoff strategies. Go for the whoppers that jump right out as big ideas. Finally, combine the strategy score and the payoff rating into a rank order for all the strategies. Your top strategy will be at the top of the list.

To get you started, Tables 13.1 and 13.2 are illustrations of how my staff and I scored the strategies in our example above, then gave them a strategy payoff ranking.

Ranking Your Personal Strategic Action Plan

Now you're ready to brainstorm strategies for each of your top four objectives, test score your selections, and rate each strategy by payoff, then assign an overall rank to each strategy for each of your four objectives (Tables 13.3 and 13.4). When you recopy your best overall strategies—voilà: there is your four-part *Real Estate Rainmaker* Action Plan for the next year!

Table 13.3
Strategy Scoring and Ranking Worksheet

Strategy	Doable?	Objective?	Research?	Budget?	Measurable?	Total

Table 13.4
Big Payoff Action Plans Worksheet and Overall Rank

Strategy	Total	Payoff	Overall Rank

Tomorrow, I will show you the money. You'll learn how to put a sharp pencil to your overall marketing budget, as well as particular action plans. To be ready, you'll need to bring along the marketing expense section from Morning #1 (Figure 10.2). We'll use it as a base to build your new *Real Estate Rainmaker* budget for the new year.

RAINMAKER CHAPTER 13 SUMMARY

Morning #4: Strategies

▶ Knowing the Difference between Objectives and Strategies.

▶ Using the Five Tests for Strategy Selection.

▶ Brainstorming Solutions to Problem Objectives.

▶ Ranking Your Personal Strategic Action Plan.

14

Morning #5: Budget

> **Make no mistake, as you add to your personal promotion budget, your production will increase.**
>
> Ralph R. Roberts
> *Walk Like a Giant, Sell Like a Madman*

I've saved the best for next to last. Today, I'll show you the money. Your budget is where your ***Real Estate Rainmaker*** Marketing Plan all comes together. Nothing brings an action plan into sharper focus than the numbers.

But don't be a slave to the figures. They will change. In fact, if this is your first time and your numbers are projections, expect the figures to be inaccurate. That's okay. What these first figures do is sharpen your focus. This morning's exercise will help you zero in on the issues, the expenses, and the reality of the objectives and the strategies you have selected. You then can adjust your sights accordingly—do more if the money allows, do less if need be, or stretch a strategy over eighteen months or two years. Next time around the budget track, you will be smarter, and more of the numbers will be closer to your actual budget bull's eye. Just remember, marketing results and budgets are always a moving target. Don't expect to be perfect.

Learning How Much You Should Invest

The first question I'm most often asked is "How much should I spend on marketing?" My first answer is "How much do you want to invest?" My second answer is "How much is a prospect worth to you?"

All rainmakers are in a different place, a different stage of their career. Every rainmaker has a different set of objectives that call for growth or maintenance or pulling in the horns. So, the answers are yours alone.

Six Rules of Thumb

Here are six helpful budgeting rules based on percent of sales:

1. One guideline is to budget 10% to 20% of gross commission income (GCI) for marketing.

2. Another is to ask "What percent did I spend last year?" Use the percent of sales figure from Morning #1 (Figure 10.2). Multiply the figure times the income goal you have set (e.g., $100,000 GCI × 15% = $15,000 budget). You've got a best guesstimate for your **Real Estate Rainmaker** Marketing Budget. Divide by 12 and you get a monthly figure (e.g., $15,000 ÷ 12 = $1,250/month).

3. The National Association of REALTORS® surveyed broker/owners nationwide and asked them how much their *company* spends on advertising and marketing. The national average was 13% of company dollar in 1996 (not gross revenue), 14.6% in 1994, 16.1% in 1991 (National Associations of REALTORS®, *Residential Real Estate Brokerage: Income, Expenses, Profits,* 1997, p. 14). Consider yourself the manager of a one-person company, and you could use 13% to 16% of GCI as your budget rule of thumb.

4. The RELO network surveyed its brokerage members in 1996 and asked what percent of expenses their companies spent on advertising. The answer: 14.4%.

5. In a joint study of 5,000 top producers in 1996 by *Real Trends* newsletter and the NAR, 1,539 responding top producers (30+ units and/or $3+ million volume) said they spend on average 8.8% of GCI on marketing themselves and their listings. Median marketing budgets ranged from 4.2% for $86,000 GCI producers to 12.3% for $225,000 GCI producers. The NAR concluded: "as the amount of money sales agents spend on marketing increases, their level of income grows proportionately" (National Association of REALTORS®, *Recruiting and Retaining the Best,* 1996, p. 11). Clearly, when you spend more, you make more.

6. The National Association of Home Builders reports that the average builder spends 6% on marketing and advertising. A significant additional amount is spent on building, landscaping, furnishing, and staffing model homes. When the budget includes model home expenses, new construction marketing averaged 12% of gross income in 1997.

Generally, I recommend you spend at least 10% of your gross income on your marketing program as a minimum or maintenance budget. If growth is your goal, expect to invest 15%. If aggressive growth or penetrating a new market is called for, plan to invest about 20% of GCI. The key is to set yourself a budget. The most successful real estate agents usually spend between 10% and 20%. If your goal is to gross $100,000 a year, at a 10% marketing budget, you know you're going to spend about $10,000 over the year on marketing and advertising. If you have a goal of $500,000 a year GCI, then you're going to spend $50,000 at 10%, which is about $4,000 a month to reach your goal. This percent-of-sales approach is the simplest and easiest way to set a budget.

Figure 14.1 illustrates how to calculate your simple percent-of-sales budget. Now fill in the numbers for your percent of sales budget (Figure 14.2).

Figure 14.1
Calculating Your Percent-of-Sales Budget

Multiply your objective GCI by your marketing expense percentage.

$100,000	GCI objective
× .10(10%)	Marketing expense percent of sales
= $ 10,000	Annual marketing budget
÷12	Months in year
= $ 833/month	Monthly marketing budget (guideline)

Understanding a Transaction-Based Budget

A variation of the percent-of-sales budget is the transaction-based method. Rather than figuring a percent of your total commission dollars, the transaction method uses the number of transactions (units or sides) you will need to reach your goal. To establish your marketing budget, first, set your transaction goal. Second, calculate your marketing cost per transaction (Figure 10.2). Finally, build your marketing budget based on the investment that generates the number of transactions needed to realize your income objective for the year. The transaction-based budget method for a rainmaker might look like Figure 14.3.

Get your average marketing cost per transaction figure you calculated in Morning #1 (Figure 10.2). There, you divided your total transactions into your total marketing investment for the

---

Figure 14.2
Percent-of-Sales Budget Worksheet

Multiply your objective GCI by your marketing expense percentage.

$	GCI objective
×	Marketing expense percent of sales
= $	Annual marketing budget
÷12	Months in year
= $	Monthly marketing budget (guideline)

Figure 14.3
Transaction-Based Budget

---

1. Calculate how many transactions you need to reach your gross commission income objective.

$ 100,000	GCI objective
÷ .021 (70% split)	Your commission split
	[Assume 3% per side or .03: 100% split = .03; 80% = .024; 70% = .021; 60% = .018; 50% = .015]
= $4,762,000	Total volume objective
÷ $150,000	Your average sales price
= 32 units/sides	Total transactions objective

2. Calculate how much you must invest in marketing to reach your total units/sides transaction objective.

32 units/sides	Total transactions objective
× $312	Average marketing cost per transaction
= $9,984	Annual **Real Estate Rainmaker** Marketing Budget

---

year to get your average marketing cost per transaction. Use that figure. It's close enough to make your marketing budget rain results. Over the years, you will work to minimize that cost-per-transaction figure through efficiency and economies of scale, what economists call *productivity*.

Now fill in the figures for your own transaction-based budget (Figure 14.4).

Using the Database
Customer-Value Technique

Another refinement of the percent-of-sales technique is the database customer-value budget. This technique estimates the number of sides you can expect from your Trophy Database and how much you should spend on customer direct marketing to produce that business. Because direct marketing to your Trophy

---

Figure 14.4
Transaction-Based Budget Worksheet

---

1. Calculate how many transactions you need to reach your gross commission income objective.

   $ _____   GCI objective

   ÷ _____   Your commission split

   [3% per side: 100% split = .03; 80% = .024;
   70% = .021; 60% = .018; 50% = .015]

   = _____   Total volume objective

   ÷ _____   Your average sales price

   = _____   Total transactions objective (units/sides)

2. Calculate how much you must invest in marketing to reach your total transaction objective.

   _____   Total transactions objective (units/sides)

   × $ _____   Average marketing cost per transaction

   = $ _____   Annual ***Real Estate Rainmaker*** Marketing Budget

---

Database is easily repeated, this value figure will be of great interest to a buyer of your practice in the future.

Figure 14.5 is an example of how it works. Now fill in the figures for your own database customer-value budget (Figure 14.6).

Building a Zero-Base Budget

Another budget method that makes good sense, but can be a complicated pain in the neck, is called the objective task method or zero-base budget. The task method is particularly good for an aggressive expansion strategy where tomorrow has little relation to yesterday, or for new agents with no previous year numbers. In a nutshell, you ask yourself, "What will it take to get to where I want to go?" Then list the tasks to produce that outcome, put a cost to each task, and the bottom line is your project budget.

If you wish to put a sharp pencil to a zero-base budget, then you must make a very specific, itemized list of every task that

---

Figure 14.5
Database Customer-Value Budget

1,000	Names in Trophy Database
×.08	Average annual turnover in database [Years of residence: 5 years = .20 (20%); 6 years = .17; 7 years = .14; 10 years = .10; 12 years = .08; 15 years = .07]
= 80	Average moves per year from database
×.30	Your average capture rate (30% market share)
= 24	Transactions per year from database
×$3,150	Average GCI per transaction (GCI ÷ units past year)
= $75,600	GCI from database marketing
×.10	Percent-of-sales budget figure (10%)
= $ 7,560	Annual *Real Estate Rainmaker* Database Budget

Figure 14.6
Database Customer-Value Budget Worksheet

Now fill in the figures for your own database customer-value budget:

_____	Names in Trophy Database
× _____	Average annual turnover in database [Years of residence: 5 years = .20 (20%); 6 years = .17; 7 years = .14; 10 years = .10; 12 years = .08; 15 years = .07]
= _____	Average moves per year from database
× _____	Your average capture rate (market share)
= _____	Transactions per year from database
× _____	Average GCI per transaction
= _____	GCI from database marketing
× _____	Percent-of-sales budget figure
= _____	Annual *Real Estate Rainmaker* Database Marketing Budget

---

Figure 14.7
Telephone Hotline and 12-Month Prospect Follow-Up Strategy

ARCH Telecom 800 Powerline	$ 295 (one-time activation fee)
800 number charges (service fee, calls & reporting)	660 ($55/month)
Newspaper advertising	5,200 ($100/week)
Home magazine advertising	2,400 ($200/month)
Graphic production	345
Follow-up mailings	+ 2,340 ($0.50/piece)

[60 new prospects/month = 60 pieces × 12 mos. + 60 pieces × 11 mos. + 60 pieces × 10 mos., etc. = 4,680 follow-up pieces/year]

Subtotal =	11,240
10% contingency	+ 1,124
TOTAL ZERO-BASE BUDGET	**$12,364**

---

makes up a strategy. Next, assign a cost to every item. The sum is your budget for that activity. Add all the activities together, and you get the total marketing budget.

Figure 14.7 is an example using the tasks from a telephone call-capture hotline and direct mail follow-up strategy.

As you can see, the challenge with this approach is working up numbers for *every* strategy in advance. With the zero-base method, it's almost as difficult to do the budget as it is to do the marketing itself. That is why only large companies with large research, budgeting, and accounting departments—or big ad agency budgets—use this method. Typically, a solo rainmaker cannot afford the time—let alone having the interest or talent— to use the zero-base budget method in its full glory. I recommend sticking with the simplified percent-of-sales approach above.

Adjusting for Exceptions to the Rules

Like all rules, these budget rules are made to be broken. Now that you have the basic budgeting idea down pat, you may want to adjust your figures to meet your particular situation.

If you are new to the business or don't keep good records, you don't have any budget figures to use from last year. In that case, throw a dart toward your income objective and use 10% of sales as your marketing budget. Also, be sure to match your means with your method and select marketing strategies based on a beer budget, not on champagne taste. Most probably, you will take advantage of the low-cost and no-cost (sweat equity) ways to leverage your time into money using the techniques in Chapters 3 to 9.

On the other hand, if you are aggressively expanding into new markets or new customer niches where you haven't gone before, or you have targeted a market where the competition is fierce or well established, then you'll probably want to increase your percent-of-sales figure to stimulate growth. As a rough rule of thumb, I recommend doubling your percent-of-sales budget in the first year of an aggressive growth strategy.

Upon analyzing their figures, some **Real Estate Rainmaker** followers discover that they have spent almost all their money in recent years promoting listings and new business lead generation. But they have not given much attention to prospect follow-up systems or to developing systematic business from a referral base where the real money and profits are made.

Instead of allocating a balanced 60%–20%–20% budget toward all three steps of lead generation, prospect follow-up, and long-term contact, they have spent 95% on generating new business from market strangers, 0% on follow-up, and 5% on long-term contact. To correct that neglect, I recommend investing steadily more into follow-up and referral generation by rerouting a "catch-up" budget to steps 2 and 3, such as 80%–10%–10% the first year, then 70%–15%–15% the second year, and so on, until the budget is in better balance.

Once you have roughly allocated your overall budget among the three steps, you are ready to fine-tune the numbers under each step and assign money to specific strategies. Use your final action plan and big payoff rankings to split up your marketing dollars under each step into appropriate amounts for each big payoff strategy, say, a half or a third or a quarter for each campaign if there are two or three or four strategies under the step. Remember to keep it simple. Put the money on the big payoff ideas first. As those strategies produce business, you'll be able to fund more ideas later.

There you have it! This ends our fifth morning session on budgets. Take the afternoon off—you've earned it. I'll see you back here tomorrow morning to pull all the pieces together into your personal *Real Estate Rainmaker* Marketing Plan.

RAINMAKER CHAPTER 14 SUMMARY

Morning #5: Budget

- ▶ Learning How Much You Should Invest.
- ▶ Six Rules of Thumb.
- ▶ Calculating Your Percent-of-Sales Budget.
- ▶ Understanding a Transaction-Based Budget.
- ▶ Using the Database Customer-Value Technique.
- ▶ Building a Zero-Base Budget.
- ▶ Adjusting for Exceptions to the Rules.

Morning #6: Case Studies

> "You can't make one thin dime giving people what they need. You've got to give 'em what they want."
>
> Angel Martin
> (Stuart Margolin),
> *The Rockford Files*

Nothing quite illustrates a *Real Estate Rainmaker* Marketing Plan better than seeing one. The only thing better than one is four. This chapter offers four representative case studies of final plans.

As tempting as it is to fit your round practice into the square hole of these case studies, avoid the temptation. Use them as a guide only. Note how they are structured. These are specific, concrete, feet-on-the-ground examples. My advice is to read them now, but imagine yourself in their shoes. Now that you are grounded in the *Real Estate Rainmaker* techniques outlined in the previous chapters, you probably are bursting with terrific ideas of your own—so many, in fact, that they will guide you for several years.

After you have read the case studies, you'll be ready to assemble your own *Real Estate Rainmaker* Marketing Plan.

Four Real Estate Rainmaker Case Studies

Here are four case studies:

1. Newbie Buyer's Agent.
2. Neighborhood Generalist.

3. Top-Producing Lister.

4. Mega-Agent Team.

As you read these representative case studies, keep an eye out for how the previous five morning sessions contributed to the final marketing plan: benchmarks, objectives, customers, strategies, budget. In the end, marketing is as much art as it is science. Look for the creative nuances and variations.

———————————— **NEWBIE BUYER'S AGENT** ————————————

Profile

I'm new to the business. This is my first year. Just got my license six months ago and finished sales training with my broker last month. My deal with my spouse is that I give this a try for two years. If I can't make a go of it, I'll go get a real job.

In sales training, they made us do some prospecting calls. I've listed my sister-in-law's house and I landed one buyer who I hope will buy something if I just stick with him. We're all learning at the same time. I was a teacher for 11 years and this is a lot like being in the classroom. Buyers have a zillion questions. But it's fun. I like it. I just hope I can make some money doing it. I like working with buyers. They're so appreciative of everything I do for them. Sellers scare me.

Benchmarks

Houses around here cost about $90,000 to $110,000, give or take. There are a lot of handyman specials, real fixer-uppers. Also quite a few HUD foreclosures and houses owned by banks. I live in a close-in old neighborhood, small lots, completely built out. Some rentals. That's why we moved here. We like the mix. Shopkeepers get to know your name. There are a lot of singles and also foreign-born immigrants. It's a real melting pot. The kids can walk to school or the parents stand by the corner with the kids until the bus comes. The houses are two-bedroom, one bath mostly. The three-bedroom, two-bath places usually have an addition. Seems like pretty good turnover. Lots of for-sale signs.

I've taken one listing for $97,000 (my sister-in-law's house). When it sells, my commission will be 50% of 3%, or $1,455. Until I get some business closed, I need to really market myself on a shoestring. The one thing I have is time, and I love to talk.

Objectives

Goals? Gee. I guess I'd like to be a million-dollar agent someday. That would mean closing about 10 deals. I want to work with buyers for now. I'd be happy if I could close six transactions in my first year.

Strategies

Concentrate on first-time buyers.

Big Payoff Action Plans

LEAD GENERATION

1. *Sit open houses for office listings in exchange for buyer leads.* Follow up by phone and mail until they buy or die.

2. *Walk neighborhoods and knock on doors of FSBOs to introduce myself as the "first-time buyer specialist."* Offer to help FSBOs with property profile sheets, interest rate quotes, and reports for buyers in return for FSBO's "extra" buyer prospects. Then follow up first-time buyers. Put names and addresses into sphere database.

3. *Telephone renters of single-family houses and area apartments with rent high enough to afford buying a house.* Use tax records to identify non-owner-occupied homes. Call renters to offer a choice of two "special reports": one for renters whose lease is up within four months *(BUYERS: Money-Saving Secrets for First-Time Buyers),* one for renters

whose lease is up in more than four months *(YES YOU CAN BUY: How to Buy a House in Today's Market)*. Ask which report is right for them.

PROSPECT FOLLOW-UP

4. *Follow up duty desk prospects from ad and sign calls using contact management software.* Relentlessly pursue first-time buyer prospects that call about properties in my area. Mail letters, postcards, and flyers. Call them offering informative reports, private consultation with a lender, and computerized search for homes in their price range. Ask for buyer referrals.

LONG-TERM CONTACT

5. *Cultivate listing agents in my office.* Several established agents in my office prefer to work with sellers only. Build a referral relationship where they give me the first-time buyer prospects they don't want to work from their ad and sign calls and open houses.

6. *Cultivate local loan officers who specialize in my area.* Collect lender names from colleagues, title companies, settlement services, and so on, and establish a reciprocity relationship to exchange first-time buyer referrals in my area. Volunteer to staff lender's home buyer seminars and follow up lender's telephone hotline prospects.

Budget

My budget is pretty tight. But I can invest $1,200 in marketing, $100 a month.

──────────────── **NEIGHBORHOOD GENERALIST** ────────────────

Profile

I want any customer with money. Buyers. Sellers. I'll take them all. In fact, over the years, try as I might to change the mix of my business with more sellers, I pretty much end up with a 50/50 mix, even-Steven. Seems like for every seller there is a buyer and for every buyer there is a seller.

What I want is just more business. Not a lot more. A lot more business would drive me crazy. This business is crazy enough as it is. I want a life. I've been in the business for six years. I do it all by myself. No assistants. No spouse.

My market area is different. Mostly, it's single-family with some townhouses, but there are several apartment complexes, too. My clients are middle-income families and are mostly first- or second-time homeowners. Lots of young families. Schools are real important to my clients. When their second child arrives, the townhouse folks tend to move up into a single-family in the same school district. Also, divorces are big. That may sound a little funny, but it's true. Sad but true. Often, they sell the family home and both buy a townhouse to stay in the district for the kids. A fair number of turnovers are military moves. We're a bed-room community to an Air Force base where officers come for two years of advanced technical training.

Benchmarks

For each of the past three years, I've closed 20 transactions for $3 million volume: 10 listings, 10 sales. Average price in my area is $150,000. Gross commission income last year was $45,000. We're a 3% market and I'm on a sliding split from 50% to 70%. Last year, I spent about $5,000 on marketing and advertising, or 11% of GCI. The best thing I did was compile a membership directory for my high school athletic boosters club. My oldest daughter is a crackerjack soccer player. That gave me a mailing list of 127 other parents in the club whom I see often at games and meetings.

Here's how I get business now: I prospect for listings. I've got 500 on my mailing list: a sphere of 200 names, including 70 past clients, and a geographic farm of 300 names. Seven out of ten listings came from that list last year. My listings generate their own market of buyers through ad calls, sign calls, and open houses. You'd probably call me traditional. But that's what works in my area and it suits me.

Objectives

Next year, I'd like to increase my overall business 25%, taking it up to 25 transactions, $3,750,000 production and a GCI of $56,250. Time to start saving more for college.

Strategies

1. *Double my database.* Last year, I captured seven listings from my database of 500. By increasing the base to 1,000, I'm confident I can increase my listings because many of the townhomes were new construction three to four years ago and are coming on the market for the first time as resales.

2. *Target dual-commission trade-up sellers.* Over the years, I've noticed how folks tend to stay in the area when they move up. I want to capture more of that double-deal business.

3. *Cultivate more referrals from my past clients.* With seventy past clients still in the area, I want to target extra efforts to generate referrals from their friends, relatives, co-workers, and neighbors.

Big Payoff Action Plans

LEAD GENERATION

1. *Add addresses to database.* Hire a temporary to use a combination of our city directory and tax records to enter 500 additional names into database, specifically 300 townhouses (higher turnover) and 200 single-family homes (higher price). Flag home style in customer record for easy selection. Names will come from two subdivisions that were new homes three to four years ago.

2. *Volunteer to publish boosters club newsletter.* Prepare on desktop publishing software a calendar listing all high school games, tryouts, and awards banquets four times during school year and mail to booster club members. To cover the cost, I'll sell three ads to local suppliers and include a fourth ad for my real estate services.

3. *Develop "sell-and-buy" trade-up program.* Offer special reports in direct-mail campaign targeting townhouse owners. Detail benefits to homeowner of working with one agent to sell and buy across town, such as better understanding of seller's needs, negotiating both sale and purchase contracts, coordinating closings to avoid double moves, etc. Use "two-for-one" slogan and run ads with photos of happy couples in front of both the "before" and "after" houses that I helped them sell and buy. "Two Houses. One Call."

PROSPECT FOLLOW-UP

4. *Send more direct mail to prospect database.* Increase mailing frequency from quarterly to monthly, alternating a newsletter and a postcard to all 1,000 names, including active prospects and sphere database. Feature information especially of interest to sellers and just listed/just sold postcards. Ask for seller referrals.

5. *Attend "New Duty Assignment Night" sponsored by military housing office.* Arrange with housing office to staff a table-top display about home selling at periodic "New Duty Nights," where outbound military families come to learn about relocating. Prepare a special "Military Marketing Package" with helpful information on everything from home sale fix-ups and accepting buyer's VA financing to free destination relocation kits and home finding referrals.

LONG-TERM CONTACT

6. *Obtain testimonial letters from six past referral clients.* Color photocopy letters that say "We're glad you were referred

to us. Service was great." Insert testimonial into envelope with a "Thought you'd be interested" handwritten sticky note, and mail six times during year to all seventy past clients. Educate clients about importance of referrals. Ask for referrals.

7. *Build referral relationship with divorce attorneys.* Experience shows many divorce referrals lead to three transactions: family home sale and purchase of two other homes. Occasionally, there is the sale of a second home for a fourth transaction. Contact family practice lawyers who will refer their clients for a property price opinion before selling. Cultivate relationship by adding attorneys to mailing lists, especially just sold postcards.

Budget

My goal for next year is 25 transactions. Last year, I spent $250 per transaction on marketing. Next year, my transaction-based marketing budget is going to be $6,250 ($250 × 25 transactions). As a percent of sales, next year's marketing budget is still 11% of projected GCI, but 25% more dollars than last year. In addition, I plan to reroute some of the property advertising money into direct mail, specifically targeting my expanded database and 70 past clients, whom I haven't cultivated enough.

─────────────── **TOP-PRODUCING LISTER** ───────────────

Profile

I don't do buyers. My specialty is listings, only listings. If I generate a buyer, I hand them off to my buyer's agent assistant. After fourteen years in this business, if I never drive another buyer around in my car, I'd be happy. But if a listing client couple wants to buy a house, and if I like them, I give them an MLS printout of ten possibles, tell them to drive by and pick the three they like best. Then I'll take them to see the inside of those three properties with the expectation we will write an offer that day.

With sellers, once I put the listing in the MLS, every agent in town is working to sell my listings. That way I can handle 25 to 40 listings at once with one marketing/transaction assistant. I'm in control of my time—as much as anybody can be in this business—and I make a good living.

Benchmarks

I know from experience it takes about 24 inquiries to sift out 6 truly interested prospective sellers to get 2 listing appointments, and out of 2 appointments, I usually close 1 listing. (As you can see, my assistant keeps very good records.) Last year, to close 29 listings, I went on 58 listing presentations out of 174 interested seller prospects sifted from 696 homeowner inquiries. My inquiry-to-closed-listing ratio is 24:1. I also closed 13 buyer sides.

These are my numbers from last year:

Production:	$8,400,000
Average sales price:	$ 200,000
Average commission:	$ 4,200 (70% split of 3%)
Gross commission income	$ 176,400
Nonmarketing costs	(47,600) (27%)
Gross income	$ 128,800
Marketing expenses	(35,200) (20%)
Net income	$ 93,600 (53%)
Marketing Budget:	$35,200 ($176,400 GCI × 20%)
Lead generation	$24,600 (70%)
Prospect follow-up	$ 5,200 (15%)
Long-term contact	$ 5,400 (15%)
Marketing cost per side:	$ 840 average ($35,200 ÷ 42 transactions)
Transactions/sides:	42
Listing sides:	29 (70%)
Buyer sides:	13 (30%)

Sources of business:

Ad/marketing:	17 (40%)
Referrals:	17 (40%)
Repeat:	8 (20%)

Contact database:

Market strangers:	14,000
Active prospects:	400 (Every day, one added and one removed to sphere list)
Sphere contacts:	1,000 (People I've met)
Past clients:	360 (Still live in area)
Past listings:	210 properties (I was last broker to market property)

Objectives

1. *Increase transactions.* I want to increase my transactions to a total of 52 (24% increase). Specifically, I want to increase my listings by 10, from 29 listings sold to 39 listings sold (and keep buyer sides at 13 units). Total production will be $10.4 million. GCI will be $218,400 and net income will be $126,800 (an increase of $33,200, or a 35% raise).

2. *Increase net income.* I want to work smarter and increase my net income by reducing my percentage spent on marketing from 20% to 15% (25% decrease), at the same time increasing my GCI 24%. My goal is an income statement that looks like this at year end:

Gross commission income	$218,400
Nonmarketing costs	(58,900) (27%)
Gross income	$159,500
Marketing expenses	(32,700) (15%)
Net income	$126,800 (58%)

Strategies

1. *Presell listing prospects.* To increase my listing production and profitability, my strategy is to improve my current

24:1 inquiry-to-listing ratio to an 18:1 inquiry-to-listing ratio. To accomplish this strategy, I plan to reroute marketing dollars into more prospect follow-up to "presell" listing prospects before the listing presentation. (If I had closed 1 listing out of 18 prospective seller inquiries this past year, not 1 out of 24, my listing production from 696 homeowner inquiries would have increased 34%, from 29 closed listings to 39 closed listings. My overall production would have increased from 42 sides to 52 sides. This year's goal exactly.)

2. *Generate more referrals.* To increase my profitability and net income, I want to increase my low-marketing-cost referral listings from my referral database from 17 to 27 transactions (59% increase). Besides repeating some of what I did last year, I plan to reroute marketing dollars into more long-term contact to generate more seller referrals.

Big Payoff Action Plans

LEAD GENERATION

1. *Advertise for sellers.* Replace one-quarter of all property ads with direct-response ads targeted at sellers that feature specific offers for special reports that appeal to trade-up sellers, outbound relocation sellers, and downsizing sellers. No additional cost.

2. *Develop "just sold" direct-mail system.* Double the impact of sold listings by mailing the same "just sold" postcard twice two weeks apart that feature recently sold listings (proof of results). On the second mailing, include a "sellers wanted" home seller response offer because the sold listings generated "extra buyers." Higher quantity press run reduces unit-printing cost to spread dollars farther.

PROSPECT FOLLOW-UP

3. *Increase home seller prospect follow-up.* Automate a 30-in-10 follow-up blitz of targeted phone calls (10) and direct

mail pieces (20) over a ten-week action plan to every potential seller who visits a house held open by buyer's
agent.

4. *Develop seller "Market Update" report.* For sellers who want
   to list in six to twelve months, offer a weekly mail, fax, or
   e-mail subscription to a "Market Update" newsletter. The
   update features one page of MLS statistics and charts re-
   porting total listings on market, average prices by area,
   listing-to-sale prices, average time on market, absorption
   rates, expired listing percentage, and interest rates. Convince prospects I am most knowledgeable agent in market.

5. *Introduce prelisting "preferred seller pack."* When sellers are
   "ready," they will receive a special pack of materials
   courier-delivered the day before the listing appointment
   containing testimonials, my recent sales, pricing and fix-
   up videos, explanation of selling process, and documents
   to gather prior to listing appointment. My goal is to turn
   two out of three listing appointments into a one-stop
   close.

6. *Develop "expired" property database.* Market research indicates that as many as 80% of expired properties are sold
   within two years of an expired first listing. Collect database of expired listings from the past two years and
   "farm" the list by mail and phone until homeowners move.

LONG-TERM CONTACT

7. *Obtain "property" testimonials from past sellers.* Solicit testimonial letters from past sellers about my success marketing their old property. Use these letters to build
   "repeat" business from current owner of the property because I was the last broker to successfully market that
   property (even though they bought the house through a
   co-op broker).

8. *Develop five-piece thank-you system for professional referrals.* Write a series of five different thank-you letters to be

mailed to business-to-business referral sources. Using contact management software, thank-you letters will go out automatically upon receipt of referral, listing appointment, signed listing agreement, purchase contract, and closed settlement. Include $25, $50, and $100 gift certificates in last three letters of series, if allowed by RESPA regulations.

9. *Create "Do a Friend a Favor" direct-mail campaign.* Cultivate seller referrals from past clients, sphere, and active prospects with three mailing pieces that spell out the information I need about prospective sellers: Who?, Why selling?, When want to move?, Where moving to?, and, What they want to sell? On alternating months, mail three-piece series twice during year.

10. *Host two client appreciation events.* Plan an event for consumers and one for professionals during year to show my appreciation for their referrals. As many attendees will know each other, illustrate where they fit on a "referral tree" with easel boards, color-coded name badges, and public introduction of largest group of "referral relatives" within my friends and family circle. Use "rain forest" theme. Rent restaurant for the event.

Budget

Total marketing budget will be $32,700 ($2,500 less than previous year). This budget is based on 15% of sales of $218,400 GCI. Marketing cost per transaction will be $630 ($32,700 ÷ 52), a reduction of $210 per transaction from previous year. The overall marketing budget will be allocated:

Lead generation (60%)	$19,000 (− $5,000)
Prospect follow-up (20%)	$ 6,500 (+ $1,300)
Long-term contact (20%)	$ 6,600 (+ $1,200)
Total Marketing Budget	$32,700

—————————— MEGA-AGENT TEAM ——————————

Profile

Real estate is a potato chip business. Reaching one level of production is never enough: I always want more. I always want to take it to the next level. After years as a broker/owner, I'm still a manager, but now everyone on my personal team is my employee and I'm loving it. The key to this business is customer service and building relationships.

Because my system only gives Gold Team service that's "worth its weight in gold," all our customers get the same high level of care. Customers benefit from our team's combined expertise and our complementary skills. Most important, I don't have to be personally involved with a customer. That means I can take a vacation or go to a conference or even sell the practice, and our customer relationships won't be affected if I'm not there. The Gold Team takes care of business with our state-of-the-art computer system and eight assistants (three buyer's agents; three coordinators for listings, closings, and marketing; and two support staff).

After careful research, I selected a single geographic area of eighteen desirable communities with the highest turnover (6%) and above-average prices ($260,000) just inside the ring road. With only 11% market share (211 transactions out of 1,920 moves), we have lots of room to grow before we dominate this move-up area of 32,000 homes. The key to our marketing is the geographic concentration of neighborhoods. All our promotions target this area, especially our eight-page Gold Team tabloid newspaper we print and mail to every household monthly. Our newsprint tabloid and 800 property hotline are the vehicle and engine that drive our marketing campaigns.

Benchmarks

Transactions:	151 (79 listings sold, 72 sales)
Average price:	$260,000

Average commission:	$7,800 (100% of 3%)
Production:	$39,260,000
GCI:	$1,177,800
Sources of Business:	
Ad/marketing	74 (49%)
Referrals	63 (42%)
Repeat	14 (9%)
Marketing budget:	$129,558 (11% of GCI)
Marketing/side:	$858/transaction
Sign installs:	57 new signs (79 sold listings – 14 carry overs + 19 expired – 27 current listings)

Objectives

1. *Increase transactions by 10% to 166 sides or 15 more transactions next year.* This will produce a GCI of $1,294,800 from a volume of $43,160,000.

2. *Increase referrals and repeat transactions by 15% to 89 from 77 transactions next year.* Our source-of-business goal is ad/marketing: 77 (46%); referrals/repeat: 89 (54%).

Strategies

1. *Concentrate on working with sellers in Gold Team market area.* Our *Gold Team* tabloid does a super job of attracting buyers for our listings.

2. *Increase hands-off state-of-the-art marketing techniques that allow Gold Team assistants to handle more transactions without adding employees.* Automating lead generation and prospect follow-up will be essential to cope with higher transaction volume. Hotline is good example. Prerecorded property descriptions greatly reduce info-only calls to staff, but caller ID automatically captures number, name, and address of every prospect for follow-up system.

3. *Leverage word-of-mouth referrals among neighbors by systematic cultivation of past clients.* Use our market area

concentration to advantage by encouraging residents to pass along our name.

4. *Target cooperating real estate agents representing buyers from outside our area to build referral relationships.* Build relationships with agents by sending them outbound referrals of our sellers moving out of the Gold Team area to their area, in return for their sending us inbound referrals of their sellers moving out of their area into the Gold Team market. Collect database of co-op agents from past three years of Gold Team transactions.

Big Payoff Action Plans

LEAD GENERATION

1. *Mail Gold Team tabloid to 32,000 households monthly.* Recover some cost by selling classified ads to local service providers. Annual cost of printing and mailing: $81,000 (21¢/copy for 384,000 copies). Use tabloid to announce new marketing promotions, provide useful content for sellers and buyers, and advertise listings.

2. *Experiment with advertising in neighborhood media.* Place direct-response test ads on shopping carts, transit stop benches, bus route timetables, high school newspaper, billboards, supermarket bulletin boards. Test response offers for free reports, website address, seminars, and Gold Team tabloid.

3. *Upgrade website design.* Add consumer content stories written in Q&A format and direct-response offers for free reports. Increase number of ways consumer can contact Gold Team for more information: Q&A e-mail service; free subscription to tabloid; seminar reservations; enroll in Personal Shopper program; a "How are we doing?" suggestion box; upgrade graphics, moving marquee type, music, virtual home tours using PhotoShare™; more links to community information sites.

4. *Install brochure box on every yard sign.* Preprint on back of every flyer a response advertisement asking sellers to

respond for free reports. Hire kids of seller to keep brochure box full by paying them in $2 bills ("One now, four more when it's sold."). Encourage drive-by lookers to take brochure by using Talking House™ sign and three-minute prerecorded message from AM radio transmitter in every listing.

PROSPECT FOLLOW-UP

5. *Host weekly seminars alternating for sellers and buyers.* Promote seminars in Gold Team tabloid featuring a no-pressure approach and informative classes where sellers and buyers can learn about today's market, how to avoid the greatest mistakes when selling or buying, and free in-file credit report. Enter each attendee into contact management program for mail and telephone follow-up by Gold Team telemarketer. Free subscription to tabloid if out of area.

6. *Capture more buyers with Personal Shopper program.* Offer prospects from hotline, seminars, ad and sign calls an opportunity to enroll in the Gold Team Personal Shopper program. To qualify, they must accept a free consultation from Gold Team buyer's agent and a session with loan officer to be preapproved. Prospective buyer can call Price Hotline anytime to get information on any recent sale or property for sale. Personal Shopper will alert prospect to new listings by e-mail or fax before house is advertised or held open. Shopper will personally preview suitable listings in advance, provide prospective buyer with market value analysis and property evaluation, and help negotiate best price before someone else buys prospect's dream house.

7. *Capture more sellers with "wish list" and "just sold" mailings.* Prepare postcard mailings for seller prospects. Wish list features a description of properties (community, house size/style, price range) Gold Team Personal Shopper buyers are looking to buy. Just sold postcards feature recent sales, and explain how Gold Team has many buyers enrolled in Gold Team Personal Shopper program who are

qualified to buy right now if prospect knows anyone interested in selling.

LONG-TERM CONTACT

8. *Systematically obtain testimonials from all buyers and sellers.* Ask every customer to write a short letter answering the question: "What did you like best about the Gold Team's service?" Ideal testimonial uses the word *team* and mentions a neighborhood in the letter to emphasize our team approach and local neighborhood specialization. Use letters in ads, tabloid, and follow-up. Get signed permission to use letter for promotional purposes.

9. *Plan intensive after-sale follow-up for every buyer and seller for one year.* Develop series of contacts to be used with all customers—six phone calls (3–10–30–60–180–365 days after closing)—asking if their needs have been met and recommending local services listed in Gold Team tabloid. Send photo or rendering of "old" house to sellers, change-of-address labels to sellers and buyers. Mail twelve newsletters plus closing anniversary and birthday greetings. In January, send photocopy of settlement sheet for tax purposes. With every contact, ask for referrals. Insert referral stuffers in all outgoing envelopes.

10. *Mail "new neighbors" card to 20 houses on street after closing.* Introduce new buyers (with their permission) to new neighbors. Invite neighbors to a "meet your new neighbor" potluck party at buyer's house arranged by buyer's agent. Use family photo with names on card whenever possible. Note if buyers were "referred by so-and-so" to Gold Team or if they are members of Double Nugget Club of repeat customers. Ask for referrals by offering to help neighbor's friends or relatives buy or sell in the area.

Budget

Marketing budget will be $142,428, or 11% of GCI.

Assembling Your *Real Estate Rainmaker* Marketing Plan

You are now ready to assemble and prioritize your own script for success. Use these case studies as a launching pad for your **Real Estate Rainmaker** Marketing Plan tailored to your profile, to your benchmarks, to your objectives, strategies, big payoff action plans, and to your budget. That way you'll be off and running in the right direction—financial independence for life.

Go back to the previous week's notes and bring forward these nine worksheets:

- Marketing Expenses Benchmark (Figure 10.2): *Benchmarks* (Morning #1).
- Mission Statement (Figure 11.3): *Objectives* (Morning #2).
- Marketing Objectives Summary (Figure 11.5): *Objectives* (Morning #2).
- Target Customers Summary (Figure 12.4): *Customers* (Morning #3).
- Four Big Payoff Action Plans (Table 13.4): *Strategies* (Morning #4).
- Percent-of-Sales Budget (Figure 14.2): *Budget* (Morning #5).

The nine worksheets you have in hand *are* your **Real Estate Rainmaker** Marketing Plan. The next step is to convert your plan into a Do List of large tasks and smaller, specific activities all with due dates.

Eating an Elephant One Bite at a Time

In the early 1980s, Dr. Janelle Barlow, then an outstanding trainer and now president of North American operations for Time Manager International based in San Rafael, California, (www.tmiworld.com), taught me how to attack a large task. "There is only one way to eat an elephant," she said. "One bite at a time." I've used that technique on every task I've faced, large and small, ever since, from running my company to writing this book. On my digital clock sitting on the shelf over my desk I keep an elephant cookie cutter just as a reminder.

To manage your time using Barlow's elephant technique, separate your Action Plans into *tasks* and *activities*. Tasks are large projects that require several steps to complete. Activities are one-shot items, such as a phone call or letter or meeting. Next, assign a due date to each task or activity. Using these dates, prioritize exactly which task needs attention now and work on that elephant-size task first. When a spare moment pops up in your day, turn to the one-shot activities. Interestingly, although I concentrate solely on the bigger tasks, many times, when I turn to the one-shot activities list, I discover some have been done already, almost without thinking about them.

Now your job is to apply the same elephant-eating Do List technique to your Marketing Plan.

Creating a Vision for the Future, and a Plan for the Day

Turn to your four Big Payoff Action Plans (Table 13.4), which are divided into General Business and the three **Real Estate Rainmaker** steps: lead generation, prospect follow-up, long-term contact. Assign a due date to complete the task of each individual Action Plan. For each Action Plan task, list the needed activities to accomplish the task. If someone else will be responsible for actually completing the task or activity, indicate who it will be.

Let's take an example. Your Lead Generation Action Plan task is: *Turn yard sign brochure boxes into a seller lead generation medium.* The needed activities include:

- Order 10 brochure boxes with brackets for sign installer.
- Order 50 each of three different direct-response Special Reports for sellers.
- Write and design three test ads for the back of property highlight flyers.

- Print 300 copies of each ad on copier paper (900 total) to be used for flyers as needed.

- Arrange with home seller's kids to keep brochure box stocked with flyers.

Cost (brochure boxes, reports, printing, kids): $285 (see Table 15.1).

If your worksheets need a bit of polish, especially the new task/activity lists, retype the key sections onto a clean document using the case study outline as a guide: profile, benchmarks, objectives, strategies, big payoff action plans, budget. A clean copy is especially useful if you will share the Marketing Plan with staff members. Put any additional worksheets and notes in an appendix, ready for next year's planning sessions.

At last, you have turned your vision of the future into a daily Do List plan with specific tasks, activities, priority due dates, and task budget.

Congratulations! You made it through the week and you now have a road map to guide your practice. Do you realize how far you've come? Pat yourself on the back—you've earned it big time.

Implementation is now the magic word. Just do it, as they say at Nike. Part Six lists some Trophy Database strategies and resources that have worked for other ***Real Estate Rainmakers*** on their journey toward a practice that yields business year after year regardless of market fluctuations.

Table 15.1
Brochure Box Action Task Budget

Projected additional revenue (2 listings @ $2,250)	$4,500
Cost of marketing listing ($250/unit on average)	(500)
Gross additional revenue	$4,000
Action Plan marketing cost	(285)
Net revenue projection	$3,715

RAINMAKER CHAPTER 15 SUMMARY

Morning #6: Case Studies

▶ Newbie Buyer's Agent.

▶ Neighborhood Generalist.

▶ Top-Producing Lister.

▶ Mega-Agent Team.

▶ Assembling Your *Real Estate Rainmaker* Marketing Plan.

▶ Eating an Elephant One Bite at a Time.

GROWING YOUR
PRACTICE TO SELL

Building a *Real Estate Rainmaker* Trophy Database

Technology won't
put agents out
of business.

Agents with
technology will put
agents without
technology out
of business.

Quoted by John
Rinehart, president,
Rinehart Realty, Rock
Hill, South Carolina

In Chapters 10 to 15, you created a marketing plan and budget. In this chapter, you'll learn the nuts and bolts about how to plan and select database software and five strategies to grow your business into an autopilot practice that is transferable to a successor.

Building a Trophy Database Is Your Top Job

As leading trainer and business coach Mike Ferry says, "There are two types of people in the world. Ones you know and ones you don't know." A rainmaker's Trophy Database subdivides the "ones you know" into three sublists: Core List, Prospect List, and Circle List. Everybody else—the "ones you don't know"— are entered in a fourth, Wannabe List.

By the way, this list actually is a database. It's not in a shoe-box or card file, it's not in your day-timer, and it's not in dusty case files in the storeroom. It's a computerized database that will generate mailing labels. Minimum customer records include name, address, city, state, zip, and phone for a start, plus the sublist status of every customer record. Then, the records grow much more sophisticated. Here are the basics.

Core List. The core of your Trophy Database is past customers. Call it your Core List. These are people who have actually completed a transaction as your client, or who have sent you a referral that closed. If you've been in the business for, say, 10 years, and you've closed 20 units on average every year, you'll have a past customer Core List of 200. In addition, the Core List includes noncustomer referral sources that are just as valuable as past customers. These past customers and referral contacts who consistently send you referrals are sometimes called ambassadors, advocates, even apostles or disciples.

Circle List. Around this Core List is assembled the social circle of people you've met, but who have not recently shown an interest in real estate services. Call it your Circle List for circle of influence (also, "sphere of influence" or "friends and family" circle or "personal" list). Your Circle List includes friends, relatives, neighbors, co-workers, and potential business-to-business referral sources. Your Rolodex or holiday card list and your accounts-payable suppliers are a good beginning for your Circle List. Both your Core List and Circle List are "warm" lists.

Prospect List. Just outside your Core and Circle Lists is your collection of active prospects. Call it your Prospect List. These are potential buyers and sellers you have met or who have responded to your marketing: call-capture hotline prospects, word-of-mouth referrals, ad callers, yard sign inquirers, duty desk callers, website visitors, open house guests, seminar attendees, publicity responders, in short, all your marketing-generated active leads. These prospects are inquiries you've talked to, perhaps even met, and put in your active prospect pipeline, but you've not yet signed them. Your Prospect List is a "hot" list.

Wannabe List. Surrounding your three "who you know" sublists is a database of compiled names. Call it your Wannabe List (also, "farm" list). On this list of market strangers are folks you've targeted as people you want to do business with, but you've neither met them nor have they responded yet to become your prospect or client. These targeted customers are your FSBOs; expireds; your geographic, demographic, and Internet farms; directories, rosters, and membership rolls; referral networks; church, club, and school contacts; even strangers in your aerobics class. Your Wannabe List is comprised of market strangers you've targeted because you wannabe their real estate agent. The Wannabe List is a "cold" list.

Like a whirlpool, your **Real Estate Rainmaker** Trophy Database is in constant motion. On the outside, quiet eddies of warm and cold contacts steadily cast off prospects toward the center. The hot prospects in the center are stirred round and round ever hotter. Inexorably, inevitably, the hot prospects are pulled nearer and nearer the center. With every marketing effort, the prospects pick up speed until ultimately they rush into an appointment ready to buy or sell—where all you do is close. Some prospects shoot right into your arms with the first contact. Others circle for weeks, gradually coming closer and closer. Still others drift for months, even years, until they are drawn into action by your relentless database marketing.

When We Die, Whoever Has the Trophy Database Wins

So where do you start? Start by assembling your information for entry into your computer's contact management software program. Collect name, address, and phone for all your past customers, active prospects, circle of contacts, and targeted market strangers.

On the most basic level, your Trophy Database must maintain a customer profile, an ever-growing well of information about each customer. The database will collect not only their personal data, but also their household information, their property description, their entire contact history, with a record of every outgoing mail piece and phone notes logged every time you talk to them. These notes will prove critical for your follow-up action plan and also create an invaluable case history file that your staff will hand you as you run out the door to a presentation appointment with a prospect you've never met. Free-form notes along with structured data fields will be very important.

Assembling Invaluable Customer Information

As your database grows, your initial, bare bones information—name, address, and phone number—soon will have the names of spouses, kids, pets, their birthdays, anniversaries, and special interests, building on Larry Kendall's F.O.R.D. method (family, occupation, recreation, dreams). Also, you'll collect property information such as date of purchase, sales price, assessed value, interest rate, loan amount, and loan type, and a full property description identical to an MLS profile.

In a nutshell, you'll need to keep two types of information: personal and property. Some information will relate to the name of a person and follow that person wherever he or she lives. Other information will relate to an address, regardless of who lives there. When the owners of a property change, you'll want to keep their personal record intact, but be sure to transfer listing property information from the seller's record to the buyer's record. Remember, the purpose of this information is a profile of both the customer and the client property. Both profiles must be available instantly as a report printout for your case history file, as well as a searchable database to select individuals or groups of contacts and print letters or mailing labels for target marketing. Fields can be for data (fill in the blank) or pull-down menus (preset selections) or open notes areas. Many software packages offer most of these fields, but be sure to check before you buy. Also, being able to transfer property data easily between your software and your MLS, the Internet, or other applications will be crucial.

Data Fields for Customer Records

Personal information will include:

- Customer: first name, middle initial, last name, suffix.
- Home: address, phone, fax, e-mail.

- Customer work: address, phone, fax, mobile, pager, e-mail; employer; title; date of employment.
- Spouse: first name, middle initial, last name, suffix.
- Spouse work: address, phone, fax, mobile, pager, e-mail; employer; title; date of employment.
- Kid(s): first name, middle initial, last name, suffix; birth dates, number of kids.
- Dates: date referred, desired move date, date began house hunting; birth date, wedding anniversary.
- Recreation, hobbies, interests.
- Marital status.
- Rent or own.
- Previous zip code.
- Number of commissions from this customer (combined direct and referral).
- Source history: source of business (advertising, referral, repeat client); original, most recent.
- Referral source: who referred this contact.
- Marketing history: ad response code(s) and date(s).
- Contact history: dates, conversation notes, scheduled action plans.
- List status: Core, Circle, Prospect, Wannabe (compiled).
- Desired property features: bedrooms/baths, price, etc.
- Desired destination area.
- Working with another agent? (Y/N).
- Met with lender? (Y/N).
- Lender name, company, address, phone.
- Plans to be a FSBO? (Y/N).
- Able to offer seller financing? (Y/N).
- Seen houses they like? (Y/N).
- Available down payment? ($/%).
- Maximum monthly payment? Rent?
- Et cetera: complete personal record.

Property information will include:

- Address.
- Date property purchased.
- Purchase price.
- Assessed tax value.
- Desired sales price.
- Occupancy: residence, second home, rental, etc.
- Date of lease end.
- Date listing to expire or did expire.
- Mortgage balance.
- Loan type.
- Interest rate.
- Available equity or down payment.
- Property type: single-family (SFDU), multifamily, land, farm.
- House Style: colonial, Cape Cod, ranch, country, Victorian, Mediterranean, split level, bilevel, duplex, town house, etc.
- Number of bedrooms, sizes.
- Number of baths, sizes.
- Total rooms.
- Building square footage.
- Property square footage.
- Et cetera: complete MLS property description.

QUICK CHECKLIST PRIMER FOR DATABASE SOFTWARE SHOPPING

Fortunately for rainmakers, there are many software choices for off-the-shelf real estate database and contact management packages you can use immediately. At the core, most are designed to do the same thing: maintain a database of detailed profiles about people and properties and your contact history. But each has its own personality; each software tackles the Trophy Database challenge from a different angle. The more you study them all, the more informed you will be about their subtle differences, and, most important, the smarter you will be about the power of a Trophy Database.

Here are five popular residential brands. For more detailed information, visit their websites and talk with other users. For an invaluable shopper's session, make it a point to attend one of Rolf Anderson's excellent "three-ring shoot-outs" at a convention comparing the Big Three: Top Producer, PREP, and On-Line Agent (See Resource Guide under Database Software).

☑ *Top Producer:* Widely considered the industry leader with the most registered users. Add-ons: Top Connector (MLS), Top Locator (mapping), Top Presenter (printed and multimedia presentations), Top Financial (reports), Top Office (brokerage). Network and franchise versions available.

☑ *PREP Real Suite:* Four modules available separately or as a suite: Prospecting (database), Presentations (printed presentations), Productions (multimedia presentations), Financial (analysis and report tools). Version 4.0 uses Microsoft Outlook environment. Rich in quality content: property flyers, postcards, and so on.

☑ *On-Line Agent:* Networkable, CMA module for downloading MLS data, multiple report options, module with preformatted presentation templates. Selected by Century 21 (Power-Pack 21), RE/MAX (Agent 2000), and Realty Executives as the endorsed software for those franchises.

☑ *Exceed98:* A new program for Windows building on publisher's DOS experience with *RealAide* program. A template built on Microsoft Office, Exceed98 is integrated with MS Access, MS Word, and other widely used Microsoft products. MS Office purchased separately.

☑ *Howard & Friends:* Real estate contact manager, financial module, CMA/presentations with auto download feature in one package. Track listings, closings, referrals, people, prospects, appointments, correspondence. Postcard and letter libraries with mail/merge.

"Internet Farms" Fast Becoming a Valuable Asset

Because e-mail addresses are not as readily available in directories as postal addresses, and because e-mail contact is virtually free to a rainmaker, e-mail addresses are increasingly valuable. Make it a practice to collect e-mail addresses, and ask clients how they prefer to be contacted (e-mail, phone, mail). To expand your e-mail list, use these tips from Allen F. Hainge's CyberStars™, a select group of top producers with a significant Internet presence:

1. Ask. Every chance you get, ask for customer's e-mail address: open house registry, ad call, sign call, buyer information request, relocation kit request, and so on.
2. Put response forms on your website.
3. Offer a free report or premium on your website. E-mail requests should also be required to give complete contact information, not just e-mail address.
4. Include e-mail request option in print ads for faster response to get free premium.
5. Send postcard to your database asking for e-mail address. Consider a sweepstakes or prize drawing available to all respondents to increase response. Also ask for birthdays, anniversaries, and website address.
6. Get e-mail addresses from all agents and professionals in your Bird Dog network.

Caution: E-mail addresses are notorious for deteriorating much faster than postal addresses because people change Internet service providers more frequently than an address changes on a property. Be sure to delete undeliverable e-mail addresses regularly so you know everyone on the list receives your messages. If *they* provided their e-mail address, assume it is okay to send them e-mail. Otherwise, if you compiled the e-mail address from other sources, web etiquette recommends that you include an option on the e-mail message for the prospect to be taken off the list. Avoid sending unsolicited, repeated, or annoying e-mail to strangers. This is called "spamming," and is outlawed in several states.

Remember Your Mission

The sole purpose of your Trophy Database is to make money, using the information to increase your business and the value of your practice. Ultimately, a *Real Estate Rainmaker* database is designed to target a specific customer who is most likely to move, and to develop a predictive customer profile that identifies additional likely prospects in the upcoming months and years. Information is the key to your survival and success. In marketing, we call this technique *database marketing* or *data mining;* a rainmaker invests in a career to develop customer information so rich that the rainmaker will always outperform any market fluctuations.

Another benefit from a Trophy Database is it will generate more prospects than you can work. Nothing is more empowering for a rainmaker than to be able to pass up bad listings and difficult buyers, or even select locations or price ranges that suit your marketing plan. Naturally, to say no to business becomes practical only when you have more leads than you can handle. Your broker referral network will also benefit as you refer out extra prospects after selecting only those customers that fit your goals.

Quick Checklist of Tips on Trophy Database Hygiene

Here are four proven rainmaker tips to clean your lists.

☑ *Do it.* The waste of printing and postage to mail to undeliverables is a far greater cost than the time it takes to correct your list.

☑ *First class.* Once or twice a year, mail a first-class postcard (least expensive) and print on the card Return Service Requested, Do Not Forward. If the prospect has moved, the post office will put the correct address on a sticky label and send the card back to you at no charge. *Tip:* The post office charges a return fee if you send the postcard standard/bulk rate, not first class.

☑ *Ask them.* Never threaten your customers with the ultimatum "If you don't respond, we'll delete your name." Instead, ask them, "If you wish to remain a preferred customer, please take a moment to let us know," or "Is a real estate move in your plans for this year?" On the reply card, include an option to "Please remove me from your preferred customer list." That way, if they don't respond, you can keep them as a contact in your database, or not, at your discretion. *Never* delete a name from your database unless you learn it is no longer valid. Otherwise, keep it and simply relegate the contact to the Wannabe List for occasional mailings.

☑ *Four hats.* The purpose of list hygiene is to reduce the cost of "nixies," undeliverable addresses. Another cost-reduction strategy is simply to target your best customers. Imagine that you're flipping customer playing cards into four hats based on the amount of business they have produced. Figuratively, toss each customer into the hat that reflects the number of commissions that customer has brought you to date, either directly or through referrals. #1: Three or more commissions from customer to date; #2: Two commissions; #3: One commission; #4: None. Assign a code in your database records that notes the customer's value. If you must allocate a limited budget, spend it on the top hats: first on #1, then on #2, and so on.

Five Rainmaker Strategies to Grow Your Practice

Strategy #1: Constantly Increase Your Trophy Database

This is the single biggest moneymaking idea you can put into practice. As the old saying goes, "Even though you're second in line, pretty soon you'll be first in line if you're standing in enough lines." The key is how many folks you can get in touch with and stay in touch with, because marketing is a numbers game. You've got to have the numbers on your side to overcome any market.

If you only prospect to 50 people in a 10% turnover market, the most you can expect is 5 deals in a year. On the other hand, say you expand your database to work a list of 500 people. If homeowners still move at a 10% rate, 50 of your target prospects will move this year. You're still the salesperson you've always been who captures 50% of your market. But now you're closing 25 deals in a year.

The only thing you've done is increase the size of your Trophy Database. Take that same concept another level higher. Imagine you're working 1,000 people and 10% move—that's 100 people a year. You still capture 50% of that market. Now you can afford a personal assistant to help with 50 deals in a year. The more people you stay in touch with, the more people you market to, the more money you'll make. The first secret to growing your practice is to grow your database. I can't emphasize this strategy enough.

Strategy #2: Turnover Rate Is Critical

Whether you're building a list for the first time or you're re-examining an old list, the most important secret to success for a Trophy Database is a simple concept: your rate of turnover. Turnover is simply the percentage of people who move in a year. If you have 100 people in your database, and 10 people move, that's a 10% rate of turnover.

Turnover of 5% or higher is a must for your Trophy Database. If you capture an impressive 50% market share from your database, you still must have twice as many prospects and 20 times the household moves every year to reach your closed units goal. Put another way, at a 5% turnover, if you want to close 25 deals this year from your database, you'll need 1,000 names to reach your goal (25 units ÷ .05 turnover = 500 prospects ÷ .5 capture ratio = 1,000 contacts needed). Work out your own figures and set a database goal that matches your unit volume objective.

The magic multiplier is the turnover rate. Imagine that you're starting a Trophy Database list from scratch. There are 500 people in subdivision A and 500 people in subdivision B. Which group should you target?

Look at the rate of turnover. In Group A, 5% move every year, or 25 families. You're still the salesperson you always were. At a 50% market share with Group A, you'll close 12½ deals per year out of 500 prospects. If you get $2,500 a transaction on average, you'll make $30,000 from Group A in one year. Now analyze Group B. These people move at a rate of 10% per year. That means, out of the 50 moves, you get 25 deals worth $60,000 a year.

Look at what has happened. You're still working 500 homes. You're still mailing 500 pieces monthly. You're still calling 500 people. You've invested the same time and money in both groups. But because you did your turnover homework and targeted Group B instead of Group A, you've *doubled* your money and realized a $60,000 return, not $30,000. You've worked smarter, not harder.

Strategy #3: Upgrade the Quality of Your Data

A classic business-boosting technique for a listing database is the "Previous Zip Code" survey. Target an area with substantial turnover, for example, a new home subdivision just coming on the resale market. Ask the recent subdivision buyers where they moved from, specifically their previous zip code. The answers can produce a gold mine of information. You'll be amazed how many buyers already live in nearby areas. In fact, nationally, almost 60% of buyers already live in the county where they buy. You'll also develop an insight into the proportion of long-distance relocation buyers—and discover whether that is a lucrative buyer group for you to target.

Use your survey results as a powerful tool in your listing presentation. A lead-in script would be something like this, recommended by Chuck Bode, an outstanding Residential Sales Council trainer with N. P. Dodge Real Estate Company in Omaha, Nebraska: *"I know who is going to buy your house. I just don't know their name."*

Based on the trend of zip codes you gathered, tell prospective sellers that you will send a just listed message to the zip code(s) where people live who are most interested in buying in the seller's neighborhood. It's a terrific listing contract closer.

This rainmaker technique is called a *feeder farm*. As you spot the move-up trends in your area, you will always know where to promote a new listing. Also, you'll benefit from cultivating customers for life who use you repeatedly as they move up or down the homeowning ladder—and tell all their friends. Feeder farm information is a natural repeat-business builder.

Strategy #4: Understand Reverse Feeder Farms, or "Where They Move To"

A variation of the *move-from* feeder farm, which identifies where buyers come from, is the *move-to* feeder farm, which identifies where sellers move to.

To do this analysis, simply mail a first-class letter to the *old* address of all the homeowners in an area who sold within the prior year. Mark the envelope under your return address Please Do Not Forward, Return Service Requested. The post office will return the letter to you free, plus apply a sticker with the seller's *new* address on the original letter. The post office wants to help mailers correct their lists to minimize incorrect addresses in the future.

Compile the new zip codes. The seller move-to results should complement your buyer move-from results. Note the percentage of sellers who were local relocations within your market area, and how many were long-distance relocation referral opportunities. Once a move-to geographic trend emerges, you can use a Hot List of other brokers' new listings in the move-to area to whet the appetite of potential local sellers in your Trophy Database. Nothing unearths a potential listing faster than showing the owners what their money can buy in today's market.

Tip: This Return Service Requested technique works best when you use an official-looking window envelope with a live first-class stamp. Avoid a hand-addressed envelope (new owners may forward it) or postcard (letter carrier or new owner sees what it is and forwards it or tosses it without returning to you) or advertising mail (letter carrier may toss it, mistaking it for undeliverable bulk mail). In case someone does open the letter, be sure to enclose a pleasant note congratulating them on their move, and suggesting that your marketing has generated more buyers for homes in their old neighborhood. Ask them if they know any of their old neighbors who would be interested in selling.

Strategy #5: Collect "Orphans" by the Drawerful

When salespeople leave the business, they abandon their customers. No matter if the salesperson had only one customer or 100 or a 1,000, the salesperson spent time and money to cultivate those past customers and a circle of influence. The salesperson built a level of trust and understanding to get prospects to believe the salesperson was their neighborhood real estate specialist.

When salespeople leave the business, an astute rainmaker can take advantage of those abandoned customers and turn them into your own customers. One of the great secrets to why prospecting works is that the competition quits. After all, once the follow-up stops, a terrible thing happens: Nothing. A rainmaker can seize this real opportunity to acquire these abandoned customers.

Start by asking your office manager if you can activate the files of old customers whose past agent is no longer with the company. The office, as well as you, will benefit from increased referral and repeat business. This "orphan win-back" technique can be a gold mine, especially with properties originally listed by your office but purchased through a co-broker. Who else is in the best position to successfully market that property but you and your company? You did it before. Go for it again.

RAINMAKER CHAPTER 16 SUMMARY

Building a *Real Estate Rainmaker* Trophy Database

- ▶ Strategy #1: Constantly Increase Your Trophy Database.
- ▶ Strategy #2: Turnover Rate Is Critical.
- ▶ Strategy #3: Upgrade the Quality of Your Data.
- ▶ Strategy #4: Understand Reverse Feeder Farms, or "Where They Move To."
- ▶ Strategy #5: Collect "Orphans" by the Drawerful.

Exit Strategies to Cash In or Cash Out

> When a rainmaker becomes a reign maker, the system is complete.
>
> Dan Gooder Richard

The ultimate test of any rainmaker is to be able to pass on the reign. The next rainmaker may be a partner, an adult child, an assistant—or it could be an outside buyer, perhaps an office colleague either established or newly arrived, or a local competitor, or a new licensee with a business background.

Whoever takes over the reins to drive your practice must get something tangible, something of value, but most important, that person must get a system he or she can step into and continue driving down the road to more business.

Before a practice can be sold, a rainmaker must accomplish these four goals:

1. Document with accounting records a consistent level of business activity using profit/earnings financial statements.

2. Deliver a computerized database of all referral sources.

3. Demonstrate the loyalty of these sources with sales histories and source of business logs.

4. Agree to work with the buyer during a transition to cement awareness and loyalty to the new rainmaker.

In a word, you need a *system*. Think of Pizza Hut, for example. No matter which store you go into, every sign looks the same, the menu is the same, the prices are the same, even the pizza tastes the same. How do they do that? A system. Every procedure, every policy, every detail is systemized and written down in manuals. Workers can be hired to do jobs at the lowest level of pay, not the highest. With some training, any manager can step in and take over. An owner/operator can open a new store and simply plug in the system by following the manual.

The **Real Estate Rainmaker** system provides you with the same systematic approach to business generation. Whoever takes over your practice can step in with some training and take over the marketing functions without missing a beat. That is your goal: a business development system that is transferable.

Be Paid to Walk Away

By practicing the **Real Estate Rainmaker** principles—building a Trophy Database of customers, keeping a record of results, putting in place a transferable system with a proven and profitable earnings stream—you have a sellable practice. Remember our holiday litmus test? Could you cash in by going on holiday or working part time, and have the business go on? Could you cash out by selling the practice entirely, and have the business continue? The ability to turn your business over to the next rainmaker is the driving purpose behind everything you do year after year. Transferring the business to someone else is the ultimate holiday test.

The distinction between *cashing in* and *cashing out* is an important one. If you want to keep your finger in the business, stay in the area, keep receiving referral fees, but work fewer hours, then a "book of business" installment sale based on referral fees for future business may be best for you. If, on the other hand, you want to step out of the business, retire or leave the area, and never look back, then a "multiple of profit earnings" sale with a fixed price and funded by cash or a bank note may be a preferable way to structure your exit strategy. There is no one right way—just the deal that best suits both you and your buyer's needs.

QUICK CHECKLIST OF PROSPECTIVE BUYERS

Since 1993, Pat Dearing, Co-Regional Director of RE/MAX of Georgia, has taught hundreds of agents in his groundbreaking three-hour class, "Plaques Are Not Profit" (formerly, The ME, INC, System, written with Elaine Shreiber), on how to develop a real business practice that can be sold in the future. Dearing says his business management system with complete workbook is incredibly easy, has zero learning curve, and is so simple it takes only about thirty minutes a month to use. "If you wrote the check, you've done 90% of the work," Dearing told me. (See Resource Guide under Selling Your Practice.)

From experience, here is Dearing's short list of three prime buyer prospects:

☑ *Colleague.* The best prospective buyer is an existing agent who does not want to go through the growth curve of growing a practice. The agent might be someone in your office, a competitor, or an experienced agent new to the area.

☑ *Businessperson.* Another prospect is a person entering the real estate business from being a middle manager or small business owner who is used to a salary and doesn't want to start at the bottom.

☑ *Assistant.* With more and more practices using one or several assistants, grooming an assistant to take over the practice is another good bet.

Where do you turn for help to find a buyer? Again, there is no single answer. Some real estate brokers, such as Windermere Real Estate based in Seattle, have recognized the benefit of helping their agents sell their practices to each other and keeping the business within the company. Other top producers have simply worked out a deal directly between themselves. Still others have used the services of a top agent or businessperson, such as Bob Bohlen at Prudential Preview Properties in Brighton, Michigan, to act as a paid business broker to prepare a sales presentation, solicit prospective buyers, and negotiate the sale.

Whichever path you take, there are some costly mistakes that experience has proven can be avoided. Below are some of the key issues and solutions to help you step out of the business and help the buyer step into it in a way that's transparent to the public.

Costly Mistakes to Avoid When Selling a Practice

Mistake #1: Staying a Part of the Business When You Really Want Out

If your intention is to get out of the business, retire, or move out of the area, then selling a practice based on a percent of income over time is a mistake. You're still in the business. During the first year, sellers are still on top of the transactions and payments. In the second year, buyers begin to feel they've generated the business on their own efforts and question paying. By the third year, auditing the sales may be difficult and collecting can be a problem.

Solution: Stay involved in the business. Keep your license active. Cultivate your contacts with your past customers and referral sources. Just spend less time at the practice. Concentrate on business development and the aspects you enjoy most. Cash in, not out.

Mistake #2: Thinking Value Is Based on Production Volume, Not Net Earnings

In real estate, we are programmed to think in terms of production: closed units, listings, sales, commissions. The tendency is to attach value to that production. But there may not be any value to that production if all the money is thrown away in expenses. Which would you rather do: earn $200,000 but have no money to pay taxes, or earn $100,000 and make a $30,000 profit?

Solution: Although there is value in active listings and buyers or property under deposit, true value is based on the net profit earnings record of the business, according to Pat Dearing of RE/MAX of Georgia. Focus on profit, not on production. One of the value models Dearing suggests is to set a sales price using a factor that is a multiple of profit earnings.

Mistake #3: Selling an Image That Is Not Transferable

Reinventing and reprinting marketing materials can be costly. If your corporate image is so highly personalized it must be totally redone from square one, then potential buyers will wonder whether they can create their own image with the money they would otherwise spend buying the business.

Solution: Imagine your photo being replaced by a buyer's picture. Imagine replacing your name with a buyer's name in your personal brochure and in your logo. Does it still work? If your styles are compatible, you will have an attractive business-boosting match.

Mistake #4: Failing to Document Sources of Referral Business

Generating business from market strangers using general media advertising is a necessary investment. But anyone can do it. Failing to carefully record your percentage of referral business and the value of specific referral sources is a critical error.

Solution: Test your Trophy Database. Are the names clean? Do the prospects still live there? Be ready to prove to the buyer with business logs and records the volume of business to be expected from your database. You'll be sharing your books and your tax returns, so be open to examination of your closed case files for the prior two or three years to verify every transaction's source of business: advertising, referral, or repeat client.

Mistake #5: Offering a Personal Practice Disguised as a Business

Some real estate practices are so intertwined with the practitioner and his or her "name"—both literally and figuratively—that future business evaporates when the seller leaves the scene. Often, the seller's personal name is also the name of a "personality business."

Solution: To provide peace of mind, suggest the buyer examine the systems behind the business. Demonstrate how procedures are manualized. How forms and letters and checklists are used. How well the system is computerized—and how the data are compatible with the buyer's system. Most important is to arrange an adequate transition period (six to twelve months to five years) that guarantees you provide more than a passing introduction to all customers, not just to the active clients under agreement.

Learn from the experience of Rich LaRue, a top producer for Realty Executives in Phoenix and now Referral Network director for the entire national franchise. In 1986, LaRue bought the $3 million, 30 unit personal real estate practice of Bill Powers, who went on to be chief operating officer of Realty Executives International. Within three years, LaRue says, he noticed the business and referrals from Powers's past customers were beginning to decline, although his own practice was growing. "We did some things right and we made some mistakes," LaRue says. One mistake was not having the seller stay in touch with his past clients.

When LaRue sold his business 13 years later ($7.5 million, 50 units in 1998) to an office colleague in 1998, part of the deal was for LaRue to stay in touch with his past clients. "It takes me about an hour a week on the phone," he says. "But it's worth it. Every referral I can generate for my colleague means it's one more referral fee for me and a sale for him. It's a win-win situation."

Mistake #6: Failing to Keep the Assistant

Many practices live—or die—by the assistant. Customers may be more attached to the assistant as a primary contact than to the real estate professional. Losing the assistant can kill a business.

Solution: Arrange to have the assistant's job continue with the buyer. Encourage the buyer to consider an incentive employment package to keep the assistant on the team. Include your assistant in the transition plan, as well as yourself. Both of you will be needed. At a minimum, provide a detailed transfer of "company memory," systems, and procedures to the buyer.

QUICK CHECKLIST OF TIPS TO SELL YOUR PRACTICE

Bob Bohlen has been the number one agent for the entire Prudential network worldwide for eight of nine years, from 1990 through 1998. He also has been involved with the sale of more than two dozen real estate practices between 1996 and 1999, and has personally bought or sold more than a dozen real estate offices between 1993 and 1999.

The first practice Bohlen brokered was a $50,000 sale the buyer paid off in nine months from net profit. The largest payout in his experience has been $750,000 for a personal real estate practice. "There are several practices across the country today," he says, "that are worth into the seven figures, well over $1 million."

Here are some of Bohlen's tips to sell your practice:

☑ Build an accurate, comprehensive database of past customers, clients, and friends.

☑ Be a lister. Your inventory and listing prospects are worth money. The more you have, the more your practice is worth.

☑ Make your listings detachable from your broker. Negotiate with your broker in the event of your leaving the company that the listings are your property, not the broker's.

☑ Have somebody besides yourself negotiate the sale of your practice on your behalf. Only an outsider can be emotionally detached from the outcome of the sale.

Lisa Burridge, a top producer now with Realty Executives of Casper, Wyoming, sold her RE/MAX office and personal practice in Evanston, Wyoming, in November 1997 after 13 years in the business. Burridge says her personal production between January and November that year was $14 million from 180 units at an average price of about $78,000. Here are some tips from her experience:

☑ *Grow your database.* Part of the value of a practice is your database, your past customers. The number of names on the database is important. The more names, the more value. If you don't have a computerized database to keep track of your contacts, then you can't prove its value to a potential buyer. Burridge took care to write a letter to all 2,800 people on her database to recommend they work with her buyer.

☑ *Maximize your listing inventory.* A big percentage of your business value comes from your listing inventory. Get as many listings as you can. Pump up your listings in the year of your sale. Part of the future value is how many listings you typically carry from your marketing and database, and part of the immediate value is how many listings you actually have at time of sale. Burridge contacted all her sellers by phone and letter personally, then sent a joint letter with her buyer. Finally, the buyer followed up with a personal phone call to every seller. Together, they didn't lose a listing. Every seller stayed with the new broker.

☑ *You don't have to be a top producer to sell your practice.* When Burridge moved out of state, then moved back to

Wyoming a year later, this time to Casper, she looked to buy a practice each time. She would have bought just a database. It didn't have to be a super heavy-hitter practice, she says. Even a middle-range agent in the business for 20 years would have been good. "Everyone has something to sell if they are organized," she believes.

☑ *Doesn't take long to sell.* Burridge's sale took five weeks from start to finish. From solicitation letter of prospective buyers to purchase offer was three weeks, then two more weeks were needed to close the sale. "Once the decision to sell is made, it's not a long drawn-out deal," she said. "Time is of the essence."

Tony DiCello, a top producer in the Boulder, Colorado, market, sold his practice of 16 years in April 1997 with Bob Bohlen's help and went on to open several Keller Williams market centers and be a one-on-one coach for the Mike Ferry Organization. In the year before DiCello sold his RE/MAX practice, his personal production was $32 million from 154 transactions. Here are some of his tips on selling a practice:

☑ *Stay in touch with your people after the sale.* Monthly mailings. Even if it's just a simple postcard with both your pictures on it. Between DiCello and his buyer, they had over 50 years of real estate experience. Don't stop at just one letter announcing the sale. Continuously reinforce the buyer as "The Guy." Eighteen months at least; DiCello and his buyer agreed to 36 months. When they compared their two databases—the buyer had 1,500 names and DiCello had 2,500 contacts—there were only about 50 duplicate names.

☑ *Find a compatible buyer with a like personality.* DiCello had seven interested parties and three actual bidders. To decide, he asked himself: Which buyer would give the best service to my clients? How would my clients benefit most? In the end, he sold to a buyer who was most like him, a male agent about the same age, who had a similar demeanor and business style. The decision benefited DiCello's clients *and* kept referral fees coming.

☑ *Don't forget to contact your referral sources, in addition to listings.* Eyeball to eyeball is best, but at least do it on the phone. Not just a letter. DiCello and his buyer talked about a client party, but they became too busy. In hindsight, a party would have been a chance to say goodbye and meet the new buyer.

☑ *If you want to still be paid, don't walk away.* It's still your business if you want referral fees. As soon as you stop contacting clients, the business stops. DiCello discovered that when they stopped mailing their every-21-days postcards (18 times per year) for three months in a row, their leads fell off. As soon as they got the mail out, their leads picked up. Staying in touch with the old database is critical. In the first three to four months after a sale, DiCello suggests mailing two times a month. He almost forgot that part. "We both got too busy to be successful," he said.

Maria Bunting is chief operating officer for Windermere Services Company, the operations side of a megabroker firm based in Seattle. For the last five years of the 1990s, she has counseled her agents that their book of business is valuable, especially if they collect in-depth customer information. When it's time to retire or slow down, agents can reap residual business from their years of work. Here are some of Bunting's helpful tips:

☑ Get what you want in writing.
☑ Have an attorney, not just your real estate broker, review the agreement.
☑ Always involve your CPA because how you receive the dollars affects how you are taxed on those dollars.
☑ If you're the seller, be sure to maintain your real estate license to be able to receive future referral fees.
☑ Investigate if your real estate broker expects to receive a percentage of future referral fees.

☑ Valuation is on a case-by-case basis. There is no formula, although referral fees and some money up front are the most
common structure for a deal.

Four Rainmaker Exit Strategies

Here are four proven exit strategies. Choose the one or combination that best fits your business and your needs.

Exit Strategy #1: Asset Sale

Negotiate with a buyer to purchase your equipment. An *asset
sale* is the most basic type of exit strategy. Make a list of all your
business-owned office equipment, computers, and telephones.
If you own your office space, that real property asset less the
outstanding mortgage could be included in the sale. Typically,
all your liabilities, such as an office lease or car lease, tax payments or outstanding payables, will remain your responsibility
separate from the sale, unless specifically agreed to be assumed
by your buyer. After all the bills are paid, you will also pocket
the cash balance in your business checking account.

Although there is some value in these tangible hard assets, especially because they make up a working system, understand
that equipment and computers are *used*, and potential buyers
often discount their value and offer only a fraction of the original price—if anything at all. Remember, an asset sale can stand
alone separately or can be an add-on component of any of the
other three exit strategies.

Exit Strategy #2: Pending Business Sale

The simplest illustration of selling a practice is to sell your *pending business,* which is the business you already have on the
books. Pending business is the existing transactions expected to
close less a discount for fall-through contracts (see Figure 17.1).
The business you have on the books at any moment includes

Figure 17.1
Pending Business Worksheet

As of (___date___)

Listings pending settlement	$_____	(_____ units)
+ Purchases pending settlement	$_____	(_____ units)
+ Active listings	$_____	(_____ units)
+ Active buyer representations	$_____	(_____ units)
= Pending business subtotal	$_____	(_____ **units**)
− Less fall-through discount	× _____	(%)
= Discounted subtotal	$_____	(_____ **units**)
× Commission split	× _____	(%)
= Net pending business	$_____	

---

pending contracts under deposit waiting to close for your listings and your purchases. Pending business can sometimes also include active listings and active buyer's representation agreements, based on the assumption that a certain percentage will go to contract and settle. (In some practice deals, the seller is required to work prospective sellers or buyers until they sign a ratified contract before the transaction is considered pending business, and part of the sale. In other deals, the practice seller simply works all prospects and business under deposit through to closing personally, and the transactions are not part of the sale.)

After your checking account cash and your tangible hard assets, your pending business is what you would be entitled to if you left the company today. Payment could be a lump sum, or, more typically, the rainmaker receives a split percentage of the closed commissions. Unlike an asset sale, pending business is often a key component of value that is combined with one of the last two exit strategies.

Exit Strategy #3: Future Book of Business Sale

The *book of business* strategy is another simple rainmaker technique to sell (or acquire) a practice, and probably the most universally accepted. In its simplest form, rainmakers sell the rights to all future business produced by their **Real Estate Rainmaker** system over a period of time, say, one to five years. In return, the rainmaker receives an up-front payment and/or referral fees for any transaction involving, or referred by, an individual on the agreed database list. Assets and pending business are additional. Advertising-generated non-database business during the period is not included in the referral fee calculations.

Because your Trophy Database contacts will become steadily more familiar with the new rainmaker, the referral rate could remain fixed at, say, 30%, or be scheduled to diminish year by year. For example, all transactions caused by the registered list of contacts in the first year earn a 30% referral fee, in the second year a 20% referral fee, in the third year a 10% referral fee. (From a buyer's perspective, a preferable fee schedule might be 25%, 10%, 5%.) No fee is paid in the fourth year or later. For a seller who wants a faster exit, a variation of the book of business deal might be 50% of all database-procured business in the first year and 25% of all second-year business, period. Transactions that qualify for payment are verified against the rainmaker's database by comparing the annual list of clients to the names on the agreed database.

Business brokers call this book of business exit strategy an installment sale. The seller is paid in installments for transactions as they occur. Clearly, the installment book of business strategy (also, "referral fee strategy") favors the buyer. All the risk rests with the seller. If the buyer doesn't close many (or any) deals—which is completely beyond the control of the seller—the seller gets little or nothing. Additionally, in the book of business strategy, the seller is paid only for repeat transactions involving prospects registered on the customer database and direct referrals from registered clients.

Both parties should reach an agreement on the gray area of third-tier clients to avoid any misunderstanding. Should the seller receive payment for referral-from-a-referral transactions, such as third-generation new clients referred by "unregistered" second-generation new clients who originally were referred by "registered" database customers? Typically, the practice buyer does pay for unregistered second-generation business referred directly by registered old clients, but does not pay a fee for repeat or referral business from those second-generation clients as the years pass. How to track new customer referrals from the registered Trophy Database list—and separate them from advertising-generated business—clearly is an important aspect of any negotiation.

One arrangement that makes the book of business approach work best is to have the seller remain involved, perhaps as a senior partner, a *rainmaker emeritus.* One ideal scenario is where the selling rainmaker attends listing presentations and buyer-qualification appointments with the new rainmaker. The "team" explains to the prospective clients that the prospects are getting the best of both worlds. The rainmaker emeritus will always be there, but in the background. The direct daily details of the transaction will be handled by the new rainmaker. *"If there is ever a negotiation or a crucial question, I will always be right here to help,"* says the rainmaker emeritus.

In this way, both the selling rainmaker and the new rainmaker receive the benefit of each other's presence. The selling rainmaker is assured to receive the maximum closed deals and referral fees. The new rainmaker is reinforced during the transition by the selling rainmaker to guarantee customers are "sold" on the new practitioner. Also, in the transition-partner scenario, the selling rainmaker's role is greater, which opens the door for a possibly larger referral fee percentage than the common broker-to-broker 20% to 30%.

Exit Strategy #4: Multiple of Profit Earnings Sale

To understand the *multiple of profit earnings* strategy, it's helpful to understand how real estate companies and other businesses, such as medical, dental, or legal practices, are sold. As a rainmaker, you are the owner of a one-person company with a **Real Estate Rainmaker** system so refined, the system itself will produce business even after you are gone.

For real estate companies, a multiple of earnings formula is commonly used to set a price by multiplying a factor by adjusted earnings (also, "adjusted cash flow"). How are earnings calculated? The business broker's standard formula is called EBITDA: Earnings Before Interest, Taxes, Depreciation, and Amortization. Your practice's earnings are the net after subtracting all expenses from the gross commission income. The EBITDA earnings formula doesn't include the addition of any interest income earned from keeping your cash in an interest-earning account, or the subtraction of taxes due on your net income, or depreciation of any equipment.

During negotiation, the *A* from EBITDA can also stand for adjustments, and it's critical to the sales price. Adjustments might include business on the books, debts, lease(s) for space or equipment, salaries (assistants to be hired or fired), hard assets (computer, telephone system, printer, copier, fax machine, furnishings, etc.). Adjustments could also include exceptional marketing expense needed to bring the rainmaker's business into the buyer's system (an advertising fund for direct mail announcements, photography, reprinted materials showing the new "partners," etc.). The rainmaker buyer will put a value on these adjustments and typically use it to negotiate a discount off the average annual earnings.

Real Trends newsletter reported in November 1997 that the going market for brokerage companies based on earnings multiples roughly falls into three brokerage sizes, with the value varying "market to market and buyer to buyer depending on the strategic value to the buyer and competition for the deal from other buyers":

- Large firms in metropolitan areas: Multiple is high end of 4 to 5 times EBITDA.

- Large firms in medium to small markets: Multiple ranges from $3\frac{1}{2}$ to $4\frac{1}{2}$ times EBITDA.

- Local acquisitions by privately owned firms: Multiple ranges from 3 to $4\frac{1}{2}$ times EBITDA.

You may find it helpful to use a range from a low of three times to a high of five times profit earnings to give you a beginning ballpark idea of the value of your personal practice.

The rationale for the EBITDA multiple of profit earnings price calculation goes like this: Because the buyer rainmaker does not need the seller rainmaker, the seller's earnings are now available to pay off a loan taken to finance the purchase. If the sales price, for example, is $150,000 (three times annual profit earnings of $50,000), it is supported by the fact that the annual principal and interest on a five-year $150,000 loan at 10% interest is $45,000 ($30,000 principal, $15,000 interest annually). Quite manageable with $50,000 in cash flow earnings, which is calculated after assuming the new buyer takes home the old seller's salary, as long as the cash keeps flowing.

Pat Dearing at RE/MAX of Georgia had a husband-and-wife team who came to him after only four years in the real estate business using Dearing's simple system of forms, logs, and a customized one-write peg-board bookkeeping system from McBee Systems (Parsippany, NJ). Sitting with their prospective buyer, the couple turned the pages of their record binder and stopped at the profit earnings page. Pointing to the bottom line, the sellers said, "When you buy this business, if you do what we've done the way we've done it, you can make this much profit. We've created a system. You just have to do it, just continue the system. The only variables you bring are your personal style and skills. They're both in your control."

In Dearing's experience, the prices he's known for real estate practices (as of the writing of this book) range from $75,000 at the high to $10,000 at the low end. The critical elements are how much profit the practice generates, and finding the right buyer. "The bottom line is," Dearing says, "whatever you get beats walking away from your practice and getting nothing."

To begin setting a value on your practice, step outside real estate and pretend you're selling a restaurant, Dearing suggests. Ideally, you may want a fixed price up front. The buyer takes out a bank note and makes payments over time at a fixed rate per month. A straightforward sale. No need for auditing. Say the sales price is $50,000. The buyer invests $20,000 cash and takes out a note for $30,000 to be paid to the bank at $1,000 a month for thirty months. The seller is paid cash at closing. Nothing is tied to future business, and there is no need to audit sources of business and client names against a registered list. That way, the seller is never overpaid or underpaid for the practice based on an ongoing partnership. The price is fixed. The bank collects on the note. You retire without worry.

Figure 17.2 is a worksheet for a multiple of profit earnings sale. Do the math to determine if this strategy is for you.

Once the sales price is determined, the negotiations may continue over a payment schedule. In short, if payment is all cash, the seller is assured the full amount up front. However, if payment is scheduled in installments, the sales price may be increased to adjust for the risk of nonpayment to the rainmaker. A common formula is to treat this additional increment to the sales price as an employment contract between the buyer and the retiring rainmaker, in return for the services of the rainmaker to stay on as a "partner" for a specified transition period.

Figure 17.2
Multiple of Profit Earnings Worksheet

Average annual earnings (before
interest, taxes, and depreciation) $ _____

Less adjustments:
– Pending business $ _____
– Debts $ _____
– Leases $ _____
– Salaries $ _____
– Hard assets $ _____
– Marketing expenses $ _____
= **Adjusted annual earnings** $ _____
× Multiple of profit earnings   _____ × (factor)
= **Sales price** $ _____

Quick Checklist on How Bob Bohlen
Markets a Real Estate Practice

Here are the ten steps Bob Bohlen of Prudential Preview Properties has developed to market a real estate practice.

☑ Bohlen assembles all data related to the agent and the agent's practice for the prior five years, including profit and loss statements.

☑ He then analyzes the value of the practice using his specially developed, proprietary software program. The model takes into account current listings, pending contracts, buyer's agent agreements, listing price to sales price ratio, expired listing ratio, average sales price, and commission rate, among other factors, such as intangibles for community involvement and professional designations.

☑ Profit and loss are projected for the next five years based on previous five years to put a value on the practice.

☑ A computer analysis is used to evaluate the production of local agents and create two lists of prospective buyers, one group in the local area and another group in the surrounding fringe market area.

☑ Potential buyers are then sent a FedEx letter from Michigan that generically describes a practice in their area that may be for sale soon. Interested prospects must respond by a deadline.

☑ Respondents sign a legal, binding confidentiality agreement, and must supply information about their practice sufficient to create a statistical analysis.

☑ Bohlen creates a pro forma operating statement that merges seller's practice with buyer's practice so prospective buyer knows what to expect from sale and what value the acquisition would have to buyer's practice.

☑ The merged pro forma operating statement is sent to each prospective buyer with a tender sheet complete with proposed offer, deadline to respond, and expected settlement date.

☑ As part of the negotiation, a system for the transition period is spelled out where seller and buyer agree to cooperate on a list of items, such as a client party and follow-up letters to database contacts and mutual advertising. Transition could be from six to twelve months or as long as five years, depending on seller's interest in staying involved in practice.

☑ Final terms commonly range from all cash up front to a little up-front cash plus an earn-out payment based on performance of both parties. Typically, the entire process from FedEx letter to closing takes less than a month.

Mergers and Acquisitions

Now you know the endgame. Your first step is to put your *Real Estate Rainmaker* system in place. Be sure leads are being generated by every available media; the database is expanding; follow-up is automatic and perpetually getting better; long-term contact with past customers and a growing circle of contacts is producing a steady flow of referrals and repeat business. In short, your practice is growing in its production, profit earnings, and system.

Soon, you will be ready to expand the business to the next level in quantum leaps. One way is to acquire other practices in your market. As you look around for valuable candidates, negotiate the deals, and manage the transitions, you will gain invaluable experience toward the day when you cash in or cash out as well. The best approach to mergers and acquisitions is to stick your toe in the water and build expertise through your own experience. As you discover things you value in practices you buy, you can also instill those same values in your own practice.

Whatever exit strategy you use, the fundamental truth remains: a *Real Estate Rainmaker* system is a valuable business asset. So valuable it is worth paying for. So valuable it is clearly quantifiable for a buyer. So valuable it can become the ultimate driving goal for a rainmaker.

Don't delay. Start now. As the famous Sgt. Preston of the Royal Canadian Mounted Police is reported to have said, "The scenery only changes for the lead dog." Make it happen. Be a leader. Launch your own *Real Estate Rainmaker* system today. And look forward to the day when you can cash in or cash out with a huge step toward your financial independence for life.

As I wrote in my introduction, imagine a real estate practice . . . where you are the *Real Estate Rainmaker.*

RAINMAKER CHAPTER 17 SUMMARY

Exit Strategies to Cash In or Cash Out

- ► Exit Strategy #1: Asset Sale.
- ► Exit Strategy #2: Pending Business Sale.
- ► Exit Strategy #3: Future Book of Business Sale.
- ► Exit Strategy #4: Multiple of Profit Earnings Sale.

18

Real Estate Rainmaker Resource Guide

Real Estate Rainmaker is a book about marketing, not sales. That is why this Resource Guide focuses primarily on marketing tools, not sales tools. Because Trophy Database software is so critical, that category is listed first. All other categories and their entries are in alphabetical order. Suppliers with multiple products are listed once under their primary product category unless multiple references are easier to find. For your convenience, phone numbers, addresses, and websites are listed when available. Naturally, call first. Contact information often changes; check directory assistance or an Internet search engine for the current information.

DATABASE SOFTWARE

Exceed98. Exceed98 agent automation exploits the power of Microsoft Office. Offering agents or offices contact management, contracts, transaction management, MLS, scheduling, e-mail, faxing, financial functions, correspondence, network ability, 32-bit architecture, and data synchronization. *Exceed 98, 2050 South Oneida, Suite 111, Denver, CO 80224-2555, (303) 757-3903, (800) 757-3903; fax (303) 758-7670; e-mail @rockymtnsoft.com; www.rockymtnsoft.com.*

Howard & Friends. Track your listing, closing, referrals, people, prospects, appointments, correspondence, card and letter libraries. Contact management, financial package, and CMA/presentations with auto download in one package. *OnTrac, 9898 South Eden Pointe Circle, South Jordan, UT 84095, (801) 254-4636, (800) 588-8609; fax (801) 253-9939; e-mail sales@otcs .com; www.otcs.com.*

On-Line Agent. Software for agent and broker productivity, office management, contact management, and listings presentations. *Moore Data Management Services, 100 Washington Square #1000 Minneapolis, MN 55401, (612) 661-1000, (800) 328-6367; fax (612) 661-1704; www.moore.com.*

PREP Real Suite. Pat Zaby's PREP™ Software produces four fully integrated programs for prospecting, presentations, contact management, and financial functions. PREP Suite 4.0 features Internet integration, e-mail access, mass e-mail, HTML content and mail, web browsing, 32-bit application, new designs, and more content. RS Council recommended. *PREP Software, 3333 Earhart #150, Carrollton, TX 75006, (972) 991-1998; fax (972) 991-1992; www.prepsoft.com.*

Residential ACT! & Trans/ACT!. Custom real estate version of popular contact management software. Windows compatible, networkable, Internet and e-mail ready, auto letter writing, attach photos, MLS data transfer, loan qualifier, financial calculator, and more. *Real Estate Computer Solutions, (303) 321-3341, ext. 21; fax (303) 321-2219; e-mail info@recsnet.com; www .recsnet.com.*

Top Producer. Real estate sales and marketing software features prospecting, follow-up, scheduling, photo imaging, CMAs, buyer presentations, Internet ready, networkable, data synchronization, and more. Add-ons: Top Connector (MLS), Top Locator (mapping), Top Presenter (printed and multimedia presentations), Top Financial (reports), Top Office (brokerage). RS Council recommended. *Top Producer Systems, Inc., 1100 SW 27th Street, Renton, WA 98055, (604) 270-8819 ext. 8288, (800) 444-8570; fax (604) 270-8218; www.topproducer.com.*

AD WRITING SOFTWARE

Classified Simplified PRO. 18,000 phrases creates ads in minutes. Save and track ads. Office and single-user version. *Power-Mate Technologies, 55 N. First Street, San Jose, CA 95113, (800) 581-1943; www.powermatecorp.com.*

Re/Ad. Property ad writing program for real estate created by Hal Douthit, columnist and publisher of 19 homes magazines and 13 newspapers. Individual agent version and office version with multiple agent links. *AdWriter/Douthit Communications, 165 E. Washington Row, Suite 314, Sandusky, OH 44870-2998, (419) 621-2142, (800) 646-7323; fax (419) 621-2134; e-mail sales@adwriter.com; www.adwriter.com.*

ASSISTANTS

Ed Hatch. Seminar: "Finding, Hiring, Training an Effective Personal Assistant." *Ed Hatch Seminars, 8215 Mandan Court, Greenbelt, MD 20770, (800) 334-2824, (301) 474-1125; fax (301) 474-3524; e-mail edhatch@aol.com.*

Personal Assistant System. One-hour cassette for agent on how to hire, manage, and compensate assistant. Three cassettes train assistant on phone, control attitude, time management, and approaching job as a profit center. Plus workbook and diskette. RS Council recommended. *Christine Doyle Seminars, 5894 Steele Road, Burlington, WI 53105, (800) 700-3695, (414) 767-1234; fax (414) 767-1237; e-mail czdoyle@wi.net; www.christinedoyle.com.*

Monica Reynolds. Specializes in training assistants. Provides hiring, training, profit center assistant systems, and Powerline. Books: *Multiply Your Success with Real Estate Assistants* (with forms on diskette), *The Real Estate Assistant* (six assistant training cassettes, manual, and diskette), *The Profile Center* (seven assistants interviewed), *The REALTOR® Toolbox* (forms and systems on five diskettes). *Monica Reynolds Seminars/800 Power Line. 5412 Merrywing Circle, Austin TX 78730, (512) 425-9709 or (512) 425-9736, (800) 789-9995; fax (512) 425-9701; e-mail mreynolds@simpletel.com; www.monicareynolds.com.*

CALENDARS

Kinko's. Deluxe twelve-month flip calendar with twelve photos, yearly calendar with single photo, oversize calendar with photo, rendering, or collage. Various options for designer templates; laminating or mounting; greeting cards; stationery; placemats. *Kinko's. For locations (800) 254-6567; www.kinkos.com.*

Magnets USA. Unique marketing products "Just for real estate professionals," including magnetic calendars with exclusive Teaser Tips; Homeowner's Portfolio, a closing gift that generates referrals and repeat business; stickers and more. *Magnets USA, 817 Connecticut Avenue NE, Roanoke, VA 24012, (800) 869-7562, (800) 788-6872; fax (800) 869-7562.*

Melco Marketing. Agent calendars (8½" × 11"), magnetized, refillable; farming and prospecting tools; Time Master, time management organizers; listing and closing gifts; upscale deluxe Tele/Address books. *Melco Marketing, Inc., 8707 East Quarry Road, Manassas, VA 22110, (703) 631-0592, (800) 854-8669; fax (703)369-0492.*

Teldon Calendars. Based in Richmond, British Columbia, one of North America's largest printers of wall calendars. Many choices: premier, theme, Canadian provinces, U.S. states, presidential. Also custom cover or full custom calendars. Browse online, download PDF file or request printed catalogue. *Teldon Calendars, 250 H Street, P.O. Box 8110-8000, Blaine, WA 98231, (800) 755-1211; e-mail calendar@canadawired.com; www.teldon.com.*

CLIENT FOLLOW-UP

Client Follow-Up. Today's Living magazine (12 mailings over five years include welcome card, client satisfaction survey, and magazine every spring and fall with personalized insert). Elegant Card program (12 mailings over five years include welcome card, anniversary, and six-month-later card). Classic Print program (10 mailings over six years include survey and nine full-color prints with personalized letter). *The Personal Marketing,*

Co., 11843 West 83rd Terrace, Shawnee Mission, KS 66214, (800) 331-4294; fax (800) 234-9423; www.personalmarketingco.com.

Continuity Programs. DataLead Customer Follow-Up program is a series of 16 hand-addressed mailings over five years, including six greeting cards, three surveys, three letters, and four post-cards. All mailings have a postage-paid reply, most with personalized messages. *Continuity Programs, 4375 Pineview Drive, Walled Lake, MI 48390, (800) 521-0026; fax (248) 669-6875; www.continuityprograms.com.*

InTouch. Two series of 12 colorful oversize postcards. Select either bimonthly for two years or quarterly for three years. You receive exact copy of each postcard with client's name and phone for follow-up. *Quantum Systems, Inc., P.O. Box 140825, Austin, TX 78714-0825, (512) 837-2300, (800) 637-7373; fax (512) 837-2777; e-mail mail@quantumsys.com; www.quantumsys.com.*

CLOSING GIFTS

Ad-Soft. Home inventory with mortgage calculator, family medical records, pet information software on diskette. Opening screens feature you and your business with photos, text and complete contact information. Disk presentation holders and downloadable website version available. *Ad-Soft, 154 E. Bethel Road, Coppell, TX 75019, (800) 535-1010, (972) 393-6917; e-mail info@ad-soft.com; www.ad-soft.com.*

Closing Statements. Large selection of unique, memorable, and personalized closing and referral gifts. Catalogue. *Closing Statements, 5783 West Erie Street, Chandler, AZ 85226, (602) 940-5255, (800) 252-0620; fax (602) 940-1941; www.closingstatements.com.*

The Cookie Garden. Variety of cookies and chocolates in bouquets, tins, and containers. Catalogue. *The Cookie Garden, 1508 Miner Street, Des Plaines, IL 60016, (800) 582-9191; (847) 299-9191; fax (847) 299-7779.*

Fresh Beginnings. Gourmet chocolate chip cookies, baked and shipped the same day. Franchise and custom tins available.

Fresh Beginnings, Inc., 4001 North Coleman Road, Valdosta, GA 31602, (912) 242-0237, (800) 444-7923; fax (912) 244-8320.

Gift Baskets USA. Gift baskets for every occasion. Specializes in corporate accounts, quantity buying incentives, and will ship anywhere in the U.S. *Gift Baskets USA, P.O. Box 7084, Mission Hills, CA 91346-7084, (818) 727-1934, (877) 277-7778.*

Hospitality Pac. Wicker baskets with full-size household and personal care products, gift wrapped, welcoming message, and delivered in two to three weeks to address you choose. Deluxe, standard, and budget pacs available. *Hospitality Pac, Inc., 757 Third Avenue, New York, NY 10017, (800) 992-9260; fax (212) 593-9148.*

Images USA. Unique photo cups, clocks, tiles, and other gifts personalized with photo and imprinted with your name and number. *Images USA, 35985 Scone Street, Livonia, MI 48154, (888) 462-0630; (734) 462-4114; fax (734) 462-4114; e-mail images@images-usa.com.*

Magnets USA. The Homeowner's Portfolio™ and a wide variety of calendars, magnets, stickers, greeting cards, open house guest registers, custom-printed notepads. Catalogue. *Magnets USA, 817 Connecticut Avenue NE, Roanoke, VA 24012, (800) 869-7562, (800) 788-6872; fax (800) 869-7562.*

Planner Systems. Homeowner's Records Portfolio, real estate planners, farming tools, closing gifts, open house guest registers, and listing brochure holders. Catalogue. *Planner Systems, 21609 NE 4th, Redmond, WA 98053, (800) 752-6448, (425) 558-3951; fax (800) 243-1390; e-mail reachus@plannersystems.com; www.plannersystems.com.*

Windsor Vineyards. Award-winning winery. Custom label inscriptions and/or logo for closing, referral, prospect, and anniversary gifts. Over thirty wine varietals, champagne, gift packs, and baskets. *Windsor Vineyards, 9600 Bell Road, Windsor, CA 95492, (800) 289-9463, ext. 5361, (707) 836-5484; fax (800) 224-9732; www.windsorvineyards.com.*

DIRECT-RESPONSE REPORTS

Gooder Group. More than forty consumer brochures and handbooks for sellers, buyers, relocation, and general target audiences. Reports easily combined with existing advertising and designed to maximize response in any media. Sampler Pack with one of each report available. Catalogue. *Gooder Group—The Lead Generating Company, 2724 Dorr Avenue, Fairfax, VA 22031-4901, (703) 698-7750; fax (703) 698-8597; e-mail leads@gooder.com; www.gooder.com.*

HOTLINES

ART. Formed in 1989, a marketing system includes twenty-four-hour toll-free 888 number with caller ID, unlimited message capacity, fax on demand, advertising response reports, pager signaling, ad tracking, and personalized customer support. Demo line and fax-on-demand application (888) 245-1101. *Automatic Response Technologies, 154 Avenida Victoria, San Clemente, CA 92672, (800) 854-8765, (949) 498-7343; fax (949) 498-2591; e-mail art@fea.net.*

Powerline. Twenty-four-hour turnkey call-capture lead generation system. Effective listing presentation demo. Unlimited mailboxes for property description or direct-response reports. Fax-on-demand and broadcast fax available. For recorded information and free report, (800) 390-6223, ext. 2009. *Arch Telecom, 210 Barton Springs Road, Suite 275, Austin, TX 78704, (800) 882-0223, (512) 492-0735; e-mail sales@archtelecom.com; www.archtelecom.com.*

SoftKlone. Own your own real estate hotline (Interactive Voice Response system). Allows real estate professionals to provide voice and fax information to potential customers 24-hours seven days a week. One-time fixed price for equipment itself. *SoftKlone, 327 Office Plaza Drive, Suite 100, Tallahassee, FL 32301, (800) 634-8670; fax (904) 877-9763; e-mail info@softklone.com; www.softklone.com.*

MARKETING AND PROSPECTING TOOLS

American Dream Passport. A unique buyer representation tool that "puts signs on buyers." Designed like a passport to assist buyer registration at new homes and open houses, it identifies buyers as your clients and includes buyer do's and don'ts. *American Dream Passport, 4023 East Grant Road, Tucson, AZ 85712, (520) 327-6849, (800) 320-6660; fax (520) 325-8950; e-mail hogans@azstarnet.com; www.dreampass.com.*

Audio Business Cards. A custom-written script and professional recorded biography comes in audiocassette case with full-color photo insert. Also marketing plan, seminars, personal magazines. *Cold Call Cowboy Productions, 75–100 Mediterranean, Palm Desert, CA 92211, (800) 226-9269, (760) 568-5124; fax, (760) 779-0544; e-mail info@audiobusinesscard.com; www .audiobusinesscard.com.*

Hobbs & Herder Advertising. Custom personal brochures, personal logos, postcards, house flier master, websites, e-mail farming program, letterhead and envelope packages, TV commercial script and coordination, and two-day personal marketing conference. *Hobbs & Herder Advertising, 1221 E. Dyer Road, Suite 205, Santa Ana, CA 92705-5635, (800) 999-6090, (714) 549-8000; fax (714) 549-4055; www.hobbsherder.com.*

LetterWriter and *LetterWriter Plus.* More than 200 real estate letters on disk in each collection. LetterWriter has eight years of follow-up letters and over 70 prospecting letters to expires and FSBOs. LetterWriter Plus features letters arranged in nine unique action plans. Conversational tone makes these letters personal and real. Also, *Newsletter Writer* software with fifty newsletters ready to print. *Dave Beson Seminars, 7200 West 78th Street, Minneapolis, MN 55439, (612) 947-9111, (800) 242-3031; fax (612) 947-9110; e-mail info@davebeson.com; www.davebeson.com.*

3-Step Rainmaker Lead System®. Features marketing programs for lead generation, prospect follow-up, and long-term contact—brochures, handbooks, newsletters, self-mailers, letters, ads, website content links, and postcards. More than 16 marketing programs and services. *Gooder Group—The Lead Generating Company, 2724 Dorr Avenue, Fairfax, VA 22031-4901, (703) 698-7750; fax (703) 698-8597; e-mail leads@gooder.com; www.gooder.com.*

Magnets-N-More. Discounted advertising specialties—any item: magnets, calendars, pens, mugs, etc. Guaranteed lowest prices. *Magnets-N-More, 1810 South Broadway, Denver CO 80210, (303) 470-6666, (800) 394-6789; fax (303) 733-8799.*

Superior Real Estate Supply. Complete supply of over 1,000 marketing and business products for the real estate industry. Sell retail to members of NAR and wholesale to boards. Free catalogue. *Superior Real Estate Supply, 20805 North 19th Avenue–#11, Phoenix, AZ 85027, (602) 516-9202, (800) 234-0095; fax (602) 516-9209; www.superior-realestate.com.*

NEWSPAPER COLUMNS

Ask Howard, The Real Estate Dog. Q&A format weekly advice column written by Howard, The Real Estate Dog. Add your logo and information to set of 24 12-column-inch camera-ready ads. Protected locations. *Howard, The Real Estate Dog, P.O. Box 4817, Maryville, TN 37802, (800) 257-8371, (423) 982-0500; fax (423) 982-0519; e-mail howard@nelson-realtors.com.*

Baron Publishing. Offers ready-to-use newspaper columns and also a custom column service. Free brochure. *Baron Publishing, P.O. Box 488, Lexington, MA 02420, (800) 562-0062.*

Best Image Marketing. Writes and distributes "advertorial" columns to newspapers after subscriber review for 52-week program. Exclusivity and custom columns. *Best Image Marketing, 10336 Loch Lomond Road, Suite 130, Middletown, CA 95461-9500, (800) 762-2836, (707) 928-4434; fax (707) 928-5866; e-mail feedback@number-one.com; www.bestimage.com.*

Paul Christian's Ghost Writers. Weekly ghost-written newspaper column (price based on publication's circulation) and many other ready-to-print products: brochures, letters, postcards, and so on. *Paul Christian's Ghost Writers, 418 Third St., SW,*

Taylorsville, NC 28681, (828) 635-1773, (800) 234-1481; fax (828) 635-1931; e-mail ghostwriter@twave.net; www.theghost.com.

Real Estate Star Columns. Each thirteen-week set of weekly columns includes listing, selling, and informational articles. Available on an exclusive basis and sold with a money-back guarantee. *Newsletter Services, Inc., P.O. Box 3433, Englewood, CO 80155, (800) 231-1579, (303) 771-4008; fax (303) 771-0836.*

NEWSLETTERS

Gooder Group. Six monthly newsletter programs include full-color *Home Report*®, *NewsCards*®, *Seller Reply Mailer* and *Buyer Reply Mailer*™, two-color *HomeLetter*® (also available in ready-to-print master), and two-page *Relocation Letter*® (ready to print). *Gooder Group—The Lead Generating Company, 2724 Dorr Avenue, Fairfax, VA 22031-4901, (703) 698-7750; fax (703) 698-8597; e-mail leads@gooder.com; www.gooder.com.*

Kall Publications. Camera-ready newsletters, postcards, and clip art, plus monthly "Dear Friends" holiday letters for do-it-yourselfers. Catalogue. *Kall Publications, P.O. Box 3554, Englewood, CO 80155, (800) 345-5255, (303) 768-9927; fax (303) 768-9916; e-mail kallpub@aol.com.*

Marketing Advantage-Farmnet. Custom marketing program providing personal prospecting services supported by monthly newsletters and marketing pieces, such as notepads, personal brochures, calendars, personal custom logos. *The Marketing Advantage-Farmnet, Inc., 101 East Commonwealth Avenue–#A, Fullerton, CA 92832-1907, (714) 578-0266, (800) 655-6611; fax (714) 578-0717.*

Newsletter Services, Inc. *Home News Digest* is a monthly preprinted newsletter with three separate areas to add personal information, even rewrite front page. *Happy Home* is master proof monthly newsletter sold on a zipcode-exclusive basis. *Newsletter Services, Inc., P.O. Box 3433, Englewood, CO 80155, (800) 231-1579, (303) 771-4008; fax (303) 771-0836.*

The Personal Marketing Co. Newsletters, just listed/just sold Rapid Cards, recipe cards, mailers, business cards, client follow-up, websites, greeting cards. Mailing services. *The Personal Marketing Co., 11843 West 83rd Terrace, Shawnee Mission, KS 66214, (800) 234-0143; fax (800) 234-9423; www .personalmarketingco.com.*

Your Marketing Assistant. Newsletters, postcards, client retention, calendars, magnets, and more. *Your Marketing Assistant, P.O. Box 864813, Plano, TX 75086-4813, (800) 997-4771; fax (972) 548-6991; e-mail clfox1@flash.net.*

POSTCARDS AND GREETING CARDS

Gooder Group. Two postcard programs: *NewsCards®*, a monthly jumbo "postcard newsletter," and *Rainmaker Lead Cards™* that offer a pick-and-choose selection of 24 direct-response jumbo postcards featuring direct-response free special reports. *Gooder Group—The Lead Generating Company, 2724 Dorr Avenue, Fairfax, VA 22031-4901, (703) 698-7750; fax (703) 698-8597; e-mail leads@gooder.com; www.gooder.com.*

Image Builder Advertising. Several postcard programs, one features direct-response reports, logos, and personal brochures, stationery package, bulk mail services, just listed/just sold programs, recipe cards, and more. Catalogue. *Image Builder Advertising, 5783 West Erie Street, Chandler, AZ 85226, (602) 940-1100, (800) 241-6935; fax (602) 940-1941.*

Lentz Design. Full-color, personal marketing postcards for real estate professionals. Call to receive a free catalogue, samples, and price list. *(800) 924-3833, ext.98.*

Maggie's Mailbox. Postcards and greeting cards for real estate: keeping in touch, seasonal, anniversary, birthday, partner cards, specialty cards, blank note cards, and more. Online catalogue. *Maggie's Mailbox, 907 South Longwood Loop, Mesa, AZ 85208-2623, (800) 949-0559, (602) 830-3646; fax (800) 949-5150; e-mail maggie@maggiesmailbox.com; www.maggiesmailbox.com.*

Quantum Systems. Turnkey just listed, just sold, or farming postcard mailings. Twenty personalized Quantumcards™ mailed at low cost. Quantumcards now also available with full-color personalization. *Quantum Systems, Inc., P.O. Box 140825,*

Austin, TX 78714-0825, (512) 837-2300, (800) 637-7373; fax (512) 837-2777; e-mail mail@quantumsys.com; www.quantumsys.com.

Sendsations. Full-color postcards featuring recipes and comedy cards, also websites and e-mail postcards. *Sendsations Personal Marketing, 1074 North Industrial Park Drive, Orem UT 84057, (801) 225-2277, (800) 800-8197; fax (800) 800-8316; e-mail feedback@sendsations.com; www.sendsations.com.*

Sparrow & Jacobs. Provides personalized postcards, calendars, and greeting cards designed specifically for real estate professionals. *Sparrow and Jacobs, 2870 Janitell Road, Colorado Springs, CO 80906-4141, (719) 579-9295, (800) 237-1324; fax (719) 579-9007.*

Stay In Touch Follow-Up System®. Choose from three editions of 12 monthly full-color oversized postcards printed with your photo, logo, contact information and friendly message or blank (no message). Mailing services available. *Excellence In Action, Inc., 1420 Spring Hill Road, Suite 600, McLean, VA 22102, (800) 241-9991; fax (804) 237-3110; e-mail eaction@erols.com; www .excellenceinaction.com.*

Trilogy Co. Twelve different postcard programs with 12 cards in each set including calendar, retro, art, recipes, seasonal series, and more. Catalogue. *Trilogy Co., 900 North Shiloh Road, Garland, TX 75042, (877) 377-4332, (972) 205-1190; fax (972) 487-1379.*

PRINTERS

Aardvark Labels. Color photo business card labels, referral, photo postcard laser labels; photo labels and fun stickers; more than 200 label products in all. *Aardvark Labels Inc., P.O. Box 218, Savage, MN 55378, (612) 894-1037, (800) 553-2856; fax (612) 894-5271; e-mail info@aarvarklabels.com; www .aarvarklabels.com.*

Express Copy. Full-color real estate property flyers, business cards, postcards. Online ordering with Internet file transfer software, QuikLinx. *Express Copy, Inc., 215 S.E. Morrison, Suite 2001,*

Portland, OR 97214-2111, (503) 234-4880, (800) 260-5887; fax (503) 234-5562; e-mail xcopy@expresscopy.com; www.expresscopy .com.

Kolor View Press. Custom full-color promotional printing includes stock postcard programs, custom-printed postcards, sell sheets, brochures, business cards, and other prospecting tools. *Kolor View Press, 3046 South Delaware Street, Suite A, Springfield, MO 65804, (800) 225-6567; fax (417) 887-1822.*

Modern Postcard. Full-color custom promotional postcards starting at 500 copies. *Modern Postcard, 1675 Faraday Avenue, Carlsbad, CA 92008, (800) 959-8365, (760) 431-7084; fax (760) 431-1939; e-mail modern.cs@irisgroup.com; www.modernpostcard.com.*

SELLING YOUR PRACTICE

Bob Bohlen. Involved with more than two dozen practice sales 1996–1998. Also personally bought or sold more than a dozen real estate offices in five years 1993–1998. Top-producing agent for entire Prudential network worldwide for eight of nine years 1990–1998. *Bob Bohlen, Prudential Preview Properties, 130 West Grand River, Brighton, MI 48116, (810) 220-1500; fax (810) 220-1512.*

Plaques Are Not Profit *(fomerly ME, INC.).* A complete business management system designed for RE/MAX sales associates (examples), but good principles for all agents. Workbook and user's guide, forms, and one-write peg-board bookkeeping system by McBee Systems. Also three-hour seminar. *Pat Dearing, RE/MAX of Georgia, 1100 Abernathy Road NE, Suite 705, Atlanta, GA 30328, (770) 393-1137; e-mail pdearing@remax.net.*

Selling a Real Estate Agent's Practice, or Book of Business. Eight-page article excerpted from the book *ME, INC.* by Pat Dearing and Elaine Schreiber. Contact Pat Dearing, RE/MAX of Georgia.

TECHNOLOGY TOOLS

DirectConnect. Program designed for real estate companies utilizes voice mail technology to provide daily updates on available properties to buyers. Searches MLS for new listings, back-on-market listings, price reductions, and sends recorded voice mail message including address on daily basis to system mailbox of enrolled client whose requirements match price range and area of new listings. System comes with software, training, forms, and collateral materials. *Ralph Leino, Principal Broker, Preferred Carlson REALTORS®, 3227 South Westnedge, Kalamazoo, MI 49008, (616) 344-8599; info@precar.com; www.precar.com.*

Know the Neighborhood. Demographic information on a CD with neighborhood makeup, school rankings, housing trends, crime rates, houses of worship, and more. Go to street, click on a map to see neighborhood profile. Compare any two neighborhoods in the nation. Onscreen or color printouts. Initial CD-ROM with built-in expiration; monthly or quarterly updates. *eNeighborhoods, Inc., 200 Rittenhouse Circle, Suite 3E, Bristol, PA 19007, (800) 975-9742, (215) 785-0900; fax (215) 785-3200; e-mail info@eNeighborhoods.com; www.eNeighborhoods.com.*

Map Solutions. GeoLocator produces high-quality maps to locate present properties for buyers, sellers, and lenders. Free demo disk. *Map Solutions, 765 Coleman Avenue, Menlo Park, CA 94025, (650) 326-0120; fax (650) 326-2607; www.mapsolutions .com.*

PhotoShare. Software creates multimedia home tours using digital cameras, adding text, voice, and music. Transmit tour via diskette, e-mail, or website. For free sample, download multimedia home tour from their website. *TRF Systems, Inc., 10235 West Sample Road, Suite 200, Coral Springs, FL 33065, (800) 873-0700; (954) 345-9701; fax (954) 345-9703; e-mail sales@photoshare .com; www.photoshare.com.*

PictureWorks. Software to enhance photos for print or Internet presentations helps you catalogue, store, enhance, and share your digital photos. Create postcards, flyers on e-mail or websites, panorama photos, and virtual home tours. *PictureWorks Technology, 649 San Ramon Valley Blvd., Danville, CA 94526, (800) 403-4466; (510) 855-2001; fax (925) 855-4356; e-mail info@pictureworks.com; www.pictureworks.com.*

RESICOM. Link to your website provides online analyses for virtually any residential or commercial property in U.S. Residential Property Analyzer identifies property's past appreciation rate, equity analysis, and area demographics. Neighborhood Analyzer identifies neighborhood within county or zip code with high concentration of homes in a price range and indicates rate of appreciation. Monthly subscription. *RESICOM Analytics, 5605 Glenridge Drive, Suite 950, Atlanta, GA 30342, (888) 864-6339, (404) 459-9945; fax (404) 459-9946; e-mail info@resicom.com; www.resicom.com.*

SOAR MLS. Service dials your MLS searches automatically, then prints, faxes, or e-mails MLS information to buyer or seller prospects daily, weekly, or monthly. One-time activation fee and monthly service fee; cancel any time. Fax-on-demand free report (800) 229-7426, ext. 2301. *SOAR Automation, Inc., 777 Roosevelt Road, Suite 110, Glen Ellyn, IL 60137, (877) 762-7657, (630) 942-0877; fax (630) 942-0878; e-mail info@soarmls.com; www.soarmls.com.*

Talking House. AM radio transmitter sits inside listing. Drive-by prospects tune in on car radio to hear recorded message about property. Yard signs, scripts, newsletter, prospect presentation video, five-year warranty included, installment financing available. Celebrity voice messages option. *Realty Electronics, Inc., 195 N. Main Street, Fond du Lac, WI 54935, (800) 444-8255; fax (888) 923-6222; www.talkinghouse.com.*

Win2Data 2000. Property and tax data with mapping systems for comparables, farm areas, mailing labels, and mail/merge. One-time software fee and monthly update fee for CD-ROM or online service billed by the hour. Check website for available markets. Formerly TRW/Redy Property Data and Experian. *First American Real Estate Solutions, 5601 East La Palma Avenue, Anaheim, CA 92807, (800) 345-7334; www.firstam.com.*

VIDEOS

BCW Video. Customer videos, direct-response system. "Dress Your House for Success" (also book), "Finding a Home" (also book), "Price Your House for Success," "Let's Get a Move On!" Personalization and seminars. *BCW Video. 123 North Third Street-Suite 216, Minneapolis, MN 55401, (612) 338-4887, (800) 288-4635; fax (612) 338-7763; www.bcwvideo.com.*

Christine Doyle Seminars. A series of three consumer videos on selling your home. One each for FSBO, seller, and transferred homeowner. "How to Get Your House SOLD." *Christine Doyle Seminars, 5894 Steele Road, Burlington, WI 53105, (800) 700-3695, (414) 767-1234; fax (414) 767-1237; e-mail czdoyle@wi.net; www.christinedoyle.com.*

David Knox Productions. Several consumer videos and related training materials. "8 Steps to Buying a Home" (buyer agency and nonbuyer agency versions), "Pricing Your Home to Sell," "Preparing Your Home to Sell," "Selling by Owner," "Expired Listing," "How to Select a Real Estate Agent" (for sellers). *David Knox Productions, 7300 Metro Blvd., Suite 120, Minneapolis, MN 55439, (800) 822-4221, (612) 835-4477; fax (800) 822-2716; e-mail info@davidknox.com; www.davidknox.com.*

Success Connection. Three consumer guide videos about buying, selling and pricing. "Buying a Home," "The Seller's Role," "Pricing to Sell." Created by national speaker Rick Willis. *Success Connection, 6545 Sunrise Boulevard, Citrus Heights, CA 95610, (800) 434-8457, (916) 728-1200; fax (916) 729-5545.*

VOICE BROADCASTING

Voice broadcast allows you to leave recorded voice messages on contacts' answering machines or voice mail, terminating on live answers.

Arch Telecom Voice Broadcast. Emulates power of personal phone call. Lets you make thousands of simultaneous calls in the time it takes to make one phone call. Load phone lists 24-hours with e-mail or send disk. Real-time detail or summary report available off website or fax-on-demand. For recorded information and free report, (800) 390-6223, ext. 2039. *Arch Telecom, 210 Barton Springs Road, Suite 275, Austin, TX 78704, (800) 882-9155, (512) 492-0735; e-mail sales@archtelecom.com; www.archtelecom.com.*

Epo-Call. Once database of numbers is established, use 800 number to record message, select phone list, and schedule calls. Message storage available. Detailed call report via e-mail or fax. Initial cost plus monthly and per-minute charges. *Epoffect, Inc., 1133 Broadway, Suite 921, New York, NY 10010, (888) 805-7979, (212) 367-0813; fax (800) 511-6005; e-mail info@epoffect.com; www.epoffect.com.*

Digital Voice Broadcasting. Transfers messages directly to voice mail systems and records message in your voice on answering machines. Average 43%–56% of calls result in messages left. No setup, no contract. Charge per call made. *Digital Voice Broadcasting LLC., 1 Executive Drive, Fort Lee, NJ 07024, (201) 224-6439; fax (201) 224–0411; e-mail digvoicebr@aol.com.*

Marketek Consulting. Provides system design, consulting, hardware, software, and installation of own-your-own voice broadcasting system. Significant investment. *Marketek Consulting, 5655 Lindero Canyon Road, Suite 202, Westlake Village, CA 91362, (818) 735-5902.*

SPEAKERS AND TRAINERS

Rolf Anderson. Seminars: "Dazzling Digital Photography . . . Perception vs. Reality, Product Update, Tips!" and "The Technology Big Top: A Three Ring Showcase." *Rolf Anderson Seminars, 131 South Clark Street, Forest City, IA 50436, (515) 582-3401; fax (515) 582-3167; e-mail rolfoand@aol.com.*

Bill Barrett. Audiotapes, Agent Express Net (Internet directory on diskette with links to 700 best real estate websites), seminars: "Lead Generation Systems—The Steps Beyond Prospecting," "Masterpiece Marketing, Presentations and Servicing," "The New Way Workshop" with 200-page manual, and more. *Bill Barrett Seminars, 945 South Rochester Road, Rochester Hills, MI 48307, (800) 432-1977; fax (248) 601-9900; e-mail seminars @billbarrett.com; www.billbarrett.com.*

Dave Beson. Real-world experience and over 2,000 seminars prepare Beson to deliver leading-edge profit-making ideas every time. Life Success Systems (audiotapes and seminars): "99 Ways to Profit in the New Millenium," "No Fear Negotiation," and

"The Total Service Solution." *Dave Beson Seminars. 7200 West 78th Street, Minneapolis, MN 55439, (800) 242-3031, (612) 947-9111; fax (612) 947-9110; e-mail info@davebeson.com; www.davebeson.com.*

Chuck Bode. RS Council instructor. Seminars: "The 25 Biggest Myths of the Real Estate Industry" and "Roundtable Super Session: Residential Niche Marketing." *N.P. Dodge Real Estate Company, 12915 West Dodge Road, Omaha, NE 68154, (800) GET-BODE, (402) 330-5008; fax (402) 330-5545; e-mail getbode@aol.com.*

Howard Brinton. Entertaining and informative Star Power program includes annual conference, training (Star Power University), HomeAgent online referral network, monthly newsletter, and training cassette (Star Power Club), plus books, scrapbooks, and tapes. *Howard Brinton Seminars, Inc., 2300 Central Avenue, Suite E, Boulder, CO 80301, (800) 635-6750, (303) 449-8181; fax (303) 449-4222; e-mail hbsz@ix.netcom.com; www.brinton.com.*

Brian Buffini. Teaching, coaching, mentoring organization. Working By Referral™ Resource Library with change-of-address program, endorsement campaign, and referral directory; Oh, by the Way™ contact management software; two-day Turning Point Retreat and ClubNet personal coaching. *Providence Seminars Inc., 8380 Miramar Mall, Suite 200, San Diego, CA 92121. (800) 945-3485; fax (760) 639-2750; e-mail brian@provcom.com; www.provcom.com.*

Carla Cross. Author of *The Real Estate Agent's Business Planning Guide* and *On Track to Success in 30 Days.* Seminar: "Managers: Maximizing Your Most Valuable Asset—The People in a Merged Office." *Carla Cross Seminars, 1070 Idlywood Drive SW, Issaquah, WA 98027, (800) 296-2599, (206) 392-6914; fax (206) 392-6414; e-mail carlacrs@wolfenet.com.*

Mike Ferry. Training programs, business planning program, audio/video products for sales skills, motivation, and systems, Internet referral network, and one-on-one training. Top producers use these products, services, and systems to add more transactions to their personal production every year. Catalogue. *The Mike Ferry Organization, 177 Riverside Drive, Suite F, Newport Beach, CA 92663, (800) 448-8423, (714) 852-8517; fax (949) 852-9183; www.mikeferry.com.*

Allen F. Hainge. Former English major, now national speaker who specializes in real estate technology training, consulting, and software. Founder of Allen F. Hainge CyberStars™, real estate leaders nationwide who dominate their market through technology. To subscribe to free weekly online technology newsletter, *Real Estate Technology News & Views,* send e-mail to *news@afhseminars.com. Allen F. Hainge Seminars, 8813 Side Saddle Road, Springfield VA 22152, (703) 644-4374; fax (703) 644-2159; e-mail allen@afhseminars.com;www.leading.com/hainge.*

Ed Hatch. International speaker on sales, motivation, management, assistants, and instructor development. Audiocassette programs and print-ready Success Systems including personal promotions, forms, letters, and buyer/seller presentations. *Ed Hatch Seminars, 8215 Mandan Court, Greenbelt, MD 20770, (800) 334-2824, (301) 474-1125; fax (301) 474-3524; e-mail edhatch@aol.com.*

LeRoy Houser. Coaching programs by e-mail, telephone, and in person at monthly seminars over ten months. Programs designed for new real estate agents and veterans to lead them to level of productivity they want. Newsletter. *LeRoy Houser, All-Star Coaching/LeRoy Houser Seminars, 9512 Ironbridge Road, Chesterfield, VA 23832, (804) 796-1119; fax (804) 796-3069; e-mail leroy@allstarcoach.com; www.geeroy.com.*

Laurie Moore-Moore. Co-editor with Steve Murray of *Real Trends* newsletter; hosts annual invitation-only "Gathering of Eagles" conference for principals and owners. Seminar: "Good Grief! What's Happening to Real Estate?" *Real Trends, Inc., P.O. Box 796278, Dallas, TX 75379, (972) 250-0633; fax (972) 931-8545; e-mail rltrends@aol.com; www.realtrends.com.*

Craig Proctor. Ranked the #1 RE/MAX agent in North America in 1997, Proctor holds semiannual three-day training seminars and has packaged his "Quantum Leap Real Estate Success System" for use by other real estate professionals. Call for free report. *Craig Proctor Productions, 1140 Stella Drive, Newmarket, Ontario, Canada L3Y 7B7, (800) 538-1034; fax (905) 830-1374; www.craigproctor.com or www.quantumleapsystem.com.*

Jim Pugliese. Seminar: "Mega-Agent Magic: Secrets of Top Producers." *Jim Pugliese Seminars, 101 Guilder Lane, Guilderland, NY 12084-9693, (800) 215-5528; fax (518) 456-8980; e-mail spkrjim@aol.com.*

Monica Reynolds. Seminars: *"The Dream Team: Top Female Agents Share Business Building Strategies"* and *"The Superstar Assistant." Monica Reynolds Seminars, 5412 Merrywing Circle, Austin, TX 78730, (512) 425-9736; fax (512) 425-9701; e-mail mreynolds@simpletel.com; www.monicareynolds.com.*

Ralph Roberts. Author of *Walk Like a Giant, Sell Like a Madman* with John Gallagher. Sells the system Roberts used to become America's #1 residential agent, with more than 570 closed transactions per year. Book, cassettes, workbooks. *Ralph Roberts Real Estate, 30521 Schoenherr, Warren, MI 48093, (810) 751-0000, (800) 704-5189; fax (810) 573-9845; e-mail ralphsworld@voyager .net; www.ralphsworld.com.*

Walter Sanford. Every book, tape, diskette has the exact systems of Sanford's successful career for you to imitate. "Walter's Top 250 Letters" (book and diskette), "The Last Word on Prospecting" (book and diskette), "Real Estate Telesystems" (book and diskette), and more. *Walter Sanford Systems, 321 Redondo Avenue, Long Beach, CA 90814, (562) 434-7253, (800) 7WA-LTER; fax (562) 434-6353; e-mail walter@waltersanford.com; www .waltersanford.com.*

Joe Stumpf. Real Estate Marketing University division teaches systems and techniques to implement series of referral processes to grow your business. Audio training programs, half-day preview workshop: "How to Work $4\frac{1}{2}$ Days a Week and Net a 6-Figure Income," three-day Main Event seminar, and ninety-day and year-long eight-step business Coaching Club. *By Referral Only™, 3038 Industry Street, Suite 106, Oceanside, CA 92054, (800) 950-7325, (760) 966-2800; fax (760) 966-2806; e-mail mail@remu.com; www.joestumpf.com.*

Pat Zaby. RS Council instructor and founder of PREP Software. Seminar: "Step Two—Really Making Money with Technology." *Programs by Pat Zaby, 3333 Earhart Drive, #150, Carrollton, TX 75006, (972) 991-1998; fax (972) 991-1992; e-mail patzaby@ prepsoft.com.*

REAL ESTATE MARKETING BOOKS

Creative Real Estate Advertising Made Easy, by Mary Ellen Randall and Jamie M. Edwards, 4th edition. Direct from Real Estate Business Services (888) 750-3343.

From Ads to Riches: How to Write Dynamite Real Estate Classifieds and Harvest the Results, by Joan McLellan Tayler. Direct from Real Estate Business Services (888) 750-3343.

How to Develop a Six Figure Income in Real Estate, by Mike Ferry. Chicago: Real Estate Education Company, 1993, 198 pp., hardcover.

How to List & Sell Real Estate in the 90s, by Danielle Kennedy and Warren Jamison. Englewood Cliffs, New Jersey: Prentice Hall Career & Technology, 1990, 4th edition, 481 pp., hardcover.

How to Sell More Real Estate by Using Direct Mail, by James E. A. Lumley. New York: John Wiley & Sons, 1982, 229 pp., hardcover.

Power Real Estate Letters, by William H. Pivar and Corinne E. Pivar. Direct from Real Estate Business Services (888) 750-3343.

Productivity & Profit through Leads Management, by Pat Soltys. Soltys, Inc., 10604 Manor Ct., Suite 1, Manassas, VA 20111-2807, (800) 588-0578; fax (703) 335-5446; e-mail psoltys@soltys.com. 55 pp., three-ring binder. Describes advantages of "call coordinator" (receptionist) function in real estate office versus traditional "telephone duty desk" staffed by rotation of agents.

Includes scripts, forms, job description, training, introduction to existing agents.

101 Best Tips for Using Technology in Real Estate, by Allen F. Hainge. Springfield, VA, Allen F. Hainge Seminars, 1998, spiral bound. Direct from publisher at www.afhseminars.com or (800) 695-3794.

Real Estate Prospecting: Strategies for Farming Your Markets, by Joyce L. Caughman. Chicago: Real Estate Education Company, Dearborn Financial Publishing, 1994, 2nd edition, 226 pp., paperback.

Successful Farming by Mail and *Successful Farming by Phone,* by Steve Kennedy. Orange, CA: Calculated Industries, 1987, 224 pp., paperback. Direct from Real Estate Business Services (888) 750-3343.

Tactical Marketing, by Diane Armitage. Three-cassette audio series. Write Brain, 9888 W, Belleview Avenue, Suite 230, Littleton, CO 80123, (303) 904-4064; e-mail dianearm@earthlink.net; www.writebrain-inc.com.

The Pocket Prospecting Guide for Real Estate Professionals, compiled and edited by Ernie Blood and Bernie Torrence. Canton, OH: Homes Guide of America, 1987, 301 pp., spiral bound 4½″ × 8½″ with tabs.

2,001 Winning Ads for Real Estate, by Steve Kennedy and Deborah Johnson. Direct from Real Estate Business Services (888) 750-3343.

Walk Like a Giant, Sell Like a Madman: America's #1 Salesman Shows You How to Sell Anything, by Ralph R. Roberts with John Gallagher. New York: HarperBusiness, HarperCollins Books, 1997, 207 pp., hardcover.

RELATED MARKETING BOOKS

Direct Marketing Success: What Works and Why, by Freeman F. Gosden Jr. New York: John Wiley & Sons, 1985, 225 pp., paperback.

How to Get Clients: A Survival Manual for Executives, Professionals and Entrepreneurs, by Jeff Slutsky. New York: Warner Books, 1992, 242 pp., paperback. With his brother Marc, also wrote *Streetfighting: Low Cost Advertising/Promotion for Your Business,* and *Street Smart Marketing* and *Street Smart Tele-Selling.*

Guerrilla Marketing: Secrets for Making Big Profits from Your Small Business, by Jay Conrad Levinson. Boston: Houghton Mifflin Company, 1993, 327 pp., paperback.

Prospecting Your Way to Sales Success: How to Find New Business by Phone, by Bill Good. Telephone sales training tips. New York: Charles Scribner's Sons, 1986, 242 pp., hardcover.

Managing Sales Leads: How to Turn Every Prospect into a Customer, by Bob Donath, Carolyn K. Dixon, Richard A. Crocker, and James W. Obermayer. Lincolnwood, IL: NTC Business Books, 1995, 417 pp., hardcover.

The 200 Minute Marketing System: Tools, Tips and Techniques for the Occasional Marketer, by Rob Fey. Havre de Grace, MD: Fey Marketing, Inc., 1996, 290 pp., hardcover.

Afterword by Steve Murray

You can't take it with you. And probably don't want to. My experience helping brokers shape personal as well as corporate exit strategies, and also helping brokers market their businesses to an eager community of buyers, has taught me one thing.

The value of a business is real, tangible, identifiable, and can be translated to a bottom-line sales price. How the seller increases a firm's value, and how a strategic buyer values a business, is, of course, key to the final figure.

In recent years, an interesting shift has occurred. In years past, when a top agent wanted to build a business, that agent left the firm and started a new brokerage. Today, top agents instead are staying put in their brokerage and building a "business within a business." Technology and staff make this possible, and they also deliver the productivity that allows individual top agents to realize personal production levels the size of a small brokerage.

Today's top agents are as much businesspeople as salespeople. This shift is also encouraging a growing interest among the best agents in "selling your practice." Just like a broker who wants to sell a company, more and more top agents today are looking for an exit strategy when their time comes to retire or move on. Also, just like brokers, the value of a top agent's business depends on being able to transfer a system of business generation to a buyer who can step in and use the seller's marketing system to increase future business.

As a business broker and consultant who has been involved in scores of company expansions and sales, I recognize just how powerful the *Real Estate Rainmaker* system is for agents who are building today for an exit strategy tomorrow. Dan Gooder Richard's system gives you a nuts-and-bolts way to generate leads, follow up with prospects, and stay in contact with people long term. Put the system in place and you may be amazed how valuable your business will become to a future buyer.

Steve Murray
Co-editor, REAL Trends, Inc.

Index

Aardvark Labels, 290
Abandoned customers, 134–136, 256–257
Action plans, 208, 238. *See also*
    Marketing plan; Strategy(ies)
Activity ratios, 169–170
AddressCentral, 150
Address change, 148–150
Ad-Soft, 283
Advertising. *See* Marketing;
    Media/advertising
After-closing follow-up, 153
Aging customer base, 12–13
American Dream Passport, 286
American Home Shield, 151
Amidei, Joe, xiii
Anderson, Rolf, 249, 295
Anniversary, escrow, 154, 155
Annual report, 106
Answering machines, 108, 109
Appointment, suggesting, 97
Appraisal, 119
Appreciation events, 155–156
Arch Telecom:
    800 Powerline, 216, 285
    voice broadcast, 294
ART (hotline), 285
Ask Howard, The Real Estate Dog, 287
Asset sale, 269

Assistants, 108–109, 153, 281
Atnip, Joe, 148
"Attaboy" letters, 105
Audio Business Cards, 286
Automated voice broadcast message
    services, 109

Barbara Sue Seal Properties, 73
Barlow, Dr. Janelle, 237
Baron Publishing, 287
Barrett, Bill, xiii, 108, 153, 295
BBD principle (best/better/different), 71
BCW Video, 293–294
Before You Move, Inc., 150
Benchmarks, 161–173
    expenses, lead generation, 167
    expenses, long-term contact, 167–168
    expenses, marketing, 163–168
    expenses, prospect follow-up, 167
    and other parts of marketing plan
        (*see* Marketing plan)
    pain-in-the-neck ratio, 168
    prospecting activities, 168–172
    simplicity, 162–163
    starting with what you did last year,
        163
Bender, Larry, 74, 131
Beson, Dave, xiii, 154, 295

Best Image Marketing, 287
Billboards, 51
Bird Dog network, 137–138, 250
Blewett, Dave, 106
Blum, Gladys, xiii, 145
Bode, Chuck, xiii, 255, 296
Bohlen, Bob, xiii, 262, 265, 276, 291
Book of business installment sale, 260
Books, marketing, 299–301. *See also*
    Resource guide
Brainstorming solutions to problem
    objectives, 205–207
Brinton, Howard, xiii, 99, 296
Brochure box action task budget (Table
    15.1), 239
Brodie, Mike, 73, 155
Broker network, out-of-town, 140–141
Budget, 209–218
    adjusting for exceptions to the rules,
        216–218
    database customer-value technique,
        213–214, 215
    how much to invest on marketing, 210
    and other parts of marketing plan
        (*see* Marketing plan)
    percent-of-sales budget, 212
    rules of thumb, 210–211
    transaction-based, 212–213, 214
    zero-base, 214–216
Buffini, Brian, xiii, 187, 296
Builders, partnerships with, 136–137
Bunting, Maria, xiii, 268
Burridge, Lisa, xiii, 266
Business cards, 51, 68, 148, 286
Business Letters Unlimited, 99
Business-to-business word-of-mouth
    advertising. *See* Referral(s)
Business-within-a-business, 21
Butler, K. C., xiii, 147
Buyer(s):
    prospect problems checklist, 66
    time horizon, 11–12, 95
    trend toward buyer's agent, 7
By Referral Only™, 299

Cable TV advertising, 49
Calendars, 151, 282
Call-capture hotlines, 110, 244. *See also*
    Telephone, hotlines
Caller ID, and toll-free numbers, 40
Call reluctance, 89

Capital *vs.* marketing expenses, 166. *See
    also* Benchmarks; Budget
Case studies, 219–240
    Mega-Agent Team, 232–236
    Neighborhood Generalist, 222–226
    Newbie Buyer's Agent, 220–222
    Top-Producing Lister, 226–231
Cashing in *vs.* cashing out, 260
Cedarstrom, Marilynn, xiii, 58
Century 21, 140, 249
Circle list, 244
C.J. Brown Realtors, 150
Classified Simplified PRO, 281
Clayton, Jim, 93
Client appreciation event, 155
Closing gifts, 150, 283–284
Closing Statements, 283
CMA. *See* Competitive Market Analysis
    (CMA)
Code, promotion, 97, 107
Cold Call Cowboy Productions, 286
Coldwell Banker, 58, 73, 115, 139, 140
Commission rate per transaction,
    national average, 8. *See also* Fee(s)
Comparables, 118
Competition:
    aping offers by, 68
    assembling files on, 199
    decreasing with age of sales lead,
        29–30
    generating leads before, 5
    giant/predatory, 5, 19, 125
    out-marketing, 36
    property advertising benefiting, 8–11
    studying, 198–199
    why it quits, 92–93
Competition alert, 118
Competitive Market Analysis (CMA),
    115, 154, 249
Computerized database. *See* Trophy
    Database
Concierge service, 139
Confidentiality agreement, 276
Consolidation trend, 5
Continuity Programs, 283
Cookie Garden, 283
Core competency, 175
Core list, 244
Corporate identity *vs.* personal identity,
    74
Costs. *See* Budget

Cotton, Jack, xiv, 176
Coupons, 51, 79, 80, 82, 139
Covington, Jr., Ray, xiv, 135
Cracker Jacks, 57
Creative, 35, 71–86
    corporate identity *vs.* personal identity,
        72–74
    headlines, 76
    identity, creating, 71–72
    making it easy to respond, 78–82
    pillar of direct marketing, 35
    postscripts, 83–84
    qualifying questions, 82–83
    quick checklist, maximum creative
        direct mail, 74–75
    Rainmaker strategies, 76–84
Creative mistakes to avoid, 84–86
Crockett, Stan, 151
Cross, Carla, 296
Cross-media advertising, 40
Crumpled-letter technique, 103
CTX Mortgage Company, 135
Curb appeal, 119
Customer(s):
    acquisition costs, 126
    focus on, 17–19, 54–56, 128–131
    information, 246–248 (*see also*
        Trophy Database)
    long-term contact with (*see* Long-
        term contact)
    and marketing plan, 187–200 (*see
        also* Marketing plan)
    motivation of, 196–198
    new *vs.* lifetime, 124–125
    referrals, asking for, 131
    referrals, educating about, 130
    retention strategies, 123–142 (*see also*
        Long-term contact)
    segments, 188, 189–194
    sharing, 141
    value, 125, 127–128
Customer(s), targeting, 24–26, 54,
    189–194. *See also* Direct response
    marketing
    buyer checklist, 190
    referral checklist, 192–193
    seller checklist (Figure 12.2), 191
    steps one through four, 189–194
Customer-direct marketing. *See* Direct
    response marketing
CyberStars™, 81, 150, 250, 297

Database. *See* Trophy Database
Database America, 48
Database customer-value budget
    technique, 213–214, 215
Database marketing, 251
Database software, 279–280
    shopping for; quick checklist, 248–249
DataLead Customer Follow-Up, 283
Data mining, 251
DataQuick, 48
Davis, Hollie, 135
Dearing, Pat, xiv, 261, 263, 274
Demographic aging, 12–13
Demographics, 189, 195, 245
DiCello, Tony, xiv, 147, 267
Digital Voice Broadcasting, 295
DirectConnect, 116, 291–292
Direct mail, 48, 74–75, 79, 101–107,
    137, 194, 251
    builders program, 137
    crumpled letter technique, 103–104
    eight in eight, 104
    first class, 251
    flooding prospects with abundance of
        information, 101–107
    junk mail, 75, 194, 251
    quick checklist to guarantee
        maximum creative, 74–75
    reply-mail coupon, 79
    return service requested, 255, 256
    sample, first follow-up letter, 102
    sample, second follow-up letter, 103
    techniques, ten tested, 104–107
    zip codes, 254, 255
Direct response marketing, 24–26,
    35–37. *See also* Marketing
    boosting other media, 36 (*see also*
        Media/advertising)
    expenses, 39 (*see also* Budget;
        Marketing plan)
    first/second rules of, 24
    40-40-20 rule, 35
    handpicking customers with, 24–26, 54
        (*see also* Customer(s), targeting)
    and Internet, 45, 250 (*see also*
        Internet)
    lead generation system, 35–36
    resources, 285
    three pillars, 35
    truths of, four fundamental, 36–37
    why it works, 37

Direct response offers, 53–69, 98–99, 107
  focusing on customer's problems, 54
  handpicking customers, 54 (*see also* Customer(s), targeting)
  hard/soft, 65
  high-impact response kit, 98–99
  including in all marketing/ advertising/prospecting, 64, 107
  limiting time/supply of offer, 63–64
  making offer valuable, 61–62
  mistakes to avoid, 67–69
  quick checklist, 60–61
  stating offer clearly, 62–63
  testing offers constantly, 64–65
  translating solutions into offers, 54–56
  turning solution into premium, 56–57
Discounts, 69
Divorces, 197, 198
Douthit, Hal, 281
Downturn insurance policy, 39
Doyle, Christine, 281, 294

800 numbers. *See* Telephone, hotlines
Eight in eight, 104
E-Leads program, 42
Electronic media advertising, 49
Elephant technique, 237–238
E-mail, 45, 46–47, 80, 81, 96, 116, 140, 148, 250. *See also* Internet
  address collection, 250
  attachments, 47
  automatic response to, 46, 81
  blind carbon copy, 47
  capturing leads, 45
  hyperlink to your website, 81
  inquiries, handle with persistence, 96
  ISP *vs.* online service, 46
  mailboxes, 46, 116
  networking with, 140
  newsletters, 148
  quick checklist on how to make money with, 46–47
  signature, 47, 81
eNeighborhoods, 292
Epo-Call, 295
ERA, 73, 140
Eudora Pro, 81
Exceed98, 249, 279
Excellence In Action, Inc., 290
Exit strategies. *See* Selling your practice

Expenses. *See* Benchmarks; Budget
Express Copy, Inc., 290

Farm(ing), 13, 23, 45, 244, 245, 250–251, 255–256, 288
  e-mail database, 45
  feeder, 255
  geographic, 13
  Internet, 245, 250–251
  list, 244
  reverse feeder, 255–256
Fax, 81
Features *vs.* benefits, 84–85
Federal Express, 125–126
Fee(s):
  add-on, 20
  commission rate per transaction, national average, 8
  flat transaction, 20
  listing, 20
  referral, 140
  regulatory compliance, 20
Feeder farm, 255
Ferry, Mike, xiv, 169, 243, 296
First American Real Estate Solutions, 48
First class mail, 251. *See also* Direct mail
First-time buyer hot list, 117
Fishing upstream, 25
Follow-up. *See* Prospect follow-up
F.O.R.D. rapport-building technique, 99–101, 130, 246
  dreams, 100
  family, 99
  occupation, 99
  recreation, 100
40-40-20 rule, 35
Foster, Wes, xiii
Foster, Jr., Wesley P., xiv
Fragmented media market, 10–11
Fresh Beginnings, Inc., 283
Future book of business sale, 270–272

Gellens, Maxine, 155
Geographic farming, 13
GeoLocator, 292
Giant/predatory competitors, 5, 19, 125
Gift(s):
  closing, 150–153
  expenses, 167
  resources, 283–284

Gift Baskets USA, 284
Gooder Group, 11, 42, 91, 101, 285, 287, 288, 289
Group Inc., The, 99
Growing your practice. *See* Real estate: growing your practice

Hainge, Allen F., xiv, 45, 81, 150, 250, 297
Harker, Mary, 73, 140
Hatch, Ed, xiv, 103, 281, 297
Headlines, writing, 76, 78–82
Help U Sell, 20
Herder, Greg, 104
Hobbs, Don, 104
Hobbs & Herder Advertising, 104, 286
Holiday tests, 30, 260
Home inspection, 119
Homeowner's Portfolio™, 152, 284
Homeowner's Records Portfolio, 152
Home Tracker, 115
Horizon, longer buying, 11–12
Hospitality Pac, 284
Hotlines. *See* Telephone, hotlines
Hot lists, 244
  first-time buyer, 117
  other brokers' new listings, 255
  personal home buyer, 114–116
Household service providers, 139
Houser, LeRoy, xiv, 136, 297
Howard & Friends, 249, 280

Identity:
  corporate *vs.* personal, 72
  creating for your practice, 71–72
  photo as, 74
Image Builder Advertising, 289
Images USA, 284
Information:
  and knowledge/wisdom, 42
  personal/property, 246
  soft/hard, 99
Inquiry Handling Service, Inc., 27, 91, 93
Installment sale, book of business, 260
Interactive voice response systems, 285
Internet, 7, 9–10, 36, 39, 43–46, 49, 81, 115, 118, 154, 167, 245, 250–251
  domain registration, 44
  e-mail (*see* E-mail)
  expenses, 167
  farms, 245, 250–251

and local leads, 43
NAR's website, 115, 149
quick checklist on how to make money with, 44–46
search services for property listings, 115
statistics about prospects on, 43–44
virtual MLS, 9–10 (*see also* Multiple Listing Service (MLS))
website (*see* Website)
Internet Explorer, 46
Internet Service Provider (ISP), 46
  frequently changed, 250
Internic, 44
InTouch, 283
ISP. *See* Internet Service Provider (ISP)

Job *vs.* practice, 30
Jones, Jay, 99
Junk mail, 75, 194, 251

Kall Publications, 288
Keller Williams, 73, 140, 155, 267
Kendall, Larry, xiv, 99, 246
King Thompson Realtors, 57, 58
Kinko's, 134, 282
Klocks, Joe, 147
Knowledge:
  and information/wisdom, 42
  using to convert prospects to customers, 26
Know the Neighborhood, 292
Knox, David, 294
Kohn, Marilyn, 74
Kolor View Press, 291

L&A Direct, 93
LaRue, Rich, 264
Lead(s):
  closed loop 3-step Rainmaker system, 30–31
  importance of, 4
  management of, 31
Lead generation, 30–31, 33, 35. *See also* Direct response marketing
  creative strategies, 71–86
  media strategies, 35–52 (*see also* Media/advertising)
  offer strategies, 53–69
  pillars, three, 35
Leads Online, 11, 42, 91
Legal documents, 152

Leino, Ralph, 116
Lender preapproval, 97
Lentz Design, 289
LetterWriter and LetterWriter Plus, 154, 286
Lifetime value of customer, 127
Lilly, Harry, 74
Lilly, Lynne, 74
List(s):
  Circle List, 243, 244
  Core List, 243, 244
  first-time buyer hot list, 117
  personal home buyer hot list, 114–116
  Prospect List, 243, 244
  testing, 50
  Wannabe List, 243, 244–245
List broker, 48
Lister, Top-Producing, 226–231
Listing-only focus, two trends (1990s) endangered, 7
Long Fence and Home, 103
Long & Foster, 57, 59, 74
Long-term contact, 31, 121, 123–142, 143–158
  business-to-business word-of-mouth advertising, 136–142
  consumer word-of-mouth advertising, 133–136
  cross-town referrals, 141
  cultivating bird dogs, 137–138
  developing partnerships with new home builders, 136–137
  example (Federal Express), 125–126
  expenses, 167–168 (*see also* Budget)
  focusing on long-term prospects, 133
  maximizing lifetime customer value, 127–128
  minimizing new customer acquisition costs, 126
  new customers *vs.* lifetime customers, 124–125
  orphan win-back campaign, 134–136
  out-of-town broker network, 140–141
  referrals, creating perpetual, 143–158 (*see also* Referral(s))
  staying in touch with past customers, 133–134
  strategies (nine), 132–142
  suppliers, 138–140
  targeting inactive referral agents, 142

Loyalty ladder, 187–188
Lunch Bunch, 137

Magazine advertising, 49, 50
Magazine subscription, 150
Maggie's Mailbox, 289
Magic words to use, 86
Magnets-N-More, 287
Magnets USA, 152, 282, 284
Mail. *See* Direct mail; E-mail
Map Solutions, 292
Marketek Consulting, 295
Market fluctuation, 6
Market fragmentation, 10
Marketing:
  business card used for, 148
  budgeting for, 210–212 (*see also* Budget)
  concentrating on, 16–17
  direct-response (*see* Direct response marketing)
  vs. sales, 17, 93, 279
  tools/resources, 286–287
Marketing Advantage-Farmnet, 288
Marketing plan, 159
  assembling, 237
  benchmarks, 161–173
  budget, 209–218
  case studies, 219–240
  customers, 187–200
  objectives, 175–186
  strategies, 201–208
Marketing profile worksheet, 178
Marketing your practice: quick checklist, 276–277. *See also* Selling your practice
Market share *vs.* lifetime customer value, 124
Market share statistics, 199
Mathes, Dick, 73
Mayer, Ed, 35
McGinnis BH&G, 73
ME, INC., 261, 291
Media/advertising:
  cross-media advertising, 40
  direct-response (*see* Direct response marketing)
  electronic media advertising, 49
  fragmented market, 10–11
  pillar of direct marketing, 35
  property advertising benefiting competition, 8–11

software for writing ads, 281
winning strategies, 35–52
Media mistakes, 49–51
  failing to integrate all marketing, 49–50
  failing to test lists, 50
  timing offers to mirror market, 50
Media strategies, 39–49
  capturing calls with telephone
    hotlines, 40–42 (*see also*
    Telephone, hotlines)
  changing delivery mix to test media,
    47
  developing Trophy Database, 39 (*see*
    also Trophy Database)
  generating deluge of wholesale leads,
    40
  playing media markets, 48
  using different media for different
    objectives, 48–49
  using the Internet, 42–47 (*see also*
    Internet)
Melco Marketing, 151, 282
Mergers and acquisitions, 277–278
Microsoft, 81, 115, 249, 279
Mission statement, 113, 176–179
MLS. *See* Multiple Listing Service (MLS)
Modern Postcard, 291
Money Mailer, 139
Moore Data Management Services, 280
Moore–Moore, Laurie, xii, xiii, xiv, 297
Morris, Joyce Caughman, xiv
Mortgages:
  lender preapproval, 97
  rates, 107
Motivation, customer, 95, 194, 196–198
Multiple Listing Service (MLS), 6, 9–10,
  67, 107, 116, 117, 134, 196, 199,
  246, 279, 280, 292
  automatic online searches, 115
  expired new home listings, 137
  supplying abbreviations as part of
    Preferred Customer Program
    enrollment package, 113
  virtual, 9–10 (*see also* Internet)
Multiple of profit earnings sale, 272–275
Multiplier effect, 143
Murray, Steve, xiv, 297, 304

Naming your business: Rainmaker, do's
  and don'ts, 73. *See also* Identity
NAR. *See* National Association of
  REALTORS® (NAR)

National Association of Home Builders,
  136, 211
National Association of REALTORS®
  (NAR):
  declining membership, 5
  resource for members of, 287
  sponsoring National Homeownership
    Week, 60
  survey results, 3, 7, 9, 12, 37, 38, 54,
    55, 56, 91, 128, 129, 141, 144,
    196–197, 210, 211
  website, 115, 149
National Homeownership Week, 60
Netscape Mail, 46
Network, personal, 137–138
News articles, reprinting, 106
Newsletters, 101, 288–289
Newsletter Services, Inc., 288
Newspaper advertising, 49
Newspaper columns, 287–288
Niche markets, 57, 68
Nickel, Sandra, 73
Nixies, 252
N.P. Dodge Real Estate Company, 255,
  296

Objectives, 175–186, 201–203, 205–207
  exploring, 179–180
  marketing, 183–184
  marketing profile worksheet, 178
  problem, 205–207
  ranking, 182–185
  vs. strategies, 201–203
  tests of, 181
  understanding where to start,
    181–182
  warming up, 175
  "Who Am I?" worksheet, 177
Offer strategies. *See* Direct response
  offers
Office Depot, 149
On-Line Agent, 249, 280
OnTrac, 280
Open House Guest Pass, 113
Orphaned customers, 134–136, 256–257
Outdoor advertising, 49, 51

Pafenberg, Forrest, xiv
Paper Direct, 149
Pasmanick, Zac, xiv, 113, 287–288
Pending business sale, 269–270
Percent-of-sales budget, 212

Personal Assistant System, 281
Personal home buyer hot list, 114–116
Personal Marketing Co., 288–289
Personal network group, 137
Personal open house tour, 117–118
Personal price hotline, 117
Personal Retriever, 115
Personal Shopper Program, 113–114
Pest inspection, 119
Phone Pros, 91, 92
Phone tips. *See* Telephone
Photo as your identity, 74
PhotoShare, 45, 47, 118, 292
PictureWorks, 45, 118, 292
Pipeline. *See* Prospect pipeline
Pizza Hut, 260
Planner Systems, 152, 284
Plaques Are Not Profit, 261, 291
Portals, 44–45. *See also* Internet
Postcards, 149, 289–290
Post office, 48, 149. *See also* Direct mail
Postscripts, 83–84, 98
Powerline, 216, 285
PowerMate Technologies, 281
Powers, Bill, 264
Practice. *See* Real estate
Preferred Carlson, REALTORS®, 116, 292
Preferred Customer Program, 111–120, 146
   first-time buyer hot list, 117
   personal comparable alert for sellers, 118
   personal home buyer hot list, 114–116
   personal open house tour, 117–118
   personal price hotline, 117
   personal shopper program, 113–114
   preferred property program for sellers, 118–119
   seven sure-fire services, 113–119
Preferred property, criteria, 119
Premium offers. *See* Direct response offers
Prepaid services, 149
PREP Software, 148, 172, 249, 280, 299
Press releases, 51
Price hotline, personal, 117
Printers, 290–291
Private mortgage insurance (PMI), 157
Proctor, Craig, xiv, 181, 297
Professional(s):
   appreciation event, 156
   expenses, 168
   nontransaction-related, 138
   real estate (*see* Real estate)

Profit:
   customer retention strategies for optimum, 123–142
   multiple of profit earnings sale, 272–275
   squeeze, 8, 19–20
Promotion code, use of, 97, 107
Property advertising, 8–11, 36, 53. *See also* Media/advertising
   benefiting competition, 8–11
   traditional, 53
Property highlight sheet, 51
Property information in database, 246, 248
Property listing(s):
   expired, 137
   fee, up-front nonrefundable, 20
   focus on; two trends endangering (1990s), 7
   hands-off search services for, 115
   maximizing inventory, 266
   MLS (*see* Multiple Listing Service (MLS))
   other brokers' new listings, 255
   preferred property program for sellers, 118–119
   and selling, 21
Property standards, 118, 119
Prospect follow-up, 31, 87, 89–110, 111–120
   after closing, 153
   customer conversion strategies to maximize sales, 89–110
   e-mail inquiries, 96
   expenses, 167 (*see also* Budget)
   F.O.R.D. method to build phone rapport, 99–101
   importance of, 89–92
   launching immediately with high-impact response kit, 98–99
   mailing abundance of information, 101–107
   Preferred Customer Program, 111–120, 146
   qualifying customers, 94–98
   quick checklist of cardinal rules for, 92
   Rainmaker system, closed loop 3-step, 31
   resources, 282–283, 290
   sales secrets, 28–29, 90–92
   strategies, 94–110

telephone techniques, 99–101,
  108–110, 216
tripling your business with, 93–95
two-report-choice technique, 95–96
why competition quits, 92–93
Prospect list, 244
Prospect pipeline, 20–22, 30, 31, 133,
  144, 194
Prospect problems in search of
  Rainmaker solutions, quick
  checklists, 66–67
  buyer prospect problems, 66
  relocation prospect problems, 66–67
  seller prospect problems, 66
Prospect Profile, 97–98
Prospect ratio, 23
Prudential, 74, 131, 140, 145, 155, 262,
  265, 276, 291
Psychographics, 189
Pugliese, James, 151, 298

Qualifying customers, 82–83, 90, 94–98,
  111
Quantum Systems, Inc., 283, 289–290
QuikLinx, 290

Radio advertising, 49, 51
Rainmaker. *See* Real Estate Rainmaker
Ratios, activity, 169–170
Re/Ad, 281
RealAide program, 249
Real estate:
  business-within-a-business, 21
  competitors, giant/predatory, 5, 19,
    125 (*see also* Competition)
  creating identity (*see* Identity)
  functions of, 21
  marketing books, 299–300 (*see also*
    Resource guide)
  marketing plan (*see* Marketing plan)
  selling your practice (*see* Selling your
    practice)
  signs of declining practice, 124
  statistics about, 5, 28 (*see also*
    National Association of
    REALTORS® (NAR), survey
    results)
  superagent, 20–21, 73, 140
Real estate: growing your practice, 252–257
  data quality, 254–255
  orphan collection campaign, 256–257
  reverse feeder farms, 255–256

Trophy Database, 252–253 (*see also*
  Trophy Database)
  turnover rate, 253–254
Real estate: truths that could kill your
  business, 3–14
  customers calling only one agent,
    3–5
  geographic farming ineffective, 13
  longer time horizons, 11–12
  need for customer replacement due to
    database and demographic aging,
    12–13
  profits being squeezed, 8
  property advertising benefiting
    competition, 8–11
  sales cycles, inevitability of, 6
  seller focus no longer enough, 6–8
  trend toward consolidation, 5
Real Estate Computer Solutions, 280
Real Estate Doctor®, 73
Real Estate Focus, 148
Real Estate Rainmaker:
  case studies, 219–240
  direct marketing, 26 (*see also* Direct
    response marketing)
  knowledge, 26, 42
  "rainmaker", 15–16
  resource guide (*see* Resource guide)
  system's first critical law, 5
  tools essential to, 26
  Trophy Database, 26 (*see also* Trophy
    Database)
Real Estate Rainmaker, strategies for
  becoming, 16–32
  customer relationships, 17–19
  direct-response marketing, 24–26
  Holiday Litmus Test, 30
  knowledge, 26
  marketing focus, 16–17
  productivity, 19–20
  prospect pipeline, 20–22
  sales secrets, 27–30
  Trophy Database, 22–23
Real Estate Rainmaker Lead System®,
  3-Step, 31, 286–287
  lead generation (*see* Lead generation)
  long-term contact (*see* Long-term
    contact)
  prospect follow up (*see* Prospect
    follow-up)
Real Estate Settlement Procedures Act
  (RESPA), 130, 146

Real Estate Star Columns, 288
Real Estate Technology News & Views
   newsletter, 150
REAL Trends Inc., xii, xiv, 273, 297, 304
Realty Electronics, Inc., 293
Realty Executives, 249, 264, 266
Realty World, 140
Reciprocity agents, 141
Referral(s), 128, 132–142, 143–158. *See
   also* Long-term contact
   cross-town, 141
   fees, 140
   for-sale-by owners, 133
   mistakes to avoid, 156–157
   networking, 137–138
   out-of-town brokers, 140–141
   percentage of business, 13, 124
   quick checklist on asking for, 131–132
   and selling your practice, 268
   sources of, 128, 268
   strategies for cultivating, 144–156
   strategies for maximizing, 132–142
   targeting inactive referral agents, 142
Referral Network, 264
Regulatory compliance fee, 20
RELO, 140, 210
Relocation kit, 51, 56
Relocation prospect problems checklist,
   66–67
RE/MAX, 73, 74, 106, 113, 140, 147,
   148, 181, 249, 261, 263, 266, 267,
   291, 297
Repeat three-peat call system, 108
RESICOM, 293
Residential ACT! & Trans/ACT!, 280
Residential Sales Council, 45, 103, 136,
   140, 280
Resource guide, 279–301
   ad writing software, 281
   assistants, 281
   calendars, 282
   client follow-up, 282–283
   closing gifts, 283–284
   database software, 279–280
   direct-response reports, 285
   hotlines, 285
   marketing and prospecting tools,
      286–287
   newsletters, 288–289
   newspaper columns, 287–288
   postcards and greeting cards, 289–290

printers, 290–291
   real estate marketing books, 299–300
   related marketing books, 300–301
   selling your practice, 291
   speakers and trainers, 295–299
   technology tools, 291–293
   videos, 293–294
   voice broadcasting, 294–295
RESPA. *See* Real Estate Settlement
   Procedures Act (RESPA)
Response kit, high-impact, 98–99
Response offers. *See* Direct response
   offers
Response-oriented advertising, 13, 53.
   See also Direct response marketing
Return service requested, 255, 256
Reynolds, Monica, 281, 298
Rinehart, Geri, xiv
Rinehart, John, xiv, 243
Roberts, Ralph, xiv, 20, 298
RS Council. *See* Residential Sales
   Council
Rule of 45, 27–28, 91
Rusinak, Vicki, 101

Sales cycles:
   downturn insurance policy, 39
   eliminating, 20–22
   inevitability of, 6
Sales secrets, 27–30, 90–91
   competition decreasing with age of
      lead, 29–30
   follow-up, 28–29
   Rule of 45, 27–28
Saltman, Risa, 56
Sanford, Walter, xiv, 41, 112, 118, 154,
   298
Search engines, 45, 115
Seller(s), focusing on, 6–8
Seller prospect problems checklist, 66
Selling your practice, 259–278, 291
   be paid to walk away, 260–262
   buyer prospects, 261–262
   cashing in *vs.* cashing out, 260
   mistakes to avoid, 262–265
   quick checklists, 261–262, 265–269,
      276–277
   Rainmaker strategies, 269–275
   resources, 201
Seminars, 51, 56, 57–60, 64, 151, 281,
   295–299

Sendsations Personal Marketing, 290
Shreiber, Elaine, 261
Sight qualifiers, 82, 96
Signature, 47
Signs. *See* Outdoor advertising
Simpson, Lyndi, 74
Simpson-Oke, Joy, 74
Sloan, Bill, xiv, 73
Sloan, Peggy, xiv, 73
Slogans, 73
Smoke detectors, 151
SOAR MLS™, 115, 293
Soesbe, Linda, 73
SoftKlone, 41, 285
Spamming, 251
Sparkman, Bill, xiv, 131, 157
Sparrow & Jacobs, 290
Speakers and trainers, 295–299. *See also*
    Seminars
Star Power Club, 296
Stay In Touch Follow-Up System®, 290
Stoffer, Irene, 73
Stoffer, Jerry, 73
Strategy(ies), 179–180, 201–208
    vs. objectives, 179–180, 201–203
    ranking, 206, 207–208
    sample scenarios, 202–203
    scoring and ranking, 206
Strategy(ies): tests for selection of,
    203–205
    based on market research, 204
    doable, 204
    measurable, 205
    tied to objectives, 204
    within budget, 204–205
Stumpf, Joe, xiv, 187, 298
Success Connection, 294
Superagent, 20–21, 73, 140
Super Coups, 139
Superior Real Estate Supply, 287
Suppliers, as referral groups, 138–140
Sweepstakes, 24, 250. *See also* Direct
    response offers

Talking House, 293
Tax information for homeowners, 155
Technology, 137, 243, 291–293
Teldon Calendars, 282
Telephone:
    answering machines, 108, 109
    directory as closing gift, 152

follow-up, 108–110
hotlines, 40–42, 47, 79, 101, 110, 117,
    127, 167, 216, 285
repeat three-peat call system, 108
skills training, 92
Television advertising, 49, 51
Test(s)/criteria:
    of an objective, 181
    strategy selection (five), 203–205
Testimonials, 75, 105–106, 113
Testing:
    direct-response marketing, 36, 85
    lists, 50
    media, 47
    offers, 64–65
    Trophy Database, 263
3B System, 93–94
3-Step Rainmaker System. *See* Real
    Estate Rainmaker Lead System®,
    3-Step
Time Manager International, 237
Tip Club, 137
Today's Living magazine, 282
Top Producer, 172, 249, 280
Tours, 45, 117–118
Town name, using, 74
Transaction-based budget, 212–213, 214
Transaction fee, flat, 20
Transaction-value *vs.* customer-value
    focus, 125
TRF Systems, Inc., 292
Trilogy Co., 290
Trophy Database, 22–23, 26, 239,
    243–257
    adding prospects, 94, 97, 149
    aging of, 12–13
    and benchmarking, 170
    Circle List, 243, 244
    Core List, 243, 244
    deleting names, 252
    developing, 22–23
    farm e-mail database, 45
    hygiene, quick checklist of tips,
        251–252
    and knowledge, 26
    organizing, 243
    Prospect List, 243, 244
    and selling your practice, 158, 263,
        266
    software, 248–249, 279–28
    strategies, 239, 243–257

Trophy Database *(Continued)*
  superagent's, 21
  testing, 263
  Wannabe List, 243
Turnover, 13, 23
Two-report choice technique, 95–96

Undeliverables, 251
United Coupon, 139

Val-Pak, 139
Video resources, 293–294
VIP Club, 112
Virtual tours, 45, 117
Vision, 238–239
Vitale Sunshine Realty, 73
Voice broadcasting, 294–295
Voice messaging, 41, 108, 109, 110

Wannabe list, 244–245
Warranty, 119, 151
Wattam, Pat, xiv, 150
Website:
  created just for prospect, 118
  e-mail response form on, 46
  establishing your own, 44

home page as premium, 56
hyperlink to, in e-mail signature,
  81
and Internet *(see* Internet)
NAR's website, 115, 149
past client personal, 154
Whalen, Tony, 73
"Who Am I?" worksheet, 177
WIIFM (what's in it for me?), 53, 72
Williams, Scott, 91
Willis, Rick, 294
Windermere, 115, 261, 268
Windsor Vineyards, 284
Win2Data 2000, 293
Women's Council of REALTORS®
  (WCR), 140
Writing like you talk, 74–75
  "magic words" to use, 86

Yellow Pages, 139
Your Marketing Assistant, 289

Zaby, Pat, xiv, 40, 148, 280, 299
Zero-base budget, 214–216
Zip codes, 254, 255

About the Author

Dan Gooder Richard is the creator of the *3-Step Rainmaker Lead System* now in use by thousands of real estate professionals nationwide. Dan is a publisher, consultant, and speaker. His company, Gooder Group, is a Fairfax, Virginia–based publisher of marketing materials for real estate and mortgage professionals.

Gooder Group currently publishes seven monthly prospecting newsletters and an extensive series of handbooks, brochures, website content links, postcards, print ads, marketing letters, and more, all designed for lead generation, prospect follow-up, and long-term contact. More than 12,000 real estate and mortgage salespeople in the United States and Canada use Gooder Group marketing products every year.

Dan has published articles in *Real Estate Today* (now *REALTOR*), *Real Estate Business,* and *Relocation Quarterly.* As a seminar leader and keynote speaker at sales rallies and conventions, he has spoken in front of numerous brokerage companies and groups, such as *Real Trends* Leadership Conference, Realty Alliance, RELO, Reliance Relocation Services, ERA, SuperSession, and Genesis. Dan is known for his nuts-and-bolts presentations of successful marketing techniques that agents, brokers, and loan officers can use to make the phone ring immediately.

Before founding Gooder Group in 1983, Dan was marketing director for Long & Foster Real Estate in the Washington/Baltimore area for five years. During his years with Long & Foster, the company grew from 900 agents to 2,400 agents, from 30 offices to 59 offices, and from $859 million in sales to $2.4 billion.

With more than 20 years of experience in marketing and lead management, Dan's background includes a master's degree in magazine journalism from the University of Missouri–Columbia and positions with *Los Angeles* and *Washingtonian* magazines. He is also a freelance travel writer. Dan was born in Davenport, Iowa, in 1947. He now lives in Arlington, Virginia, with his Finnish-born wife, Synnöve Granholm.

Dan Gooder Richard can be contacted at:

Gooder Group®—The Lead Generating Company
2724 Dorr Avenue
Fairfax, VA 22031-4901
(703) 698-7750
(703) 698-8597 (Fax)
leads@gooder.com (E-mail)
www.gooder.com